Work and Nonwork in the Year 2001

Marvin D. Dunnette
University of Minnesota

WITHDRAWN
Rock Valley College
Educational Resources
Center

Brooks/Cole Publishing Company
Monterey, California
A Division of Wadsworth Publishing Company, Inc.

© 1973 by Wadsworth Publishing Company, Inc., Belmont, California 94002. All rights reserved. No part of this book may be reproduced, stored in a retrieval system, or transcribed, in any form or by any means—electronic, mechanical, photocopying, recording, or otherwise—without the prior written permission of the publisher: Brooks/Cole Publishing Company, Monterey, California, a division of Wadsworth Publishing Company, Inc.

ISBN: 0-8185-0080-8
L.C. Catalog Card No: 72-94643
Printed in the United States of America
1 2 3 4 5 6 7 8 9 10—77 76 75 74 73

This book was edited by Karen Craig and designed by Jane Mitchell. It was typeset by Datagraphics Press, Phoenix, Arizona, and printed and bound by Hamilton Printing Company, Rensselaer, New York.

Work and Nonwork in the Year 2001

Preface

Work and Nonwork in the Year 2001 is a collection of original papers that presents an overview of what work and productive leisure activities—nonwork—have been, are now, and probably will be in the future. It is written by leading authorities in the field. Designed as a supplement for courses in industrial and organizational psychology, this book fits easily into other behavioral and social science courses concerned with current thinking about the problems of work and leisure.

The chapters are arranged to give, first, an overview of work and nonwork from several important perspectives: historical (Chapter 2), cultural (Chapter 3), institutional (Chapter 4), and in the context of rapid social change (Chapter 5). Then the reader is asked to speculate with us how we could satisfy both individual and societal needs in the future world of work (Chapter 6), how we could merge work and nonwork (Chapter 7), and how we may want the pattern of work and nonwork to look in the year 2001 (Chapter 8). Finally, Chapters 9 and 10 discuss two emerging concepts, human resource accounting and the experimenting society, that lead to ways of detecting, tracking, and evaluating change in the years ahead.

Concern about what work and nonwork mean in our personal lives has never been greater than it is today, due perhaps to the increasingly transient qualities of modern life: the impermanence of material goods, our geographic mobility, the fleeting quality of many human interactions, and the increasing change in institutional and organizational boundaries.

How does this new era of transience affect people? Does it lead to alienation, fear, entrapment, atrophy, and despair? Or to involvement, challenge, freedom, growth, and hope? This book offers new perspectives on how people in many cultures throughout history have managed to respond positively to changing work conditions. We take both a rational and an emotional approach to the future, since the future cannot be viewed through rationality alone; rational man extrapolates his view from the trends of the past, and he is usually wrong. Emotional man sees the future through eyes clouded by hope; he may be wrong, too, but his hope is far more likely to make him an active agent for improvement instead of merely an observer of the passing scene. These perspectives will help us use our current knowledge to assure that work and nonwork in the future will be better suited than it is today to fulfilling both society's and the individual's needs for freedom, growth, and continued renewal and challenge.

I wish to express my sincere thanks to the chapter authors for their excellent contributions, which were written especially for this book, and to Henry Borow, University of Minnesota, and Victor Vroom, Yale University, both of whom reviewed the manuscript and offered many helpful suggestions. Jean Barsaloux aided me and the other authors a great deal during the early phases of our writing by researching the literature and helping to coordinate our efforts. Later, Leaetta Hough provided invaluable assistance in the early editing and organization of the authors' first drafts.

Finally and most important, my colleagues and I wish to thank Harold A. Edgerton for providing the initial impetus to our efforts and for planning and organizing several conferences that led to the articles in this book. We also acknowledge with gratitude the continuing financial support given to this series of conferences and to this writing project by the Psychological Sciences Division of the Office of Naval Research.

Marvin D. Dunnette

Contents

1   INTRODUCTION   1

Glenn L. Bryan, Office of Naval Research

Past Attitudes toward Work   1
Work Today   2
Work and Youth Today   4
Changes from Today's Work Patterns   5
Work in the Future   8
Plan of This Book   9

2   WORK AND NONWORK: HISTORICAL PERSPECTIVES   12

Herbert G. Heneman, Jr., University of Minnesota

Survival, Tools, and Status   14
History of Concepts of Human Work   16
The Labor Movement   18
Work Today: A Coat of Many Colors   20
Leisure and Nonwork   22
Unanswered Questions   24
Summary   26
References   27
Suggested Reading   27

3   WORK AND NONWORK: INTERCULTURAL PERSPECTIVES   29

Harry C. Triandis, University of Illinois

Work: Varying Concepts   29
Different Wines in Similar Bottles: Looking for Contrasts   35

Strengths and Weaknesses: Current Views of Work in Industrial Societies   46
Summary   49
References   51
Suggested Reading   51

4 WORK AND NONWORK: INSTITUTIONAL PERSPECTIVES   53

Robert Dubin, University of California, Irvine

Focal Institutions   54
Multi-Equal Institutions   55
Summary   66
References   67
Suggested Reading   67

5 WORK AND NONWORK: PERSPECTIVES IN THE CONTEXT OF CHANGE   69

Edward C. Ryterband, Edward N. Hay Associates, Bernard M. Bass, The University of Rochester

Population Growth and Change in Its Composition   70
The Technological Imperative   71
The Revolution of Rising Expectations   75
The Generation Gap   77
Changes in Popular Culture   78
The Decline of Traditional Institutions   81
Summary   86
References   87
Suggested Reading   87

6 WORK AND NONWORK: MERGING HUMAN AND SOCIETAL NEEDS   90

Marvin D. Dunnette and Leaetta Hough, University of Minnesota, Henry Rosett and Emily Mumford, City University of New York, Sidney A. Fine, The Upjohn Institute for Employment Research

Merging Work and Nonwork   90
A Resource Conservation Industry   91
New Careers for the Poor   94
New Careers in Community Services   94
New Careers in Health Services: The Lincoln Hospital Project   97
Man-Job Adaptation: Organizational Accommodation   103

Prognosis and Hope   105
Summary   106

Technical Addendum: New Approaches for New Careers—
   Strategic and Technical Considerations   107

References   111
Suggested Reading   111

7   **TURNING WORK INTO NONWORK: THE REWARDING ENVIRONMENT   113**

Lyman W. Porter, University of California, Irvine

The Use of Rewards in Motivating Marginal Workers   115
Applicability of Work Environment Structuring to the Regular
   Employee   126
Toward 2001   131
Summary   132
References   133
Suggested Reading   133

8   **WORK AND ORGANIZATIONAL LIFE IN 2001   134**

Bernard M. Bass, The University of Rochester, Edward C. Ryterband, Edward N. Hay Associates

Looking Backward   135
Looking Forward   136
Interpersonal Dynamics in the Future Organization   137
Managing Future Organizations   146
Summary   149
References   150
Suggested Reading   150

9   **AUDITING CHANGE: HUMAN RESOURCE ACCOUNTING   153**

John Grant Rhode, University of Washington, Edward E. Lawler, III, University of Michigan

External Reporting   154
Tax Considerations   157
Internal Reporting   158
Problems Associated with Human Resource Accounting
   160
The R. G. Barry Corporation Experiment   164
Human Resource Accounting in the Future   169

Summary   172
References   174
Suggested Reading   176

10   AUDITING CHANGE: THE TECHNOLOGY OF MEASURING CHANGE   178

Nicholas Bond, California State University at Sacramento

Time-Series Observations of Long-Term Change   180
Experiments and Quasi-Experiments   185
Alternative Change-Evaluation Models   193
Expectations   202
Summary   203
References   204
Suggested Reading   206

INDEX   207

Work and Nonwork in the Year 2001

CHAPTER 1

Introduction

Glenn L. Bryan
Office of Naval Research

Introductory chapters usually define major terms used in subsequent chapters; the term *work* requires definition here. But work, like most other English words, has many connotations. Such diversity adds immensely to the scope of the concept of work. It is fascinating to observe what other cultures regard as work and how they distinguish women's work from men's work. Similarly, it is interesting to look back over this country's history to see how attitudes toward work have changed. Our present attitudes are quite different from those of our Puritan forefathers. Undoubtedly, work in the year 2001 will be vastly different from what it is today. This book will consider what work has been, what it is now, and what it may be in the future.

In this chapter, *work* means those activities normally performed for pay. One advantage of such a simple definition is that it is general and thus avoids prolonged arguments about whether professional artists, professional athletes, and prostitutes are members of the work force.

PAST ATTITUDES TOWARD WORK

Current attitudes toward work in this country are based heavily on stereotyped notions about work in early America. We are told that settlers survived in the face of many hardships at the cost of great personal effort. Life in remote colonies and on isolated farms required everyone to do his part. Small children, the aged, and all able-bodied adults were pressed into service. Families provided for all of their own needs. Although there was some bartering and some people worked for crop shares, there was relatively little work for pay. Settlers emphasized personal ambition, dedicated effort, and self-sufficiency. Laissez faire entrepreneurship was the common dream. Everyone sought his own plot of ground, his own house, his own cow, and his own bank account. Not only were these things desired as ends in themselves but also as symbols of hard work and frugality. Except for a small, privileged leisure class, unwillingness to work was scorned and regarded as a moral defect. Loyalty was demanded and received from employees.

Of course, this is a stereotype, but one that many people today believe was true. Such is the stuff of which generation gaps are made.

WORK TODAY

But let us talk about work today. Most of today's work is performed in large industrial settings. Many of us work for organizations run by professional managers. Division of labor is generally practiced. Activity is geared to high production and large profits. Most men and women work directly with machines. Their work is accomplished on a scheduled basis during designated working hours. Most work in urban areas that have become centers of professional services, manufacturing, and trade.

The specificity of work and its temporal and physical constraints have led to the modern concept of "the job." This concept is at the core of much current dissatisfaction with work. For that reason, let us take a closer look at it.

The concept of the job is common in modern organizations. Personnel departments rely heavily on job descriptions, job analyses, job evaluations, career ladders (which are really sequences of jobs), on-the-job training, and so forth. The trouble with the job approach is that it deals with the work done as if it were independent of the workers who do it. Workers are seen as necessary evils, merely instruments that generate a valuable commodity called "work." It is not surprising that workers resent having their work valued highly while they, as individuals, are not. Little wonder that some feel insecure, faceless, or exploited.

Division of labor does not give a worker the opportunity to point with pride to a finished product that he alone has produced. The modern worker finds that not only is he unable to identify with and take pride in his product, he cannot even identify with his work. He is simply a payroll number, a cost, a kind of liability. It is the job or the performance of the job duties—that is, the work—that counts. Under such circumstances, the worker sometimes comes to regard work on the job as a necessary evil, something to be endured for a certain number of hours every week in return for money that can be exchanged for something he really values. Although this point may be somewhat overstated, it is interesting to note how often professional personnel managers discuss job satisfaction when what they really mean is *worker* satisfaction.

The concept of the job has other negative implications, which stem from the idea that most people who work have an interest in a single job. Such an erroneous notion invites those who control the job to establish policies and practices that fail to take into account the worker's other jobs.

Three types of secondary jobs are apt to influence the career decisions of the modern worker. One is his moonlighting job. More and more people are supplementing their incomes and expanding their horizons with a second, usually part-time, job. Much can be said against such a practice, but moonlighting is not necessarily bad. For example, in many cases it permits a man to stick with a low-paying, but otherwise desirable, regular job. It allows people to make the transition from one type of work to another, and it sees them through economic pinches. In many cases, the moonlight job complements formal training to constitute an effective kind of work-study program. Occupational choices often depend on the availability of moonlighting opportunities.

The spouse's job also affects career decisions. As in the case of moonlighting, the necessity to consider two jobs—both the husband's and the wife's—restricts changes in working hours, travel schedules, employment mobility, and the like. And, since most people manage to adjust their level of consumption to their current level of income, multiple jobs may make the family economically more vulnerable than it otherwise would be. Now the family's standard of living or, more important, the ability to pay the bills depends on as many as three paychecks: the regular job, the moonlighting job, and the spouse's job (not to mention Junior's summer job that may also be expected to help out with his expenses). While the loss of any of these secondary jobs would not be as catastrophic as the loss of the principal job, such a loss can have dire economic consequences to the particular family and, if it happened on a large scale, to the national economy.

Somewhat more remotely, the second career is still another job likely to be involved in the personal employment decisions of a worker. One phenomenon of modern society, at least in America, is early retirement. Many people become eligible for retirement in their forties or fifties. In many occupations, retirement is mandatory at age 65. Early retirement policies, meager retirement benefits, and today's longer life expectancy have led many to plan second careers. The prospects of a second career may affect the selection of the first career and many of the day-to-day decisions made during that first career.

Organizations must recognize the complexity of the modern worker's job situation. Blanket personnel policies instituted in favor of the majority of their employees will become increasingly unacceptable to specific subgroups. Perhaps an organization should not pursue an illusory "one best" personnel policy but instead design individual flexible policies to accommodate individual workers.

WORK AND YOUTH TODAY

The current work situation exacerbates traditional problems of adolescence and influences young people's attitudes toward employment. Tomorrow's work will, in turn, reflect those problems and attitudes.

Young men and boys confront a number of problems of identification. Reared in home and school environments dominated by females, they may see their fathers only when the fathers are relaxing in the home atmosphere. The father leaves home early on working days, returns late, defers to the mother and the children on most matters associated with the family, and complains about the "rat race." He does not provide an image of either adult male or work with which the son is eager to identify. Because the father performs in his working role outside the home, the son cannot observe his father's interactions with other adults in a working situation. Consequently, in many situations, the son is not able to model his own behavior after that of his father. Life has changed from the days on the farm where the son was pressed into service as a field hand and had extensive opportunity to see how his father organized his efforts, coped with disappointments or adversity, or cooperated with others to achieve a common goal. Similarly, the artisan and the shopkeeper always had many chores for his children to do. In the days of the cracker barrel, it may have helped young people growing up to sit with their elders and listen to their conversations and observe the conversational fate of the blowhard or the liar.

Today's young people have a job of their own that is known as "going to school." In school the student often suffers from the same distinction drawn between performer and performance that characterizes the separation of the worker from his work. The student's efforts are valued; the student himself is not. Students must prepare extensively for a life that they have limited opportunities to learn anything about, a life described to them in what may be a series of gross distortions. They are encouraged to think in simplistic terms and seek textbook solutions. During this period of preparation, which can extend from age 5 to 25, many young people feel that they are forced to watch helplessly while the world's big problems get out of control. They frequently view working adults as bumbling incompetents who have sold out to the establishment in return for a paycheck that is squandered on plastic paraphernalia intended to add zest, comfort, and entertainment to a meaningless existence.

It is popular to blame current social problems on youth, their parents, Dr. Spock, or the government. It may well be, however, that some of the problems derive directly from the working situation that has grown up in modern societies. If the present working situation does contribute to current social problems, and if it really is unsatisfactory from almost any standpoint, it follows that the world of work must be changed. This social pressure to change the nature of work may be as potent a force for change as were the technological and economic pressures of the past century.

Instead of assessing blame or figuring out where we went wrong, we should recognize that some practices have outlived their usefulness and ought to be abandoned. Let us examine what changes are likely to take place.

CHANGES FROM TODAY'S WORK PATTERNS

Extensive dissatisfaction with work is sparking a serious reexamination of many of our practices and values. Many aspects of our life style, such as working hours and school years, are leftovers from an earlier rural era. In those days, it made sense to work during the daylight hours and be exempt from school during the months farmers were busiest. But we continue to endure commuter rush-hour traffic despite modern communication, which could enable some of us to work away from the office but still keep in touch. The demise of the blue laws has permitted longer hours for stores and banks; in other concerns workers may prefer to arrange their own working hours other than eight to five, Monday through Friday. The main reason that work schedules are not more flexible is that such arrangements do not permit adequate supervision under the present system. Management cannot be sure that a worker is really working if he has not punched the time clock and is not observed seated at his desk. This problem, however, does not seem insurmountable. Fixed working hours are likely to give way to more flexible arrangements that suit individual employees.

Many firms already are turning to the shorter work week, such as four ten-hour days in lieu of five eight-hour days. Apparently the four-day week provides a wide range of benefits. By going earlier and staying later, the workers avoid heavy traffic. They save entirely the costs and efforts of one round trip each week. And, management's costs—for janitorial services and heating, for example—are substantially reduced. Clearly, not everyone can go on such a schedule. But the point is that the concept of rigid schedules and regular working hours may not be valid 10, 20, or 30 years from now.

Many ingenious suggestions for alternative working schedules have been made. One, called the "cubic day," calls for a two-person team to share a job that is done seven days a week. Each member of the team works exactly half the time, but team members, themselves, can decide who works when. One could work mornings, the other afternoons, or they could alternate days, weeks, or any other block of time. With modern transportation, there need be no standard season for vacations. Each worker could arrange with his teammate to take a vacation when it suits him best.

Another interesting suggestion is to change the length of the day so that it does not coincide with the cycles of the earth's rotation. Say, for example, that we had a 25-hour day. Those who report for work at eight o'clock would continue to do so. But obviously, eight o'clock would fall an hour later each day. Thus we would progress through the light-dark cycle. Of course, those who need daylight to work would still get up with the sun while others would be on the 25-hour day. Such a scheme would make any particular starting time (like eight o'clock) as convenient or inconvenient as any other. Consequently, workers should be more willing to stagger starting times throughout the entire 25-hour period. Staggering hours would result in better use of transportation services, parking, and other facilities.

It is a radical idea, but it frees us from a daily schedule that has most workers competing for freeway space during the same few hours.

Another likely change is the shift from production-oriented employment to more service-oriented employment. Both public and personal services are expanding rapidly. Personal services in the future will range from counseling and health care to recreation and equipment maintenance. As the number of services increases, many more workers will be cast in entrepreneurial roles, and there may be somewhat less demand for replacement consumer goods but greater demand for high-quality maintenance services. In any case, most products will be manufactured automatically, and the definition of what constitutes individual productivity will change drastically.

The age-old search for employment that allows the worker to make a meaningful contribution to an activity he considers worthwhile will go on. Since many service-type jobs expected to be needed can be performed by a single individual, perhaps the range of opportunities in the future will be very wide indeed.

Another change that appears likely is a greater emphasis on work-study on a lifelong basis. Even very young students might be given far greater opportunities to work at useful tasks under appropriate supervision. The youngest students could perform many clerical activities associated with the operation of a school; there are always envelopes to be stuffed, materials to be filed, cards to be alphabetized. Students could also be asked to assist in community activities such as charity drives and other socially worthwhile endeavors. It is important to clarify that these activities would not be undertaken as a part of their "enrichment" training; on the contrary, they would be doing it because the work was useful and had to be done. Also, they would work under a typical supervisor and not under the guidance of a teacher. Youngsters need to learn how to give and receive supervision, and there are many work-related skills and attitudes that they need to be taught. It is possible that "free schools" and communes will become the accepted models for effectively teaching youngsters how to participate fully in life at every age and to undertake important responsibilities much earlier.

Life in the future will be lived in more highly individualized circumstances. One can expect that some people, at any age, will devote a greater proportion of their lives to work than will others. Some will progress much more rapidly than others through material to be learned. Each will seek out the styles that seem best for him. Some individual workers will never prepare themselves beyond the paraprofessional ranks, while others will become professionals with all of the preparation and discipline that the process entails. Some will become artists or scholars or choose other creative occupations. Under some circumstances, people will feel freer to abandon one career and start another. Because of this freedom some probably will never settle down to realize their full potential, but others will shift careers as appropriate to their age and interests. (It has always seemed that young people should undertake first careers that require energy, risk, excitement, and travel; second careers that emphasize management, supervision, control, and execution should be undertaken from ages 35 to 55; and third careers that emphasize contemplation, scholarship, patience, wisdom, and caution should be undertaken at older ages.) In any case, efforts would be made to structure opportunities that minimize career gates, bottlenecks, and hurdles. There would be no single road to success. As a matter of fact, there would be no single hallmark of success (such as economic success), but rather each individual would define success for himself in his own terms.

If technological developments reduce the number of jobs available and if proposals such as income sharing provide (at least minimum) incomes to people independent of their actual employment, the world of work in the year 2001 will be characterized by a smaller proportion of employed people. In the narrow sense in which the term *work* has been used in this chapter, we can say workers fall into four groups: managers, technicians, service personnel, and the unemployed. But how do housewives and recent retirees fit into this grouping? They would be quick to report that they are working too, but without pay.

WORK IN THE FUTURE

Perhaps work in the future will be similar to the housewives' or retirees' work in that pay will not be directly related to the work one does. Workers might be able to structure their own jobs without today's constraining and rigid structures implied by the concept of what a job entails. People will work, but they may not be formally employed. Workers may be valued for themselves, not only for their work.

This conclusion is based on the assumption that people and circumstances will continue to generate unlimited demands for work, if not for structured employment. There always will be work that simply has to be done. We also assume that work will become more of an integrative activity, drawing together people of different backgrounds, of different ages, and with different motivations. Work will be satisfying and fulfilling. In the future, when most work will be undertaken on a voluntary basis and when everyone will be working in a highly individualized way, work will be far more diverse than it is today.

PLAN OF THIS BOOK

This chapter has been a brief overview of what work has been, is now, and will be. Remaining chapters elaborate on these three themes from a variety of contexts.

Chapters 2, 3, 4, and 5 examine concepts of work and nonwork from several perspectives: historical, intercultural, institutional, and in the context of rapid societal change. Interestingly, although approaching their analyses from widely differing frameworks, these authors come to similar conclusions about the nature of changes in work and nonwork and what the concepts of work will be at the turn of the century. For example, all authors agree that work evolved in response to specific social and behavioral patterns and to institutional norms, that the nature of an individual's work has come to be a primary means of measuring his worth, and that reactions to these traditional concepts are now setting in. The authors agree that in the last five decades work has become dehumanizing for millions, but there seem to be early beginnings of a return to autonomy, greater freedom, and individualism in work. Over the next 30 years, work will become more diverse and more challenging, individuals and organizations more adaptable, and institutional boundaries more permeable as society extends its value systems beyond the present narrow, production-oriented definitions of work. All authors agree that work and nonwork will become less differentiable as opportunities for increased work fulfillment become more numerous.

In Chapter 2, Herbert G. Heneman, Jr., traces the changes in concepts of work and nonwork from the days of primitive man to the present. Recognizing that many of the early concepts seem simplistic when compared to today's complexity, he suggests the need for broader concepts in the future and presents two that he believes merit particular attention.

Harry C. Triandis, in Chapter 3, draws a fine line between cultural differences and similarities. He shows clearly how different concepts of work and work practices can be understood in terms of their common heritage—the formation of ingroups for purposes of defending territory and coping with the environment. He demonstrates how principles derived from such intercultural comparisons can suggest what kinds of changes are needed in modern industrialized work systems.

Robert Dubin argues in Chapter 4 that modern society can no longer be understood by the traditional approach of referring its values to a single focal institution. He develops instead an analysis of several equal institutions and shows how concepts of work and work organization will be affected by the patterns of institutional interdependence of such a society.

In Chapter 5, Edward C. Ryterband and Bernard M. Bass summarize the nature of the many changes we are witnessing in current society and the ways in which such changes may affect concepts of work and leisure in the years ahead.

Though the broad trends of change in the nature of work are apparent and the direction of desired changes has been specified, only limited attention has been paid to *how* change may best be accomplished. Chapters 6 and 7 discuss mechanisms for implementing change successfully. In Chapter 6, Marvin D. Dunnette, Leaetta Hough, Henry Rosett, Emily Mumford, and Sidney A. Fine, call attention to many specific societal ills plaguing modern life—substandard education, environmental pollution, and limited recreational and health services. This chapter suggests the creation of a resource conservation industry for the purpose of merging society's needs for new kinds of work to be done with human needs for more fulfilling work. Examples of two early efforts to develop new jobs and new careers are presented, and the reasons for their poor outcomes are analyzed. The crucial role of adaptive skill training is noted, and the technology of such training is presented as one critically important way for developing a viable resource conservation industry.

In Chapter 7, Lyman W. Porter describes the behavioral technologies of behavior modification and social modeling as means of creating rewarding environments and improved incentive management systems. Porter's optimism and enthusiasm are apparent as he argues persuasively that behavioral engineering may indeed be the most certain avenue for achieving the desired goal of a psychological merging of the worlds of work and nonwork in the year 2001.

Granted that the trends we now see are predictive of future trends and that existing or new technologies can be used successfully to induce desired changes in work, what will work and organizational life really look like in the year 2001? Throwing caution to the winds,

Bernard M. Bass and Edward C. Ryterband, in Chapter 8, paint their vision of the future. Not surprisingly, they see many of the outcomes suggested in this introductory chapter as well as several of the more specific ones mentioned by the other authors, but they have integrated the several suggestions and speculations to produce a cohesive and not entirely surrealistic picture of the work and organizational worlds of the year 2001.

The reader has probably inferred that most of the descriptions and extrapolations contained in these first eight chapters are based on naturalistic observation and theoretical analyses as opposed to systematic observations growing out of experimental or psychometric designs. Naturalistic observation is well suited to the detection of major changes and for developing inductions toward general principles, but the method is usually far too imprecise and nonresponsive for detecting the impact of rapid change. Because of this methodological inadequacy, Chapters 9 and 10 have been included in order to present and promote more systematic methods for auditing social and work changes in the years ahead.

In Chapter 9, John Grant Rhode and Edward E. Lawler, III, present the latest thinking in a new area of study, human resource accounting. Changes in the nature of work are irrevocably intertwined with changes in patterns of utilizing and conserving the world's human resources. Though still in its infancy, the methodology of human resource accounting promises to be of increasing importance as a means of auditing the nature and effects of changes in work as we move toward the year 2001.

Finally, Nicholas Bond, in Chapter 10, has given us a brilliantly succinct but broad description of the myriad methods available in the burgeoning field of change measurement technology. Bond places heavy emphasis on both the problems and the hopes of conducting careful and meaningful audits of social change. He chooses not to dwell at length on the elegant but essentially impracticable methods of classic experimentation. He calls instead for the use of multifaceted and continuous observational and measurement methods so that the effects of social interventions may be detected both speedily and accurately and utilized immediately to alter the course of subsequent action strategies. By giving particular attention to the methodologies proposed by Rhode and Lawler in Chapter 9 and by Bond in Chapter 10, readers will be better equipped not only for detecting and describing the effects of change but also for planning, implementing, and auditing change to assure that appropriate standards of social utility are being met.

CHAPTER 2

Work and Nonwork: Historical Perspectives

Herbert G. Heneman, Jr.
University of Minnesota

As was noted in the previous chapter, it is very difficult to define the idea of, or even the word, *work*. Work has many meanings and facets. When pressed for a specific, simple definition, after much thought we might say, "Well, it all depends. . . ." And therein lies understanding, for the concepts of work are complex, varied, and changing.

Even industrialized nations in the twentieth century have no single concept of work. Perhaps the most basic or generic definition is "purposeful effort." But this definition is not particularly helpful since "purposeful" can have various interpretations and shades of meaning. For example, *toil* is painful or fatiguing labor; *labor* denotes physical exertion to satisfy wants; *drudgery* is dull, irksome, and distasteful work. These words are common synonyms for work. Antonyms include play, diversion, recreation, rest, and relaxation. Thus, at first glance, the concepts of work and nonwork may appear clear-cut; but if work is "purposeful effort," what is a game of golf?

Concepts of work vary with time, place, culture, and society. Work is not the same in India, China, Russia, Africa, and the United

States. Not only is work culturally defined, but, within any one society, concepts of work vary in terms of objectives, effort, perspective (such as employer versus employee), reward systems, and sets of beliefs, perceptions, and values. Indeed, even within subgroups in one society there are substantial individual differences in the meanings or concepts of work. Changes in the lives of individuals, groups, and civilizations yield changes in the concepts of work. With the increasing tempo of change in the late twentieth century, concepts of work in the year 2001 A.D. will not be the same as those in the 1970s.

Social units have existed among insects, animals, subman, and man. Some forms of work can be found in all primitive societies, and there is no simple, clear-cut line separating civilizations from precivilizations. However, verbalization, thinking, planning, storage and retrieval of knowledge, and understanding help to identify civilized societies. Civilized men try to control natural forces rather than merely adapt to them. Moreover, civilization involves social organization and moral (or religious and ethical) concepts. Using these qualities as criteria, of some 20 known civilizations the earliest is 6000 years old.

Work undoubtedly was the key to controlling nature, and many of the driving forces behind work were physical—for example, hunger and cold. The thin line between work and leisure may be illustrated by man's ability to conquer fire, his movement into caves, and the fashioning of superior weapons in what was his newly found spare time. Once man could get away from using all his time to meet his daily needs, he could devote some of his time and effort to the future.

As civilizations developed, technological, economic, psychological, and social forces became powerful determinants. Inventions, such as the arrowhead, the wheel, use of metals, writing, and painting, changed the nature of work and of civilizations. Primitive societies lack these inventions; for example, the American Indians did not have the wheel, and Australian natives lacked the wheel and the bow. Part of the greatness of the Roman empire can be attributed to the invention of concrete, which greatly altered the types of jobs in Roman society. Not all changes in work, however, stem from technical inventions; social and psychological forces are also causal factors. The Dark Ages in Europe saw few inventions, but separation of work into manual (physical work) and clerical (mental work) branches in monasteries probably had psychological and sociological causes.

It is difficult to trace the changing concepts of work through history because much of the information has been lost. Not only is there a lack of knowledge, but we in the Western world tend to be parochial. We know more about Greek, Roman, and European history than we know about Oriental, African, or Indian history. Even today, we know very little about work in China and Russia. But even limited knowledge of the changing concepts of work in the mainstream of life during the last 6000 years may give us better insight for the difficult choices we face in organizing our society and work in the years ahead.

SURVIVAL, TOOLS, AND STATUS

In the primitive era, survival was the main concern. Man had to adapt to nature and compete with other animals, including other men. His view was short-run and opportunistic; when he was hungry, he would hunt, fish, and gather whatever was available at that moment. Work was sporadic, not always consciously goal-oriented, and hard to distinguish from nonwork. Climate and geography were dominant forces, and, quite early, superstition, magic, and religion led to customs and cultural behavior even in the work situation.

Technological inventions and improvements were undoubtedly some of the major causes of change in the nature of man, work, and society. Indeed one definition of man differentiates him as the tool-using and tool-making animal. With tools man was able to multiply, capture, and control more energy in more efficient form. He could produce more than he could consume in a day and store up the fruits of his labor; he could accumulate property. He could settle down in relatively fixed sites rather than rove for the necessities of life. Changes in social and work organization followed.

Groups of humans formed tribes and developed specialization of labor. Some persons produced material property, some obtained it through plunder, war, and conquest, and others protected it. Captured human property was at first valued for food (cannibalism) and later for its productive usages. Slavery had an enormous impact on civilization. Many civilizations were made possible largely through slavery, for it allowed the conquerors to rise above toil and become the ruling classes that had time for play, the arts, and advanced practices in magic, superstition, and religion. Work became more than a means to produce goods and services; it denoted and created statuses.

Various work-related statuses developed in most cultures. Teachers, preachers, warriors, beggars, prostitutes—all fit into the social hierarchy. In the partially industrialized China of 300 B.C., class differences were well defined. There were four major classes of occupations: at the top were scholars, teachers, and officials; then came farmers, artisans, and merchants, in that order. Educated people wore long fingernails to demonstrate that they were above physical labor. Despite the lowly status of the merchants, trade prospered, and enlarged markets led to division of labor and other restructuring of work.

A variety of work forms and organizations, experimentation, and change were to continue until today. New institutions and work behavior were developed, tried, tested, and abandoned. Much of the adaptive behavior was pragmatic, but values and concepts were important, too. For example, religion provided the impetus for phenomenal work efforts in building temples, pyramids, and other edifices.

The great Sumerian civilization of 4000 B.C. provides an example of the interdependence of work and cultural development. Agriculture followed the discovery and use of irrigation, the plow, and implements of flint and iron. Attendant social organization developed. Houses of fibers and mud were constructed. Medicine and theology were very important, as were the manufacture and use of cosmetics and jewelry. Probably most important of all, the Sumerians had a writing system which they used almost exclusively for records of commerce. As occupations and careers were developed and controlled, power, prestige, status, and authority systems emerged. Owners, managers, and the managed were bound together by a web of rules. Division of labor, work specialization, and systems of punishments and rewards reinforced established work behavior. Markets, trade, transportation, and a monetary system enlarged the Sumerian sphere of contacts and influence. Work-related social structures probably evolved in the family, the community, and in other institutions of Sumerian society. These and similar developments were not, however, confined to the Sumerian civilization. In China, in South America, and elsewhere, similar cultural change was also underway, with local variations in time and place.

In the late nineteenth century, when Samuel Gompers was asked, "What are the goals of organized labor?" he replied, "More." Gompers was referring to an increasing stream of material goods and services; a similar desire for more goods and services has undergirded work concepts for thousands of years in a wide variety of cultures and civilizations. Most of our basic concepts of work were old hat 6000 years ago and have varied only in form and emphasis through time. For most work, we have improved technical efficiency; whether we have been able to improve, let alone optimize, social and psychological efficiency of work is another question. For the vast majority today, work may represent a psychosocial pollution exceeding that of our other physical resources.

HISTORY OF CONCEPTS OF HUMAN WORK

Many institutions of the past were directly related to work. Education, for example, was largely concerned with passing down "tricks of the trade." A son learned his father's work skills and habits and left the learning center, the home, by the time he had reached sexual maturity. Adulthood was reached in the teens, and one was a seasoned worker by his early twenties. Guilds, the mutual-aid groups of persons associated in a common trade, were important institutions. Guilds of masters and apprentices were in existence in Babylonia by the time of Hammurabi (2100 B.C.); wages and prices in various occupations were fixed by the Codes of Hammurabi, and by law. At least as far back as 300 B.C., guilds were also present in China in the urban centers that replaced the small villages of handicraft cottage industries. Guilds became dominant in Europe in the Middle Ages. They tended to regulate and influence both work and nonwork aspects of life and definitely were tied to ideologies and practices of the family, the church, and the marketplace. The guilds thus provided social stability and defined working relationships in villages and cities.

But the stability of the Middle Ages was to yield to the influences brought by profound technological and economic changes. The Renaissance unleashed the knowledge occupations and industries. The Reformation sanctified work and economic values. The newly released knowledge and work ideologies were mutually reinforcing. More complex work skills were needed, developed, and used, and consequently more complicated work organizations grew.

Technological, cultural, social, and economic changes occurred at a disjointed pace in most societies. Wider geographical markets made cities less important and reshaped work and society. Home workshops appeared, only to be replaced by factories. Other sources of power replaced human power, and brute strength was no longer at a premium. Women and children could operate power machinery; efficiency multiplied. Machine operators turned into machine tenders, then into machine watchers, and finally, today, we see humanless, automated work.

Industrialization and urbanization grew hand in hand and were largely unplanned. Crises and conflicts in health, welfare, crime, education, and government developed. Conflicts increased as the changing nature of work upset other facets of everyday life and traditional value systems. Industrial conflicts between labor and management became commonplace. Workers attacked machines, capitalists, and the wage system. Gradually work plant organization stabilized. Division of labor and of authority emphasized coordination and control. Planning moved to the fore, and the premium was brains, not brawn. Rules formalized the nature of work and working relationships between managers and managed. Work and working organizations increasingly became depersonalized. Concern for human values in work finally began to emerge in the proscriptive preachings of academics. Labor unions, however, led the crusade for improved working conditions.

There has been some rational inquiry into the nature of man in his working relationships, but hard data are few, and speculations are rampant. We know much more about how work was performed than about historical concepts of work. Just as there is no one concept of work, neither is there one simple, logical development of work concepts through history. For the sake of clarity and emphasis, the following somewhat oversimplified list of the major historical concepts of work is offered.

1. In his primitive state, man took his food and shelter when and where he found them. He then began to domesticate plants and animals. As his own fertility made work more demanding, he developed technology (the use of a stick to plant seeds) and work-related social concepts (division of labor—for example, whereby women tended the fields and children while men hunted and fished, made war, and captured slaves). He developed superstitions about nature and designed certain work arrangements to placate his gods and the evil spirits. As occupational and social strata developed, the lowest classes got the most physically demanding jobs.

2. To the Greek and Roman philosophers, work was punishment and drudgery doled out by the gods. Work was evil, leisure was luxurious and good. Leisure (or nonwork) permitted exercise of the mind and spirit—man's loftiest occupation. Manual labor was tiring, vulgar, degrading, and the enemy of the soul.

3. The Hebrew philosophers viewed work as a form of punishment and atonement for sins. Work was a means to a better world; contemplation alone would not suffice to attain the Kingdom of God on earth. The Christians held that work was good for man, whereas

idleness was not. Work could yield a surplus of goods and services that the Christians could share with those less fortunate—the poor, sick, ill, and needy. To the early Christian, work was a means to charity or to avarice, to goodness or sin.

4. The early Catholic philosophers distinguished between spiritual and material efforts; the lay brothers did manual work and the religious brothers performed intellectual labors. Their concept of work was that no work is best of all because it permits contemplation, prayer, and a spiritual life. Work need not be emphasized when its fruits can be enjoyed only in this life; the goal of man is found in the life to come. The Scholastics regarded work as a natural right and duty, but held that one should work only enough to provide sustenance for oneself and those in the group. One should not work to acquire goods and property. St. Thomas Acquinas ranked the types of manual work: agricultural occupations first, handicrafts second, and commerce last.

5. According to Luther, work was good for man and was a way of serving God. Work was required to meet man's needs; hence each should do his best in the vocation to which he was called. Religious work was not necessarily superior to other work, for man was saved by faith alone. Activity of any sort was blessed, while idleness was not. Calvin held that man exists only to glorify God and to help establish the Kingdom of God on earth. Thus he should work to make a profit so that he could do more to help the poor; the richer man became, the more virtuous he was.

6. The Industrial Revolution, accompanied by changes in economic and social values, stripped work of its religious connotations. Materialism advanced as goods and services increased. The working day was shortened, working conditions were vastly improved, incomes were raised, education was available to almost all, rising expectations were realized, and living standards rose to new heights. A twentieth-century middle-class family lives in material luxury undreamed of by a monarch a century earlier. Savings and wealth not only make leisure activities possible, but recreation has become a necessity.

THE LABOR MOVEMENT

The unrest, protest, and conflict of the Industrial Revolution led to many changes in the concept of work. The Industrial Revolution and capitalism brought forth the labor movement. Labor unions and collective bargaining were established, first in factories and in the extractive and transportation industries. Today labor unions and collective bargaining are spreading to teaching, nursing, government work, and almost all other occupations. Behind work rules lies a complex series of laws, administrative rulings, and the common law of the workshop—"industrial jurisprudence" or civil rights in industry. Change and experimentation will continue, with events, politics, and ideas of workers outrunning the concepts of the philosophers and academicians.

Industrial capitalism has two major purposes: to satisfy societal needs and to meet individual needs for goods and services. The urbanization that accompanied the advent of the factory led to poorer living and social conditions. The industrial revolution changed the status of the typical worker; he could no longer adjust his own work efforts to his personal desires, needs, and abilities—he was attached to a machine, a schedule, and a manager. Skill and craftsmanship lost both prestige and economic value. Standardization, monotony, accidents, and fatigue were the rule rather than the exception. Unemployment and low wages were additional sources of discontent. Relations between owners and workers became distorted and impersonalized. Workers sought solace in drink, vice, debauchery, and in their fellow workers. They sought to call public attention to their plight; they protested the new labor-saving machinery, the factory, and the wage system. Some formed mobs and rioted, destroying machines and mills. Society and the establishment fought back with repressive laws and regulations. Economic efficiency obviously is not always in congruence with happiness and well-being.

Unions are perhaps the most successful workers' groups. There are three types of unions: (1) business; (2) uplift; and (3) revolutionary. Business unionism accepts the capitalist system but seeks to reform it. Uplift unionism calls for reform in education, social welfare, and legislative action, but plays a smaller role in economic matters. Revolutionary unionism seeks to overthrow the capitalist system and, if necessary, promotes violence to achieve that goal. Revolutionary unionism is highly class-conscious.

The basic union philosophy in the United States has been business unionism with the major emphasis on pragmatic, short-run goals of higher wages and improved working conditions. However, American unions have also sought social reform. Thus American unions combine business and uplift unionism interests, with the emphasis on business unionism. Workers in the United States unite primarily for economic reasons, but also for social and psychological reasons.

There are various labor theories. Marx called for social revolution to be led by the work force. The Webbs, English socialists, theorized that unions can help introduce and maintain a system of industrial democracy in work. Selig Perlman in the United States proposed that workers combine to increase economic opportunities for their members; collective bargaining permits them to ration limited jobs. (Perlman's "job consciousness" theory is perhaps the dominant concept in the United States today.) Others have argued that unions provide workers with fulfillment, security, protection, and strength. They relieve workers of anxiety and frustration and provide them with pride, prestige, and status. In newly developing industrial nations, labor unions are generally less concerned with job rights and more concerned with national interests.

The attitudes and actions of labor unions have probably done more to shape employment concepts in American industry than any other single force. Conflict is essential to change; hopefully we can keep it within desirable boundaries and channels.

WORK TODAY: A COAT OF MANY COLORS

Today, work in different parts of the world varies almost as much as it has over the past 6000 years. The Indians high on the altiplano of Bolivia tend their land and herd their flocks today with the same tools, techniques, and work codes their ancestors were using before the birth of Christ. The great masses of the world are indifferent to the concepts of work held by the Western philosophers—Greek, Roman, Catholic, or Protestant—that dominate the American work ethic. Nor are they concerned with most of the research done by modern industrial psychologists; the experiments seem neat, sterile, and irrelevant. Industrial societies are few; the have-nots follow concepts of work different from those of the haves.

Basic knowledge of what work is and why it is important may be among our most urgently needed insights. The concept of economic man—like the concept of psychological man, sociological man, or developing man—is grossly inadequate for an understanding of work. Generally contained in such concepts is a logical progression through a list of needs. However, throughout the world, working man has not progressed up a hierarchy of needs. The parochial, chauvinistic approaches of students of work in an industrial society cannot provide complete understanding. We need better, bolder, more basic concepts of work.

Karl U. Smith (1965) has provided such a concept: work is not only the central subject matter of industrial relations but also the primary determinant of the human condition. Work and tool using shape the evolutionary development of man and define the nature of man's adaptive behavior, the nature of his personality, and the structure of his society. He argues that our fundamental values and assessments of human personality are defined by the organization of human work, which is always changing and developing. In selecting a particular mode of behavior from among the many possible modes, man learns both individual and social adaptive behaviors; both behaviors determine the overall structure of society and of man's environment. In a given society, certain work behaviors are more adaptive than others, and consequently some persons rise to the top, some groups pass others, status and compensation are determined, and work processes and roles are developed. The human environment is increasingly man-made; those who survive in this setting must successfully practice newly acquired behaviors and keep adapting to technological and social innovation. Thus Smith argues that success, in occupations of different levels of difficulty, provides our only objective yardstick for measuring intelligence of adults.

According to Smith, work pervades almost all other areas of life. It is through the economic influence of the job that the ordinary individual's needs and status in society are determined and governed. Not only are the economic influences of work important, but the fact that man spends such a considerable amount of time working is also important. Work occupies man's time to a far greater extent than other motivational behavior patterns surrounding, for example, food and sex. Smith rejects the Freudian view that work symbolizes destructive tendencies of aggression and holds that tool-using behavior —work—is its own reward; it is self-motivating. He acknowledges that education, religion, recreation, and warfare influence human behavior, but he contends that work is the central influence. He calls his concept a biosocial theory: in the three-way interaction of behavior, tool design, and environmental control, there is constant feedback between the individual and his biological and social environments.

Smith says that the most important concern of industrial societies today is to understand the degrading effects of division of labor, alienation, unemployment, and underemployment on the personality organization of individuals and on social and economic organizations.

Peter Drucker (1969) also advances some intriguing new concepts of work. His argument may be summarized as follows: Technology has greatly reduced the gaps in income distribution and living standards in industrialized societies. There remain, however, severe gaps in living standards among the races. With a few exceptions in Latin America, all of the world's nonwhite nations are poor; in the United States, poverty is also concentrated among nonwhites. Mao Tse-tung has replaced Marx as the ideological guide of the frustrated masses. Handouts and poverty programs provide only transitory relief because they treat symptoms rather than causes. To deal with these problems and to prevent them, we must recognize the fundamental changes in the nature of work to be found in the knowledge economy.

Drucker argues that knowledge rather than science is now the foundation of our economy. Borrowing a term from Fritz Machlup, Drucker estimates that the "knowledge industries" accounted for one-fourth of the Gross National Product in the United States in 1955, one-third of a larger GNP in 1965, and will account for one-half of the GNP in the decade of the 1970s. The knowledge economy creates a revolution in the life of the worker. He is no longer born to an occupation (his father's) but has many choices. Access to the best jobs comes through school rather than through experience, apprenticeships, and other old-fashioned ways. Knowledge does not eliminate work but changes its form and emphasis: Knowledge is now the basis of skills—people learn to "work smarter." The knowledge economy not only creates profound changes in workers' lives, but greatly increases occupational mobility.

Life expectancy has increased greatly in developed countries in the last century. More significant, however, the *work-life* expectancy has doubled in the last 100 years (Drucker, 1969). Thus the labor force and its earning power also have doubled. The longer work-life span, according to Drucker, is due not to advances in medicine but to changes in the nature of work. Technological advances in agriculture and industry have reduced the number of physically destructive tasks. Today's work is sufficiently productive that more people can go to school for longer periods before joining the work force. Work can be an end in itself, providing challenge, satisfaction, and a sense of achievement for the worker as well as producing goods and services for society.

LEISURE AND NONWORK

What is nonwork? Increasingly nonwork does not mean free time. We manage to fill our free time but not with the pursuits of leisure envisioned by the ancient philosophers—contemplation, reflection, and placating the gods. Our concepts of leisure and nonwork are quite limited. The generation that grew up during the Depression has even been conditioned in some ways against leisure. Personal and social values help define leisure. The general American ethic seems to be, "put time to good use." Fighting, drinking, and debauchery are bad; contemplation, adult education, religion, the PTA, and fighting pollution are good. Strong drink was the curse and opiate of the masses in the nineteenth century; today, we are mesmerized by television.

For ancient man, there was no sharp distinction between work and nonwork. Work was never a general, abstract concept. Although various primitive cultures worshiped gods of love and war, there were no gods of work. By the time of the Greeks and Romans, who had over 30,000 gods and goddesses, only agriculture, hunting, and blacksmithing were recognized in the diety. Even today, distinctions between work and nonwork are blurred. Probably the best definition of leisure is "discretionary time"; for example, on Sundays one can choose to go to church or to sleep. But discretionary time may refer to work as well. A boss might say, "I want this report done by Friday afternoon, but you can work on the other report at your leisure."

Wilbert Moore (1963) argues that many people today have more discretionary time than the ancients did. Yet we feel the pressure of time because we organize our lives according to schedules. Our economy is based on a time discipline; most people are paid for time worked. Our schedules must synchronize with those of others, whether we are homemakers or assemblers. Our time is not our own; free time is at a premium. Harold Wilensky has noted that the modern worker has now attained about the same amount of leisure as his counterpart in the thirteenth century.

Leisure and work mean different things to different people. Some people do not have enough discretionary time, some have too much. Some people seek to find satisfaction in their jobs; others seek it in leisure activities. Some define work as what we get paid for doing, but we also get paid for time not worked—vacations, holidays, coffee breaks. Moreover, the mobility of our labor force implies great discretionary choice. Only slightly more than one-half of our labor force, and less than half of the population in twentieth-century America, work at full-time jobs.

The individual cannot sharply distinguish work from nonwork because work is still integrated into the whole of life. Work concepts affect society, and vice versa. Consciously or not, the worker seeks peace, adjustment, or other satisfactions and thus it is that religion, magic, superstition, and authority have played dominant roles in man's work concepts. Man lives not by bread, ergs of energy, social status, or habit alone. The individual seeks correspondence with his own environment; both he and his environment change through time. He measures his success or failure by whether his efforts yield the results he desires.

Within a society there are substantial differences among individuals and among subcultures, and there is no generally accepted compass or yardstick to measure their complex behaviors. Some people manage to equate expectations and results; some do not. With the increasing tempo of technological, social, and cultural changes—with the population, communication, and knowledge explosions—more choices are available to workers, to people generally, and to societies. More competition and conflict may be generated. Reactions will range from alienation to revolution.

UNANSWERED QUESTIONS

Generalities do not explain the substantive meaning of work. Because there are tremendous differences among individuals, cultures, and social strata, there is an almost unlimited variety of meanings and adaptive behaviors for work. The questions we ask—Is work efficient? Is it satisfying? Is it profitable? Does one view work in short-run or long-run terms?—all reflect the individual and special concerns of employers, employees, or consumers. We must recognize differences as well as similarities in work and nonwork concepts. The disadvantaged ghetto dweller conceives of work quite differently from a research engineer. The older workers of today who entered the labor market during the Depression perceive work differently than their children do. The new urban industrial worker in an emerging, developing country has to assimilate concepts far different from those he embraced as an agricultural peasant. He must learn not only a new technological system but a new social system as well. He sees new payoffs from work, including rising material living standards. But there are also new problems and costs associated with the industrial life. Employment is a relatively new concept and social institution; employment relationships are new, changing, and complex. To use Clark Kerr's terminology, "webs of rules" develop, involving fourfold relationships among employers, unions, employees, and the public.

To the individual, work may be the means to take care of his family, educate his children, and fulfill his fondest desires. Typically, the worker does not think beyond his role; he is unaware that somehow society must answer many questions that involve acceptance of joint or common concepts. Among those questions are the following: (1) Who shall work and who shall not, and how is this to be decided? (2) What tasks shall people perform? Shall this be decided by the state, or by the market? (3) Who shall be the managers and who shall be managed? (4) How shall the goods and services provided by workers be distributed? On the basis of contribution or need? (5) Who shall be responsible for training and retraining workers? (6) How shall we distribute income to people who are unable to work—that is, the aged, the infirm, the unemployed? (7) Shall we try to build employee satisfaction as well as efficiency into our jobs? (8) Shall we seek to provide jobs that maximize people's vocational capacities? (9) Need we, and can we, legislate satisfactory employment relationships? How do we prevent and resolve industrial conflict?

These are only a few of the questions that must be answered if we are to have satisfactory work and employment relationships. Our principal barrier to their solution lies in our lack of understanding of basic work concepts. It is ironic that specialists study work from different angles—psychology, industrial engineering, sociology, economics, and physiology—and yet know very little about the worker's concepts. Those who study work concepts seem to operate in closed, seemingly unrelated systems.

New work methods are vastly superior—in terms of efficiency and supply of goods and services—to those that have gone before. Our average material standard of living far surpasses that of kings only a few generations ago. Our technological concepts are well developed and are improving at an apparently accelerating rate. There is no economic or technological reason why we cannot turn some of this wealth into satisfying higher-order objectives, such as personal fulfillment, both at work and in our time away from work. But our brief survey of historical concepts of work has not revealed a unified system of frameworks or approaches from which to study work on either an individual or a social basis. Consequently, it is difficult to know how to proceed. It is only in the last 50 years that the newly developing social and behavioral sciences have seriously begun to study work. Only a very small portion (far less than one percent) of the proceeds of work go to the study of work. Work is an integral part of life; both are exceedingly complex. We need to study the concepts of work and nonwork if we are to arrive at understanding, and possibly wisdom, in the future.

SUMMARY

In primitive societies, work was physical and necessary for survival. As man moved beyond the primitive state, technological advances and economic considerations led to new forms of work. Man used tools to capture, control, and multiply his strength so that work became easier and more varied. Division of labor led to status hierarchies. An individual's worth was defined by the nature of his work. With the advent of urbanization and industrialization, work values and concepts changed drastically.

The concept of work has changed along with philosophical and religious beliefs. In his primitive state, man probably thought little about what work meant to him; nature was fickle and survival uncertain. In Greek and Roman culture, work represented punishment; nonwork was man's most honored state and ultimate goal. The Hebrew philosophers and early Christians saw work as a form of punishment and a necessary means of atoning for sins. Not until Luther and Calvin's time did work come to be viewed as worthy in its own right, as a means of serving God. Hard work and virtue went hand in hand, and riches were signs of the magnitude of one's virtuous accomplishments.

The Industrial Revolution stripped work of its religious connotations, but status was still determined by the quantity and quality of one's work-earned possessions, and materialism flourished. The status of workers, in contrast to owners, was further degraded, and labor unions were formed. Of the three major types of unions—business, uplift, and revolutionary—the major thrust in the United States was by business unionism, which sought to use the basic methods of capitalism to gain higher wages and better working conditions for union members. Labor unions have been a major force in shaping employment and work concepts in American industry.

Today, no single concept of work is sufficiently widespread or definite to serve as an infallible guide to the future. Concepts held by early philosophers and religious leaders seem simplistic when compared with the increasing complexity of work in today's world. More fundamental concepts are needed to extend our thinking beyond the parochial frameworks of the past. Illustrative of the beginnings made in this direction are concepts suggested by Smith (1965) and Drucker (1969).

Smith sees work as the primary determinant of the human condition. Smith's biosocial theory emphasizes the instrumentality of work for shaping and defining man. Different work environments are determined by the adaptive capabilities of different individuals. Drucker states that the great discontinuities and gaps in living standards and income distribution around the world will be overcome only by revolution in the knowledge economy. With knowledge, work will change its form and emphasis; workers will learn to "work smarter," and will thereby have many more work options available to them in addition to greatly increased mobility.

Efforts throughout history to differentiate between work and nonwork have been unsatisfactory. Though any individual can usually distinguish between what, for him, constitutes the tedium of work or the fun of nonwork, one man's work is often another man's leisure. In the world of the future, work and nonwork will come to be even less easily differentiable as society develops improved systems for defining, designing, manning, and rewarding the optimal production of goods and services.

REFERENCES

Drucker, P. F. *The age of discontinuity.* New York: Harper & Row, 1969.
Moore, W. E. *Man, time, and society.* New York: Wiley, 1963.
Smith, K. U. *Behavior, organization, and work: A new approach to industrial science.* Madison, Wisc.: College Printing and Typing, 1965.

SUGGESTED READING

Borow, H. (Ed.) *Man in a world at work.* Boston: Houghton Mifflin, 1964.
de Grazia, Sebastian. *Of time, work and leisure.* New York: The Twentieth Century Fund, 1962.
Durant, W. *The story of civilization: Part I—Our oriental heritage.* New York: Simon & Schuster, 1945.
Gross, E. *Work and society.* New York: Thomas Y. Crowell, 1958.
Gross, E. *Industry and social life.* Dubuque, Ia.: Brown, 1965.
Heneman, H. G., Jr., & Yoder, D. *Labor economics.* (2nd ed.) Cincinnati: South-Western, 1965.
Herskovits, M. J. *Economic anthropology.* New York: Knopf, 1952.
Hoebel, E. A. *Man in the primitive world.* (2nd ed.) New York: McGraw-Hill, 1958.
Kerr, C., Dunlop, J. T., Harbison, F. H., & Myers, C. A. *Industrialism and industrial man.* Cambridge, Mass.: Harvard University Press, 1960.
Nosow, S., & Form, W. H. (Eds.) *Man, work, and society.* New York: Basic Books, 1962.

Schrecker, P. *Work and history: An essay on the structure of civilization.* Princeton, N. J.: Princeton University Press, 1948.

Shostak, A. B., & Gomberg, W. (Eds.) *Blue-collar world.* Englewood Cliffs, N. J.: Prentice-Hall, 1964.

Tawney, R. H. *Religion and the rise of capitalism.* New York: Harcourt, Brace & World, 1965.

Tilgher, A. *Work: What it has meant to men through the ages.* London: George C. Harrap, 1931.

Toynbee, A. J. *A study of history.* (2 vols.) Abridgement by D. C. Sovervell. London: Oxford University Press, 1946.

Weber, M. *General economic history.* Translated by F. H. Knight. New York: Greenberg Publisher, 1927.

CHAPTER 3

Work and Nonwork: Intercultural Perspectives

Harry C. Triandis
University of Illinois

WORK: VARYING CONCEPTS

How do people of different cultures and in different countries define work and nonwork? In what ways can a comparative view of work in diffcrent cultural settings help us determine the nature of work in the future? In an attempt to answer these questions this chapter explores cultural differences in the definition of work.

Work Has Social Meaning

In almost every culture, work has some significance beyond economic compensation. Work allows people to form social groups, gives people a feeling of self-respect, and offers a person a place in the pecking order of his society. Though work has social meaning in every

Helpful comments on an earlier version of this manuscript were made by Glenn Bryan, Ed Bruner, Milt Derber, Roy Malpass, Ernest Nevitt, and Christos and Steve Triandis.

culture, the emphasis on work varies. In some cultures work is a virtue, and work success is a divine sign of worthiness; in other cultures work is a necessary evil. Consider the following examples of cultural variations in the social meaning of work.

Anthropologist Raymond Firth studied the people of Tikopia and the Maori of Oceania. In several cultures, work and religious beliefs are closely related. In Tikopia *work (fekau)* is a general term used in opposition to concepts such as rest and participation in sexual activities. However, the word includes a large number of ceremonial and many ritual activities. In Tikopia work is good, and idleness or sloppiness is a religious offense. For instance, when the men of Tikopia build a canoe it must be completed promptly, since the shape of the canoe represents a divine spirit, and it would be an offense to the gods to keep its pieces separate for a long time. Efficiency is a virtue, and the people of Tikopia work early in the morning; they take breaks only long enough to drink fresh coconut milk or to smoke. They dance and play games for recreation, but the ideal social activity consists of cooperating groups of men working hard, joking, conversing, and enjoying their work. Often work is done in a spirit of rivalry between competing groups. The Maori divide occupations into sacred *(tapu)* and profane *(noa)*.

In contrast are the Siriono, who live in the Amazon rain forest. In their environment food does not keep for a long time, and they hunt every day for meat. When the Siriono are not hunting they sleep, lie in their hammocks, or repair arrows. If they find tortoises that can be kept alive near their hammocks, they will not go hunting at all.

The Siriono word for work includes activities such as building a house, gathering firewood, planting, and tilling. They have different words for hunting and collecting, since these activities lead to immediate rewards. Thus, when the Siriono must work, they do; but when they have enough food, they rest, eat, have sexual intercourse, sleep, play with their children, groom each other, sing, dance, or drink. No one is criticized for remaining idle.

Even in the United States, there are considerable differences in work concepts. A random sample of employed men in all parts of the United States was asked in the early 1950s: "If by some chance you inherited enough money to live comfortably without working, do you think you would work anyway or not?" Eighty percent replied that they would want to keep working. When asked why, two-thirds of those wishing to continue work responded in a positive way ("to keep occupied"; "to keep healthy, because it is good for a person to work";

"I enjoy what I do"). The remaining answers, however, were negative ("I would go crazy if I did not work"; "I would not know what to do with my time"; "I would feel bored"). Unskilled workers divided evenly into those who would continue working and those who would stop working. In general the less skilled appeared to be motivated by economic reasons and, given the chance, would stop working or would change jobs. The highly skilled—for example, professionals—seemed to work for the intrinsic satisfactions they derived from work-related activities.

Biological Man in Culture

Some concepts of work probably have a strong biological basis. Man's biological structure has evolved over a period of 400 million years, but his cultural variations are of relatively recent origin, perhaps only 15,000 years old. Culture is the manmade part of the human environment that molds the learned behaviors—those most often observed in man. Yet some universal, biologically triggered behaviors are present in all cultures. All men tend to defend territory, cooperate with ingroups and compete with outgroups, and form hierarchies of dominance; hence when we note such tendencies in aspects of work relations we may assume that they are basic to the species. On the other hand, man's adaptations to different environments and different supplies of resources produce varied definitions of territory, ingroup, outgroup, dominance, and cooperation. The effect of environmental conditions on the concept of work serves as an example.

Some Environmental Determinants of Work

Man survives and prospers by exploiting the resources available in his environment. Since environments differ, the activities involved in such exploitation differ from one setting to another. Man not only makes use of natural materials provided by the environment but also of human resources provided, for example, by wars, the imposition of hierarchies of dominance, and the defense of territory against invasions. War can be viewed as another kind of work, and the extermination of enemies as part of the struggle for survival.

There are definite patterns of war and homicide frequency. War is most frequent among large concentrations of population. War often occurs around the Mediterranean Basin, but is relatively rare in remote mountains or jungles or in inhospitable climates. An Eskimo writing in 1756 could not understand why white men hunted each other like seals and stole from strangers. He was glad that the climate at the North Pole was so inhospitable that white men did not wish to stay. He was surprised that the Europeans had not learned better manners among the Eskimo and proposed to send medicine men as missionaries to the Whites to teach them the Eskimo way of life. In sum, climate and population resources, as well as other aspects of the environment, may result in one or another form of exploitation.

Economic activities, such as hunting, gathering, agriculture, fishing, industry, and provision of services, also depend on the nature of the environment and yield very different types of work patterns. Different kinds of work activities, in turn, develop rather different patterns of personality and social organization. For example, the Eskimos, who live in a hunting environment where individual ingenuity is most effective, score differently on measures of perceptual style[1] than the Temne of Africa, who live in an agricultural environment requiring cooperation and conformity. The perceptual style of the Eskimos is more similar to that of males in developed societies, that of the Temne more similar to that of females in developed societies. In rearing their children, Eskimo parents stress independence; the Temne stress obedience.

Our remote African ancestors coordinated their activities when they hunted in groups. Cooperation within the primitive exploiting unit later extended to herding, agriculture, trading, and providing services. In some cultures the cooperating unit, or ingroup, is extremely small, often limited to the immediate family; in other cultures it is large. In modern corporations employees cooperate with others regardless of kinship, race, or religion. The modern corporate giants are extremely effective cooperative units that exploit both environmental and human resources.

Thus work has similar meaning in different cultures insofar as man brings to the concept of work his ancient tendencies to cooperate, to defend his territory, and to establish social hierarchies. But work concepts vary as different environments require different solutions for effective exploitation. The following discussion examines in detail these similarities and differences.

---

[1]Perceptual style refers to the way one interprets external stimuli. For example, some people tend to emphasize differences between themselves and others, other people tend to emphasize similarities. Various tests of the perceptual style of Westerners show another dimension of perceptual style: males exhibit more independence while females show more dependence, conformity, or obedience.

Basic Cultural Similarities

In most societies, cooperation takes place in the ingroup, but the definition of the ingroup varies from society to society. In some societies it is very narrow and includes only the individual's extended family. In others it is a little broader, including not only family but also friends and others who are concerned with one's welfare. In some societies religion defines the ingroup, in others race, in still others occupation. In complex societies several of these criteria exist simultaneously.

Within the ingroup, members behave cooperatively, fairly, and, in some cases, with self-sacrifice. On the other hand, responses to the outgroup vary from distrust, suspicion, or fear to extreme hatred and hostility. Thus, when an individual sees another person of different race, religion, or nationality, he tends to distrust or even fear him. This syndrome exists all over the world, where ingroup-outgroup relations are often tense and sometimes bloody.

If man is removed from his usual environment and placed in an artificial one, his behavior in the new environment reveals basic territorial responses. In a series of experiments conducted at the psychological laboratories of the United States Navy, sailors lived in pairs in isolation rooms for periods of several weeks. They did not come in contact with the outside world during that time except when they opened a passage to receive food. The men had no way to entertain themselves other than by talking to each other. Teams of psychologists monitored, recorded, and analyzed their behavior. The psychologists observed an intensive development of territorial behavior. "This is *my* chair!" one would angrily shout to the other. In many cases the experiment had to be discontinued because the relationship between roommates had become dangerously strained.

Such observations suggest that some of man's basic tendencies lie dormant but will emerge when he is placed in strained circumstances. For example, war and even sports events reveal territoriality. At the same time, however, man has evolved social institutions through a process of natural selection that rewards cooperation. Love, altruism, and self-sacrifice must have developed from such a selection process, and those who at certain times displayed more of these qualities probably had a greater chance for survival. Thus, too, man developed strong bonds with his ingroup. Whether it is an Ashanti *fie* or a Greek *parea,* the ingroup dominates man's behavior. In today's Congo, for example, government ministers grant special favors to ingroup members, in direct contradiction to all principles of modern political science.

The ingroup is not a particular group. Instead, it is the unit of cooperation demanded by a particular situation in a particular environment. In one situation the ingroup may be one's immediate family; in another it may be the modern nation. Typically, the greater the emergency and sense of common fate, the broader the ingroup. Also, if cooperation with more people yields greater rewards, the ingroup will be large. Thus, if everybody is reasonably affluent and can take care of himself, the rewards are maximized by having a broad ingroup, as is the case with modern middle-class Americans. On the other hand, if most people are poor and a potential burden to one another, the ingroup is restricted, as is typical in the countries around the Mediterranean.

The lack of resources is one of the major causes of narrow ingroups. A large ingroup implies that one is obliged to help a lot of people. If many members of the ingroup are in trouble, an individual has less chance of help from the ingroup. Limiting the size of the ingroup increases the probability of help for any member. Thus among black ghetto dwellers in America, the ingroup tends to be small and the ingroup boundary relatively unstable. Such narrow ingroups are dysfunctional in modern industry, where the unit of cooperation is often rather large. It is likely that the size of the ingroup is one of the factors that has prevented the assimilation of blacks into industry, dominated by whites.

We have already mentioned the dominance hierarchies—pecking orders—that exist in one form or another in all human societies. Such pecking orders, whether they involve the head wife of an African Mende, who regulates the activities of the other wives (and sees that the husband does not spend more than three consecutive nights with any one of them), or the foreman in a modern steel factory, have a good deal in common. Cultural factors regulate who can have how much influence over whom, and under what conditions. Sometimes these cultural patterns clash with well-designed systems of administrative practice. Thus, the rational Western bases of employment specify that a boss should hire the most competent employees he can obtain. When an institution designed to operate on that basis is introduced into a culture that operates on another system, much strain is likely to occur. Thus, the European advisor to President Joseph Mobutu of the Congo was surprised to hear the President say that he avoided his mother as much as possible because she would tell him who to have as minister to his cabinet, and he had to do what his mother said.

People in all cultures define "my work" and "your work," and hold notions about the people with whom they will cooperate, beliefs about the need to exclude from their work environments people with certain characteristics, and about ways of structuring their work activities so that they conform to the existing pecking order of their society. Thus many of the basic concepts of work, work partners, and work institutions are similar in form if not in content, in all cultures.

DIFFERENT WINES IN SIMILAR BOTTLES: LOOKING FOR CONTRASTS

Psychological Differences in Work and Leisure

Definition of work. The concept work often exists in opposition to the concept rest or leisure, but specific concepts of work and nonwork vary considerably from one culture to another. For example, the Tiv of Northern Nigeria apply the term *work* only to agricultural activities. They usually put in six hours of such work in the morning before going to the market, the courts, or engaging in other kinds of activities that other cultures would also call work but that the Tiv call by a different name. The Trobrianders of the Pacific Ocean do not have an abstract general term for work; instead they use specific words such as to fish, to hunt, to carve, or to till the garden. The Finns consider manual labor "real work" and white-collar occupations "something less than work."

War is sometimes classified as work, but the Trobrianders view war as a spare-time activity, and the Kapauku include warfare in their word similar to our word *leisure*—which, of course, also applies, depending on its use, to trade, warfare, politics, love making, and hunting in our culture.

In Burma leisure means a trip to the pagoda feast or down the river with a minimum of effort. The Sino-Tibetan people, who spend much time smoking opium, regard leisure even less actively.

The value of work. Some cultures value work very highly while others do not. There is no apparent correlation between types of cultures and degree of value accorded work, but there appears to be little enthusiasm for work when it is either too easy or too difficult. Psychologists have studied the aspiration levels of persons in laboratory situations involving very easy, moderately difficult, and very difficult problems. The studies show that the easy situations are boring, the difficult are demoralizing, and the moderately difficult are stimulating. Sociological studies suggest that lower-class (difficult situation) and upper-class (easy situation) children exhibit less concern with work success than do children born into the middle class (moderate difficulty).

In another study, university students experienced (a) small, (b) intermediate, and (c) great frequencies of success in a given set of tasks. The students' attitudes toward the concepts *effort, luck, control, fatalism, time,* and *mastery over nature* changed according to the degree of success they experienced. When the chance of being rewarded was about 50-50, the students expended the greatest effort and valued *hard work* and *effort* most highly. When they were rewarded either rarely or very frequently, the students placed more value on *luck*. In the easy situation (frequent rewards), they were more likely to see man's control of the environment as appropriate, but in the other two situations, they saw the passive acceptance of an imposed environment as more appropriate.

The implications of these findings are considerable. In an easy environment where the resources are abundant and easily accessible, such as in the South Pacific or among the younger generation of American upper-middle and upper classes, people may value luck and mysticism (that is, the idea that the goods of society are distributed by a mysterious random means that is unaffected by what one actually does; poverty is due to bad luck, riches to good luck). On the other hand, a very strong expectation that man should control his environment, coupled with the inability to obtain such control, can also lead to disappointment, frustration, and hence anger and escapism. Perhaps the current mysticism and escapism on the part of the young in today's affluent societies may be partially explained in these terms. In very difficult situations, as in parts of modern India, mysticism and emphasis on luck appear again. In situations that are intermediate in difficulty, as in late nineteenth- and early twentieth-century America, effort and hard work are emphasized.

Moderately difficult environments fall midway between the equator and the icecaps. Thus, the attitudes toward work of those in the great plains of Western Europe and of China are mostly positive. The Chinese, for instance, have always been praised for their labor and diligence. Modern China stresses the virtues of manual labor; leisure time is for political studies or participation in workers' clubs.

China's neighbors to the north and to the south, however, do not share her positive work attitudes. In Mongolia, for instance, women have always worked hard, but men tend to spend most of their time drinking tea, eating *taryk* (a kind of cheese) and *urma* (the creamy skin of the milk), and visiting and talking with each other. To the south, the Cambodians and Laotians would rather "be free"—that is, not work for others—than earn a good wage. Further south, in Malaysia, the difference in the working efficiency of the Chinese, the Indians, and the Malays is so clear that it has been institutionalized in pay differentials. These differentials have recently been attacked as unfair by the Indians and the Malays, and although they are on their way out, no one disputes the basic difference in work involvement.

In very warm climates, where effort is difficult, there is less emphasis on hard work. In Thailand, the prevailing view is that life should not be a round of duties; work must be pleasurable, and leisure must follow whenever possible. The Thais admire the nonpolarized attitude toward the world which they call *choei,* and which means that they shun ego-involvement. They work, but without interest or regularity. In Okinawa the prevailing view is that "everyone dislikes work, but rice is delicious." So, work is a necessary evil. Similar attitudes exist in the extremely difficult environment of Lapland and in the extremely easy environment of Oceania.

The differences in work concepts between the Chinese and the Indians or Malays can probably be traced to the differences in environmental difficulties. How long do such cultural patterns persist? We do not know, but it seems they go on for several generations, once they become imbedded in traditional patterns of child rearing. In the case of American blacks, such persistence of cultural pattern may be traced to the days of slavery when it was extremely difficult for a black to get anything out of his environment. Minimum effort, trust in mystical phenomena, and little concern with changing the environment developed at that time; this is beginning to change only now.

Motivations for work. People work not only for money but also because of tradition, duty, obligation, beliefs in magic, social ambition, position, and vanity. They work to obtain power, to validate their self-concept, and to achieve intellectual or aesthetic satisfaction.

In American culture there are a number of examples of those whose work is not motivated by economic considerations. Among the most obvious are the Rockefellers and Kennedys, whose work is more motivated by social ambition, position, tradition, duty—or as some would argue, to obtain power—than by financial incentives. Work has such a great value in the United States that the very rich often work hard in the role of philanthropists; rarely are they idle. Intellectuals and artists often toil endlessly on projects that can do very little other than provide self-satisfaction. Often the end product is so obscure and of such limited interest that the author or artist himself pays to have it brought to the attention of others.

Margaret Mead, writing about the Manus, describes fear of illness and death as important motivations to work. The traditional Manus believed that if one did not produce enough or pay one's debts, Sir Ghost would not provide protection from illness and death. They also believed that the failure to launch some enterprise that should have been undertaken could cause illness.

An additional motivational basis involves a highly complex set of financial arrangements, by which a young man would have to obtain money from "financial backers" to pay for a wife. In order to become the master of his household, he would have to repay the "loan." For this he had to have an income, which he could obtain by making wise investments in the wives of other villagers.

Burdened with both supernatural and earthly reasons for hard work, the Manus tended to work so hard that Mead thought many died of overwork at about age 40. However, the modern Manus, who have experienced considerable contact with Americans during World War II, have learned to use labor-saving devices, which have increased their life span. Furthermore, Europeans introduced to the Manus the concept of time; now work stops at 4 P.M., and the Manus play darts or rest. Often two men work while three others watch; there is much gambling but little inclination to earn money. Twenty-five years ago the Manus worked hard and ate well, but they did not depend on foods that required money. Today their diet is money-dependent, but work habits have changed, and they tend to be less well nourished. Thus modernization has brought mixed blessings.

Attitudes toward type of work. Attitudes toward types of work also differ from culture to culture. The Thais, for instance, prefer government work. They would not consider doing other work so long as they could get a government job, and feel that they were born to govern and prefer to leave the "dirty work" such as money-making, to the Chinese. By contrast, the Afghans find peaceful or sedentary work distasteful, and dislike working for the government. They consider war their primary vocation. Manual work is scorned in some places, such as among the Afghans, but is glorified by the current officials of mainland China, and by the Finns. In India the lowest types of jobs have to do with the touching of excrement, while in Okinawa the most menial job is that of pig killer.

Some Descriptive Differences in Work and Leisure

Work schedules. Medieval Europe probably enjoyed 160 holidays per year; although the working days were long, people worked no more than about 45 hours per week. Historians believe that there were about 175 holidays per year in Imperial Rome. Such data suggest that the concept of leisure is not so recent a phenomenon as some social analysts claim.

In many cultures today, work is done only every other day, and in others it is distributed so that everyone works some of the time as opposed to some people working constantly and others not at all. In Korea, some industrial jobs, for instance, are done by two groups of workers who alternate working and smoking. Work is measured by the lengths of pipes smoked, and if you ask a worker, "How long will this job take?" he might answer, "Between five and six pipes." By contrast, some cultures, like the Hunza of Kashmir, have no concept of deserved leisure or holidays. This pattern is found in very different parts of the world, such as among the Indians of Ecuador and in the case of about one-third of Korean farmers.

Most cultures, of course, are not as extreme in their views of work schedules as the ancient Romans or the Hunzas but fall somewhere in between. For example, the fishermen of Okinawa work about 10 days per month because of bad weather. The rest of the time they do some trading, but they usually spend most of their time visiting each other. The Ganda of Africa work an average of 4.4 hours per day. The Kapauku of Oceania work every other day but then work very vigorously; the women work about two hours per day longer than the men, but they tend to work more slowly.

In certain cultures the distinction between work and leisure is blurred. The Hunza of Kashmir, for instance, work every day of the year, from 4 A.M. until it is time to sleep around 8 P.M. However, they never hurry, and they frequently interrupt their work to eat, chat, and rest.

Some subgroups in certain cultures engage only in leisure. Thus in Korea, those who considered themselves gentlemen refused to do any manual work; if necessary, they preferred death to begging or to resorting to work considered beneath their dignity. They sat, smoked, meditated, and engaged in the arts, but could do little else according to their particular code of behavior. They grew long nails to distinguish themselves from those who did manual work. Similar, but less extreme, aristocratic attitudes toward work can be found among cultural subgroups in many parts of the world.

Work rate. Work rate varies considerably from culture to culture and thus so does the rate of spending earned income. In contrast to the average middle-class worker in an industrial society, the Mallahs of Uttar Pradesh, India, earn much in a very short period of time by exerting themselves tremendously during a short work season. The Greek sponge divers, who live on the islands of the Aegean Sea, have a relatively short season during which they work as much as 20 hours per day, often under dangerous conditions. The cultural pattern that has thus developed in some of these islands is quite unusual. The spongers receive in advance their total yearly income from the captain of a boat. After setting aside about one-third of this amount for their families' necessities, they spend the rest in a short two- or three-week period when they spend, gamble, and give generous gifts and loans. After this spending spree, they ceremoniously sail away from their families for several months. When they return, they often have no money and must exist on loans until the next working season.

Workers in traditional societies can work at their own pace, but industrial workers must follow a regulated schedule. For instance, in the Middle East, an artisan who makes brass trays will work only when he feels like it; when he finishes a tray, he sells it and starts another. In mass-production industries, however, a worker must work at the pace that machines impose upon him.

Absenteeism is common among industrial workers in most traditional societies, and is a serious problem in India, the Middle East, and Eastern Europe. The Communist regimes in the Balkans have at times instituted extreme measures to motivate workers to work regularly. During one period in Bulgaria, absenteeism was punished by condemnation to a forced labor camp.

The Communist world has partially solved the problem of absenteeism by introducing strong peer pressures and by instilling the socialist concept of work—that the individual owes allegiance to the group and must work according to group-determined goals. Production quotas increase regularly; workers receive bonuses for surpassing quotas; in some situations Party members often work hard for a short period of time and thus encourage others to emulate them; rival teams compete for prizes. Every worker is encouraged not only to produce more than others but to help others produce more. The concept of work as a competitive game is also advocated by some American industrialists.

Activities that accompany work. The kinds of activities that accompany work vary. In some cultures, work is performed rhythmically, accompanied by singing. Among the Yao of East Africa, singing is essential; among the Miao of Thailand, however, singing is taboo.

Public and private work. Some cultural groups require a certain amount of work for the benefit of the entire community and design elaborate systems to reward such obligatory work. Other cultures suffer from chronic undercontribution to the public effort. An anthropologist once noted that in Greece when a road was to be built connecting a village with a main highway, most males in the village refused to work on its construction. In Malaysia, on the other hand, when the banks of a river once eroded badly and needed repair, almost every male of the community worked to repair them, regardless of whether his property was threatened by the water.

Sex differences in work attitudes. A survey of the Human Relations Area File, which abstracts the ethnographies of several hundred cultures, suggests that in many societies women work harder than men. Even in societies where the men conform to lax working habits, such as in Mongolia and in Lapland, the women are quite diligent. In some equatorial African cultures, this difference is quite extreme. Among the Wolof, for example, the women complain that the men sit and eat. In Tepoztlan, Mexico, the men argue that harder work keeps women faithful and out of trouble. Tibetan women are so active that they have little time for pilgrimages to the shrines; the men, however, regularly attend religious festivals. Thus while the Tibetan women do most of the heavy work, such as carrying goods, handling boats, planting rice—and do so while singing songs—the men attend to their relationship with the supernatural. Among the Monguor of Manchuria, as well, the women do most of the work; the men are idle much of the time. The older wives ask their husbands to acquire additional wives to lighten the burden of their work.

Work-Related Concepts across Cultures:
A Systematic Comparison

Many of the preceding observations were not strictly comparative, but were rather general anthropological descriptions of work concepts in different cultures. However, one body of evidence, collected by a score of psychologists working with Charles E. Osgood at the University of Illinois, has emerged from the systematic, comparative study described below.

Data were collected by use of a questionnaire called a semantic differential. The format is rather simple: a particular concept, for example *work,* is judged on a set of a dozen seven-point, bipolar scales, ranging from, say, *good* to *bad.* If a person thinks that work is *extremely good,* he marks the point at the extreme good end of the scale; if he thinks it is *rather good,* he marks a point that is one space away from that end of the scale; if he thinks that it is *slightly good,* he marks a point two spaces away from the good end; if he thinks it is *indifferent,* he marks the middle of the scale; if he thinks it is *slightly bad,* he marks the point one space away from the middle, toward the bad end of the scale; if he thinks it is *rather bad,* the next point; if he thinks it is *extremely bad,* he marks the point at the extreme bad end of the scale. The dozen scales were selected to represent three basic dimensions—evaluation (good to bad), potency (strong to weak), and activity (active to passive). Each dimension was represented in each culture by equivalent scales (not translations of the scales). It is sufficient here to point out that one set of scales dealt with *evaluation*—ideas like *good, clean, desirable,* and *beautiful* underlie this dimension. In one culture the statistical analysis of the responses yielded such ideas; in another the equivalent ideas might have included *nectarlike* and *fragrant.* Although each culture may have yielded different scales for judging concepts, the clusters of the scales suggested equivalent themes. Thus a systematic comparison of the meanings of each concept was possible. Another dimension was *potency,* and this included the ideas *strong, powerful,* and *big;* still another dimension was *activity,* and it included the ideas *active, alive, hot.*

Derived from such rigorous methodology, the findings of this study suggest that there are, as anthropologists have already noted, large cultural variations in work and work-related concepts (Osgood, 1964). Compare, for example, the responses of a sample of American high school students with those of a similar sample of students from Mysore, India. First, according to the responses, the concept of *work* is much more potent in America, and slightly more active. A *worker* is rated more highly in America, and he, too, is rated more potent and active in America than he is in India. Consistent with the higher rating of work is the higher rating of *wealth, success,* and *salary* in America, whereas *festivals* are rated higher in India than in America. On the other hand, *labor unions* are rated more positively by the Indians but seen as less powerful than by the Americans.

It does not necessarily follow that when a culture evaluates *festivals* relatively low, it will evaluate *work* relatively high. Greeks evaluate both concepts much more positively than do Americans. In fact, the Greeks rate the concept of *work* abnormally high, though, like the Indians, they do not value *wealth* as much as Americans do. Finally, the Greeks see *labor unions* as weak, but they do not differ from the Americans on the evaluation dimension.

The high ratings of Americans of *work* on the activity dimension reflects, of course, this culture's extreme preoccupation with work and the prevalence of the idea that time is money. In other cultures this attitude is completely absent. However, in those societies that come into contact with Western cultures there is a fair comprehension of the time-is-money concept. For example, an anthropologist who recently studied the Zuni of New Mexico found that the Zuni use this concept when they hire people to do their agricultural work in order to have more time to engage in the more profitable activities— making jewelry, for example.

Do the semantic differential ratings obtained in various cultures reflect differences in the environment? Unfortunately, the sample of cultures in Osgood's data consists mostly of European and Asian cultures in the intermediate range of difficulty of the environment. For example, there is no Eskimo (difficult environment) sample, nor is there a sample from the jungles or islands of the South Pacific (relatively easy environment).

For the purpose of this discussion, a sample of those concepts that were related to work by high school students were selected from Osgood's list of words. The words chosen were *student, school, problem, work, examination,* and, perhaps less relevant, *salary* and *business.* Selected also was a sample of words that were related to leisure: *play, leisure, game, playing chess, playing cards, playing tennis,* and, perhaps less relevant, *lotteries.* Examined first was the similarity in the responses of the persons taking the semantic differential in various countries to these particular words. To be noted here is overall similarity—that is, similar evaluation, potency, and activity scores for all the words. By correlating the mean responses of one cultural group with the mean responses of every other cultural group, clusters of similarity among the cultural groups were obtained. This analysis suggested the existence of four similarity clusters among the countries represented in the samples:

    I. Belgium, Finland, France, Germany, Illinois (U. S.), Italy, the Netherlands
   II. Hong Kong, Japan
  III. Greece, Iran, Mysore (India), Yugoslavia
  IV. Delhi, India, Lebanon Arabs, Thailand

Since complete data concerning the other countries in Osgood's project were not available at the time of this writing, analysis and interpretations must be limited to the countries mentioned above.

What interpretation can be offered for these groupings? It is obvious that group I included developed countries. The environment is relatively easy (for the middle-class high school students tested in Osgood's project) in these countries. Group II consists of developed societies in the Far East. Hong Kong has vast masses of low-wage citizens, but has also many middle- and upper-class Chinese. It is the latter group that is most likely to be in high school. Hong Kong, as an environment, is highly developed; cars, movies, boats, and other luxuries are as accessible there as in Japan. Group III represents fast-developing countries or cultural areas. Specifically, when the data were collected, Greece and Yugoslavia had just experienced rates of economic growth that were double or triple those of the more developed economies of Western Europe; prosperity was in the air. Iran, also, is experiencing fast development; oil provides a sound economic basis and the recent land reform has created new opportunities. Mysore, India, is one of the least crowded parts of India and enjoys an excellent climate and adequate resources to make life pleasant. Near Mysore is the major industrial city of Bangalore, where India's major car and aircraft manufacturing is located. It is not surprising that Mysore and Delhi are in different clusters. Finally, the fourth cluster is relatively representative of the less developed countries.

It is useful to classify the four clusters of cultures by difficulty of the environment. Groups I and II are easy, but group I is easier than group II; group III is intermediate, and group IV is the most difficult environment. But how do people in these four kinds of cultures respond to the semantic differentials? First, they are rather similar in their responses; that similarity indicates that the concepts they are judging have about the same meaning to all of them. Thus within this framework of similarity it is possible to look at the few differences and interpret them more confidently.

There was a tendency for the cultures in groups I, II, and III to see the concept *work* as more active, and for the cultures in group IV to see it as more passive. The concept *student* was seen as active in groups I and II, very active in group III, and passive in group IV, just as might be expected from the environmental hypothesis. However, the evaluation scores do not show the same pattern: the French, Germans, and Italians, as well as the Delhi and the Lebanese samples, evaluated the concept *student* as very good. On the other hand, an interesting pattern of evaluation emerged for the concept *school.* The cultures in group I gave relatively neutral responses, group II gave somewhat positive responses, and groups III and IV gave very positive responses. The best support for our environmental hypothesis can be found in the way the concept *problem* was evaluated across cultures. In cultures of group I a problem was bad, in group II it was neutral, in group III it was good, and in group IV it was bad.

The probably irrelevant concepts *salary* and *business* suggested little. All cultures thought that salary was very good, powerful, and active, with the exception of Delhi, Lebanon, and Yugoslavia, who thought that it was passive. *Business* was very active in group I, neutral in II and III, and passive in IV.

An interesting pattern, however, emerged in the case of *examination*. Examinations are bad in groups I and II and good in groups III and IV; they are passive in I and II, active in III, and passive again in IV. Thus in environments of intermediate difficulty examinations are both good and active.

The responses to leisure-related concepts yielded only two results worth noting. The concept *leisure* was seen as good in the cultures of groups I and II and bad in the cultures of groups III and IV. The concept *game* was seen as very active in the cultures of groups I, II, and III, and as only slightly active in the cultures of group IV.

In short, though these findings do not provide overwhelming evidence for our hypothesis about the correlation between degree of environmental difficulty and responses to work-related concepts, the data do give some support.

An additional comparison was made between the evaluation of work-related concepts and two other variables: (1) the mean maximum temperature of the city in which the data were collected and (2) the difference between the mean maximum and mean minimum temperatures in that city. The top scores for the evaluation of *school* were observed in Iran, Hong Kong, and Lebanon—all rather hot places. One result was rather striking: the rank-order correlation is .82 between thinking that school is good and temperature maximum, a correlation for the sample tested that is not likely to occur by chance more frequently than once in every thousand experiments. Another finding was that the evaluation of *play* had a correlation of .51 with the difference between maximum and minimum temperature, a correlation for the sample tested that is not likely to occur by chance more frequently than once in every 20 experiments. Since 14 correlations were computed in this particular study, this correlation of .51 is suspect. Nevertheless, it may be true that when there are major variations in temperature, as in Iran, playing is more fun. Temperature itself, it appears, is not a good correlate of attitudes toward work and leisure. The relationship between climate and work must be examined in a more complex way, taking into account humidity and other factors that may influence the ease of work and the desirability of leisure. Obviously, much more research is needed to relate different aspects of the environment to cultural differences in the perception of work and leisure.

STRENGTHS AND WEAKNESSES: CURRENT VIEWS OF WORK IN INDUSTRIAL SOCIETIES

The major differences between modern industry and primitive work systems lie in the degree of division of labor and the needed coordination of activities in modern settings. The rational organization of work requires that it be divided into elements so that everyone, including those with minimum abilities, can perform his work effectively and so that all work can be coordinated as the well-articulated parts of a whole.

The production of a modern automobile serves as an example. First must be the conceptualization of a model design. Market research reports, studies of consumer buying habits, and trends in the economy are each analyzed by a different specialist; the results are fed to central management locations where decisions are made. Then the design is developed. Thousands of specialists in engineering, materials, economics, accounting, and finance work on different parts of the design. Once the final design has been established, production lines are restructured, workers are hired and trained, materials are purchased, money is made available to obtain various items as they are needed, and controls are imposed to insure quality standards. These activities are further regulated by other specialists, some in charge of the consumption of gas and electricity, others in charge of steam and water, others in charge of scrap, still others keeping track of expenditures or work-incentive programs. Once the model is produced it is tested; then begins the long series of marketing and advertising. As many as five years may elapse between the decision to build a particular new car and its realization; it is a fantastic enterprise, marvelous in its coordination.

No one really understands every detail of the modern production process. Top management considers broad legal, financial, and marketing aspects; the next management level deals with the specifics of these aspects, with production programs, and with financial auditing. Lower levels of management focus on the details of narrower problems. Finally, a worker on the assembly line may only turn one screw. Such specialization and coordination have made possible the development of extremely complex products at prices accessible to mass markets. But the ultimate cost has been the creation of millions of meaningless jobs.

Joe is one worker who was studied by social scientists. His job required him to weld 25 pieces to the metal underbody of an automobile. The movement of the conveyor belt was strictly timed and allowed Joe only one minute and 52 seconds for every set of weldings. Every day Joe had a 10-minute breather in the morning, half an hour for lunch, and 10 minutes in the afternoon. There was no way to get even 10 seconds ahead. Day after day, year after year, he welded 25 pieces to the underbody of each car. The models changed, but not his job. He felt tense, his wife complained that he came home exhausted, and he snapped at her and the children. Joe reported that he would like to get another job, but felt he could not quit this one because it paid too well.

Georges Friedman (1961) examined the effects of modern factory organization on work and leisure, and concluded that men like Joe are alienated from such work. They feel that their work is depersonalized; it gives no feeling of participation, offers few satisfactions other than material rewards, and does not use the individual's abilities to the full. The result is that the individual attempts to escape in daydreams; he loses interest in the work and focuses on his leisure activities.

Modern work arrangements lack variety, pace the work at artificial rates that conflict with the natural rhythms of the human body, do not provide enough opportunities for initiative and skill, and allow neither a sense of pride and accomplishment nor status rewards.

When job situations in the so-called underdeveloped parts of the world or in the less efficient occupations of our society are compared with the highly coordinated achievements of modern industry, it appears that modern efficiency has been attained at the expense of the worker's sense of well-being. In underdeveloped societies, work has social meaning; in some cases it has ceremonial, religious, and ritual connotations. Modern industrial manual work has lost all social significance. Furthermore, traditional, preindustrial work follows the physiological cycles of the individual; modern rational work, scientifically structured by management, forces the individual to conform to proscribed work patterns.

An anecdote will help illustrate this last point. A few years ago a toy manufacturing company had a high turnover among workers in its toy assembly department. The company hired a psychologist to study the problem. After talking with the workers, the psychologist recommended that the company give the workers the option of regulating the speed of the conveyor belt. The industrial engineering department of the company refused to accept this recommendation, claiming that it had studied the job in detail, knew exactly the proper speed for the conveyor, and asserted that the workers would produce very little if they were given the chance to regulate this speed. The psychologist presented a steep bill to the company and left. Faced with an enormous bill for a recommendation that was not going to be adopted, the president of the company decided to give the consultant's suggestion a try. A rheostat was installed that regulated the belt to three speeds: low, medium, and high. Medium speed was the pace the industrial engineers considered normal; the other two speeds were 25 percent lower and higher, respectively. The workers were delighted with the change. They began their day by setting the rheostat at low. After about an hour at that speed they turned it to high, where it stayed until about half an hour before lunch time; then the workers reset the speed to low. After lunch, they again started at low and then went directly to high. The result was a higher production rate.

Noteworthy here is that rarely did the workers use the medium speed; that speed, originally set by the engineers, was unrelated to normal rhythms. In the morning and after lunch, people tend to respond more slowly, but after they really wake up, they are inclined to work vigorously. This natural variation in work rhythms was ignored by the engineers who had imposed a work environment that did not fit the human condition; hence many workers had preferred quitting to staying in an uncomfortable job.

Needed: Some New Concepts

How can the job be made to fit the human dimension? In preindustrial societies where the per-hour income is very low, people work at their own pace. They stop or start, depending on how they feel; they do one job for awhile and then another; they use their ingenuity, imagination, and skill to a considerable degree; they derive many satisfactions from accomplishing their tasks; and they gain rewards in their social hierarchies that reflect their efforts. The social meaning of work derives from other social contacts such as the worker's other activities within his ingroup. But modern industrial society has divorced the job from other social relationships, and so many of the rewards associated with work are missing. Job specialization has increased production but it has created alienation.

How can the benefits of higher production be combined with the benefits of work tailored to the human scale? There must be new forms of organization and new concepts of work. Some modern analysts have advocated that job enrichment, job rotation, and automation will provide a partial solution. Automation has some very positive features: it increases the scope of a worker's activities, it makes his work more varied, it allows him to pace himself at more normal rates, and it allows him to use his imagination and skills to a greater extent. On the other hand, it forces workers to assume much greater responsibilities than they are often willing to assume. The job tensions associated with the operation of extremely expensive equipment are significant, and many workers prefer a less demanding job. It thus seems unlikely that automation will be widely adopted in underdeveloped cultures. First, these cultures have an abundant supply of low-wage labor, and, second, they have little money for the foreign exchange needed to obtain the automated equipment.

In developing new concepts, we must keep in mind that man needs to derive social meaning from his work. If the worker sees his company as his territory, if he sees his work group as part of his ingroup, and if he feels comfortable in the hierarchical arrangements of the company management, he is likely to experience less alienation. If he can use his abilities, exercise his judgment, have sufficient responsibility, and experience self-realization on the job, he is more likely to be more satisfied and to give more effort. If rewards for high effort are readily available from both the hierarchy and the ingroup, he will put forth high effort. If the environment is sufficiently challenging so that it is not too easy, and sufficiently rewarding so that it is not too difficult, his effort will increase.

SUMMARY

On the surface, cultures appear to differ greatly in their definitions of work. However, regardless of culture, men are similar in that they defend their territory and form ingroups characterized by internal cooperation and dominance hierarchies. These fundamental similarities underlie the nature of work in all cultures, but the varying demands of different environments induce differences in cultural perceptions of territory, the nature and size of ingroups, meanings of dominance and cooperation, and the form of intergroup competition. Thus societies form different cultural norms about "my work" or "your work," about who may appropriately be included or excluded from work groups, and about work structures that conform most accurately to existing societal pecking orders.

Cultures differ also in a number of work-related concepts, such as definitions of work, value and importance accorded to work, motivations for working, and attitudes toward different types of work. Degree of environmental difficulty appears to be a powerful determinant of the value accorded work. When the environment is either extremely easy or extremely difficult, cultures tend to emphasize mysticism or luck. Cultures existing in environments of intermediate difficulty tend to value hard work highly because they perceive a definite connection between effort and the rewards, both tangible and intangible, of conquering or coping with the environment.

Cultures differ also in a variety of work practices, including: (1) appropriate amount of work; (2) time periods allotted for work—continuously, infrequently (seasonally), or almost never; (3) the pacing or rate of work—steady daily effort or short periods of concentrated effort, or machine versus individual pacing; (4) activities that may accompany work—talking, singing, socializing; (5) whether work is done in private or in public; and (6) appropriate work for a person's sex and age.

Though most cultural differences in work have been inferred on the basis of naturalistic observations of particular cultures, Charles Osgood has made much more rigorous and systematic observations. He used a semantic differential as a means to compare a number of cultures in the nature of meanings they attributed to work-related concepts. His statistical analyses yielded four groupings of countries; concepts within groupings were highly similar, but they differed sharply from group to group. Interestingly, work-related concepts were most highly valued in countries whose environments are intermediate in difficulty; countries with less positive views toward work were those where environmental demands were either very easy or very difficult.

What do these patterns of cultural differences and similarities in work concepts mean for an understanding of modern industrial work systems? Present work systems differ primarily from primitive work systems in the current emphasis on work specialization and the necessity for work coordination, which have made possible the manufacture of extremely complex and sophisticated products at prices accessible to mass markets. But industrial progress has created millions of meaningless jobs. Modern work arrangements lack variety; pace work at artificial rates that conflict with natural body rhythms; provide little opportunity for the exercise of initiative and skill; and provide the worker little sense of pride, accomplishment, or status.

A search for solutions to problems wrought by dehumanizing modern work systems should lead to the development of more flexible systems that encourage employees to design their work so as to regain social meaning from it. The environmental-difficulty hypothesis points toward making work less routine or easy. If the environment is made more challenging, but not too difficult, work may once again become sufficiently rewarding to assure deeper worker involvement, increased effort, and feelings of personal worth.

REFERENCES

Friedman, G. *The anatomy of work.* Glencoe, Ill.: Free Press, 1961.
Osgood, C. E. Semantic differential technique in the comparative study of cultures. *American Anthropologist,* 1964, **66**, 171–200.

SUGGESTED READING

Berry, J. W. Temne and Eskimo perceptual skills. *International Journal of Psychology,* 1966, **1**, 207–229.
Breer, P. E., & Locke, E. A. *Task experience as a source of attitudes.* Homewood, Ill.: Dorsey Press, 1965.
Herskovits, M. J. *Cultural anthropology.* New York: Knopf, 1955.
Morse, N. C., & Weiss, R. S. The function and meaning of work and the job. *The American Sociological Review,* 1955, **20**, 191–198.
Triandis, H. C., Feldman, J., & Harvey, W. Person perception among black and white adolescents and the hardcore unemployed. (Rep. No. 5, SRS No. 12-P-55175/5.) Champaign, Ill.: Department of Psychology, University of Illinois, 1970.
Triandis, H. C., Feldman, J., & Harvey, W. Role perception among black and white adolescents and the hardcore unemployed. (Rep. No. 6, SRS No. 12-P-55175/5.) Champaign, Ill.: Department of Psychology, University of Illinois, 1971.(a)
Triandis, H. C., Feldman, J., & Harvey, W. Job perceptions among black and white adolescents and the hardcore unemployed. (Rep. No. 7, SRS No. 12-P-55175/5.) Champaign, Ill.: Department of Psychology, University of Illinois, 1971. (b)

Triandis, H. C., Feldman, J., & Harvey, W. The perceptions of implicative relationships among black and white adolescents and the hardcore unemployed. (Rep. No. 8, SRS No. 12-P-55175/5.) Champaign, Ill.: Department of Psychology, University of Illinois, 1971. (c)

Triandis, H. C., & Vassilou, V. A comparative analysis of subjective culture. In H. C. Triandis et al. (Eds.), *The analysis of subjective culture.* New York: Wiley, 1971.

CHAPTER 4

Work and Nonwork: Institutional Perspectives

Robert Dubin
University of California, Irvine

What impact do the institutions of society have on work? How may social institutions encourage or impede changes in work concepts? What new work-related social patterns are emerging in developed industrial societies? These are difficult questions; furthermore, the answers are only speculative.

Social science theories typically are built on historical data. Consequently, they have a tendency to model the past, and possibly the present, and may have little predictive accuracy. The theory of social institutions underlying this chapter, however, represents an ahistorical view that generates different predictions about the relations between work and social institutions in the future.

Special thanks to Marvin D. Dunnette, who has contributed substantively to this chapter through his perceptive review beyond the normal call of editorial responsibility.

FOCAL INSTITUTIONS

Simple societies contain one focal institution that dominates other social institutions. Behavior in the subordinate institutions derives from position and participation in the focal institution. For example, if the family is the focal institution, the individual's work behavior cannot be in conflict with his role in the family setting. The political institution may be similarly keyed to the familial institution when, for example, only family elders or males have the right to participate in community polity decisions. Such societies are, therefore, able to achieve coherence and unity because all social behavior patterns are determined by the focal institution.

Historians view the production institution of modern Western societies as focal for all other institutions. In modern urban-industrial societies, religious institutions are not only supportive of but subordinate to the industrial institution (Weber, 1947; Tawney, 1926). The family too has become subordinate to the demands of work, and life styles are shaped by consumer products.

During American capitalism's great boom periods, muckrakers and other social critics accused industrialists of greedily assuming social and political power both in pursuit of economic goals and as a consequence of achieving them (see, for example, Lundberg, 1960). Recent studies of power elites have also argued that social power nurtures itself and is sustained today by the military-industrial complex. Even Keynes (1936), though appearing to suggest the preeminence of the governmental institution (with its emphasis on economic development through such policies as taxation and public welfare), called for encouraging and sustaining the production institution. Galbraith (1967) and Boulding (1953) have shown that the structure of modern society is patterned after modern industry.

Critics of production-institution theories argue that other focal institutions compete for precedence. For example, the humanistic movement in psychology, beginning at least with Freud and reaching its climax in the various schools of group dynamics, has asserted that the real focal institution in society is the company of intimate associates. At first, group dynamics served the production institution by proclaiming the virtues of self-knowledge and interpersonal competence as necessary to organizational effectiveness and increased productivity. Lately, however, group dynamics embraces the possibility that intimate group life, as in a commune, is really the focal institution of society and seeks to enhance personal interaction and shared experience through such means as nude encounter groups (see, for example, Howard, 1970; Reich, 1970).

This brief and incomplete survey of diverse analytical approaches to the study of social institutions indicates that all are anchored in the belief that each society has a focal institution. According to these theories, the focal institution may vary among societies, or may change during the history of a society, but social unity is always dependent upon the dominance of a single focal institution.

I assert that the focal-institution model is inadequate. The alternative model I propose has special utility as an analytical tool for the study of relations between work and social institutions.

MULTI-EQUAL INSTITUTIONS

Society's major institutions are basically independent of each other, and they therefore impinge upon social behavior very differently and in a far more complicated way than assumed by advocates of focal-institution theories. Institutions interact but essentially compete with each other and reinforce their isolation. Modern society is thus institutionally heterogeneous but no less capable of functioning.

The multi-equal institutional model is based on the four characteristics of the institutional structure in modern urban-industrial society: (1) the physical segregation of institutions, (2) the temporal segregation of institutions, (3) the functional segregation of institutions, and (4) the organizational structure of institutional operations.

Physical segregation. The institutions of a modern, complex society are physically separated and, therefore, functionally segregated from each other. Work is separate from family life; the home and place of work often are miles apart. Religious functions may be carried on at considerable distance from either work or family activity. Education has been moved out of the home, and, at least during the period of formal education, takes place within its own physical setting. Political decisions are often made at centers far removed from the areas affected by those decisions. Except for watching television at home, most recreation takes place elsewhere.

Primitive societies carry out all institutional activities within a very limited geographic area and often use the same physical structure or locality for a variety of practices. For the individual participant there is never any sense that physical separation of institutions from each other might suggest their functional segregation as well. The citizen of an urban-industrial society, however, must move from one institutional setting to another. Thus the effort required to travel from place to place may become so great that, if given the opportunity, the individual may choose not to participate in a particular institutional activity.

Temporal segregation. The institutions in which modern man participates are also segregated in time. Nonwork periods follow work periods. Within the daily cycle, a period of nonwork follows a regular shift of work. In the longer weekly cycle, time off from work falls on the weekend. The annual cycle includes an even longer period of time —the vacation—away from work. Participation in one institution utilizes large blocks of time, and few opportunities exist for moving back and forth among different institutional settings within a short period of time.

The temporal segregation of institutions also means that an individual interacts with different groups of people as he moves from one institutional setting to another. Thus, society as a whole becomes less integrated since the same people seldom participate in the same institutions at the same time.

Furthermore, the temporal segregation of institutions provides a time frame for anticipating deferred gratification. From any point within a work period, for example, a worker can estimate exactly how much time must elapse before the onset of a nonwork period. The temporal segregation of institutions provides the individual a very important means for estimating the passage of time before he will have the opportunity to move into another institutional setting. Because it can be measured accurately on a time scale in both work and nonwork institutions, deferment of gratification no longer implies an indefinite point in the future. Thus, if it is clear that family participation or recreation may be enjoyed at a predictable time in the future, some of the unsatisfactory aspects of work may be endured patiently. Or conversely, the deferred gratifications of returning to work after a prolonged absence may have positive consequences for worker motivation.

Functional segregation. Institutions have become increasingly specialized. Work activities have clearly moved out of the family and home setting, as have many of the responsibilities of providing for the education and welfare of family members. Food stamps, unemployment checks, and many other welfare services have replaced help that was previously provided occasionally by both close and distant relatives. The citizen soldier with his weapon above the fireplace has become the professional or conscript soldier. The religious edifice and the professional religious ceremony have replaced the family altar.

Functional specialization has had three consequences for institutions. First, each institution becomes insular—that is, internally consistent with regard to its basic values and the behaviors designed to exemplify or achieve these values. Second, institutions become increasingly divergent from each other with regard to values and behaviors. For example, profit and love may not be reconcilable within a single institution, but separately profit may be one goal of the production institution, and love one goal of the family. Third, institutional specialization provides the mechanism by which new institutions are born and is thus an important source of social change and behavioral innovation. For example, when welfare and educational functions outgrew the family institution and acquired separate institutional identities, the creation of the two new institutions as well as the modification of one old one restructured the entire social system. In a similar way, the welfare capitalism of the nineteenth and early twentieth centuries in the United States lost much of its relevance when business and industry specialized further in the production of goods and services, and left welfare activities to the collective-bargaining or specialized welfare institutions.

Indeed, the most convincing evidence of modern life's rationality is the increasingly functional specialization of institutions, each with a corresponding set of values and associated behaviors, and the relative ease of recognizing the necessity to create new institutions to meet emerging needs or to perform functions sloughed off by existing institutions as they become more specialized.

For the individual, institutional specialization has two primary consequences. First, his life is neatly compartmentalized into recognizable institutional spheres that are somewhat independent of each other. A man can be an authoritative business manager during the day and a student under his professor's authority in the evening without feeling any inconsistency between the two roles. The second consequence is greater social autonomy. The individual is no longer bound to the values of a dominant institution. Values and required behaviors are relative; every behavior is justified by its appropriate institutional setting. But at the same time, the citizen must realize that values of one institutional area do not carry over into others.

Organizational structure of institutions. Institutions have unique organizational characteristics. In order to participate in an institution, an individual must meet the special requirements of its organizational structure. Furthermore, there may be considerable variability between organizations performing similar institutional functions. Thus, even within one institution, the individual's behavior varies according to his role. A small drugstore's owner-pharmacist serves both as a trained professional filling prescriptions for medical purposes and as an entrepreneur selling a variety of goods and running a business for profit.

The Cement that Binds

If institutions are isolated from each other, how then is society knitted together? Durkheim (1933) perceived two different bases for social unity. First, a broad consensus of the dominant values of a society weld society into what Durkheim calls *mechanical* solidarity. Aware, however, that institutions are segregated, Durkheim saw institutions as the constituent parts of society, united through the interdependence of parts to the whole. He called this second form of social unity *organic* solidarity.

Mechanical solidarity, or the consensual basis for social unity, relies on a focal institution that dominates all value systems of the society. How then can social unity be maintained in a society of multiequal institutions? Is the interdependence of institutions sufficient to bind them together in social unity? The answer lies in two central issues: (1) the meaning of interdependence among functionally specialized institutions; and (2) the grounds for social unity when a high level of functional specialization of institutions has been attained.

Interdependence among functionally specialized institutions is best understood by analogy. Ecological chains of life link food and other resources to individual biological species, which in turn are interrelated. The resources and species obviously do not operate at a level of consensus about their relations to each other; nevertheless, the chains of interdependence linking them are complex, and a break at any point in the chain affects the entire ecological balance. Functional specialization and institutional segregation also generate a chain of interdependence. Any failure of a given institution, or a change in its function, will affect other institutions. What sociologists call the "unintended consequences of purposive social action" illustrates the nature of institutional interdependence. For example, the transfer of productive activities out of the home and into the factory ultimately created a way of life for women left at home that can lead to boredom, a sense of purposelessness, and sometimes deviant individual behavior. Also, at least in the United States, the movement of the wife and mother into the labor force has had unanticipated consequences on the family. Third, women have increased their demands for equal rights in the labor force as well as in other areas. Thus, a change in one institution often generates one or more responses in another, and, together, the change and response keep the institutions in balance.

The changes in institutional functions and their unanticipated consequences in other institutions are largely incremental. Fundamental and revolutionary changes are seldom planned or, if planned, rarely produce the anticipated revolutionary consequences. For example, the predicted consequences of the introduction of automation into the productive institutions have yet to be realized in family life, leisure, and political behavior after almost two decades.

We may view institutional interdependence at one of two levels. In his daily life, the individual determines the interdependence among the institutions in which he participates actively by the way he allocates his time and energy to them. On a grander scale, institutional interdependence in society as a whole not only insures the performance of existing essential functions but allows the creation of new institutions to serve emerging functions.

Some degree of consciousness about interdependence among institutions is necessary to both the individual and society. The individual must choose the institutions in which to participate, decide the order of participation, and be aware of what is functionally required by society. Society as a whole must at times be able to distribute social resources and citizen time expenditures among the existing institutional spheres. For example, draft of males for military service is a social allocation of citizen time.

The individual and collective awareness of institutions may also be the foundation for the resistance to institutional change. An individual's participation in an institutional setting often leads to his behavioral commitment to the institution. The form of an institution and its accompanying behaviors may therefore survive long after the function has changed or disappeared. Many practices in the production institution are no longer truly functional. For example, certain welfare practices such as providing for hospital care, medical costs, and old-age security are still retained by most work organizations even though most welfare functions have been separately institutionalized.

Implications for Work

What are the relationships between work and multi-equal institutions? What value will work and citizenship have in the future? And how will the interdependence of institutions advance or impede change in work functions and in places of work? The following discussion considers these questions.

Meaning of work. So long as the productive institution dominated, advanced industrial societies defined good citizenship by the work the individual performed and differentially assigned status to occupations and professions. Financial rewards for different occupations and types of work also varied, and those without paying jobs—the unemployable, the unemployed, children, women, the elderly, and the infirm—received relatively low social esteem.

The affluent society, however, has introduced a new dimension for evaluating citizenship. A good citizen is now a healthy, active individual who consumes a wide variety of goods and services (see Jones, 1965). The affluent society even insures that everyone, including the poor, can consume at a level satisfactory to accepted notions of equity. The idea of a right to consume underlies all demands for public support of good housing, good health, and good environment. In the United States the growth of welfare services led to the idea of a guaranteed annual income unrelated to productive work.

As good citizenship is increasingly defined as good consumerhood, the relation between citizens and productive work will change. All utopias foresee man's release from the need to engage in productive labor (see Bellamy, 1898). In the more traditional utopias, man was free to engage in the leisure pursuits of the rich—art, literature, music—the only historical examples of nonwork activities. What the early utopians did not foresee is the overabundance of goods and services in an affluent society and the constant need of a market capable of consuming these goods and services.

The emerging social system, however, accommodates the problem of consumerism. The consumer is valued as a good citizen. Society approves of what Veblen (1918) called "conspicuous consumption" because it moves the goods from the market and keeps the economy going. The ability to consume and the willingness to do so has become a valued indicator of the state of the economy, regularly measured by the University of Michigan Survey Research Center in its quarterly survey of consumer buying intentions. Consumerism is not limited to capitalist societies but is just as characteristic of socialist societies.

The revision in the meaning of work will have a profound impact upon education. The traditional goal of formal education is the preparation of citizens for a productive role in the society. At the most basic level, education inculcates work discipline, regular attendance, obedience to authority, appropriate behavior within hierarchies (student-to-teacher becoming worker-to-supervisor), and measuring of self-esteem in terms of productive activity. Beyond learning the necessary disciplines that allow effective transitions into productive work, students learn basic language and math skills. Most schools also provide some specific technical skill training.

The future may bring revolutionary changes in education. For example, all technical skill training may be transferred from the educational institution to the work institution, where it can be very specific to an industry or occupation. In the late 1960s and early 1970s Ralph Nader's "Nader's Raiders" began educating consumers and trying to keep producers honest. This was a precursor of the broader movement to educate for consumerhood. The emergence in the 1970s of consumer protection groups in both the private and public sectors points to greater consumer education in the future.

The daily schedule of school may also be modified. If life style rather than occupational competence were to become the primary socialization goal of education, residential schools may be provided for all students in the society.

Changes in the meaning of work will affect work cycles in the life history of the individual. In the modern industrial world the individual typically works approximately 45 to 48 years. The need to work for a living now dominates the most vigorous periods of the life cycle. If citizenship is defined as consumerhood, however, the point in the life cycle when work activity is required may shift from the vigorous period of life. For example, the individual might enjoy the ages 20 to 30 developing himself as a consumer of nonworking time, later making a productive contribution to the society. Alternatively, the work-nonwork cycle could be successive intervals of productive work and nonwork. The individual could work only every other year, determine in advance a lifetime work cycle by choosing his own schedule of work and nonwork periods.

In brief, the changing meaning of work in a modern, affluent, industrial society brings: (1) a shift in the definition of a good citizen from productive individual to wise consumer; (2) a significant modification in the function of the educational institution; and (3) redefinitions of the work-nonwork cycle.

Organization of work. Rapidly changing technologies—in the materials and production processes used and the methods by which products and services are delivered—in modern industry and commerce create problems in two areas: (1) the introduction of new recruits into the labor force and the utilization of the unskilled already within the labor force, and (2) the abandonment of technically obsolete physical plants and locations.

Because modern technology resides in the plant and office, not in the classroom, the schools cannot produce technically sophisticated workers in the vocational education programs as they exist today. In highly technical fields, such as accounting and engineering, a new employee must undergo intensive training in the particular operations of his employer, whose methods may differ significantly from those taught in schools. Work organizations thus cannot expect, much less demand, that the skill training of their labor forces be done in the educational institutions. Indeed, when social conditions require the employment of uneducated adults, the irrelevance of the school becomes even more marked.

The transfer of technical training to the work organization will continue. Notions of cost-related efficiency and benefits have plunged industrial and commercial organizations into the role of educators. New recruits and those employees of an organization with enough seniority to have a claim on retraining will benefit most. As technology continues to change at a faster rate and in more industries, work organizations will become even more isolated from the educational institution.

Work organizations will have greater geographical mobility in the future. Improved transportation and communication systems have now removed geographic limitations; furthermore, a greater flow of capital has reduced the need to use obsolete facilities. Lease-back arrangements (through which a company leases all of its physical facilities for only the period of required use) have also given the corporation greater geographic mobility.

Increased mobility in the American and European labor forces means that labor supply is a considerably less limiting factor in plant location. The family and production institutions are no longer so intertwined that the ties of family would keep employees from following industry to new work locations. Segregation of the production institution would not, by itself, increase mobility with regard to industrial location, but, in conjunction with economic and technological considerations that encourage locational shifts, institutional segregation facilitates mobility.

Adaptive responses of work organizations. What adaptive options are available when the production institution is segregated? First, segregation of the production institution allows greater variation in the shape, structure, and function of both work and work organizations. Organizational boundaries will become less fixed as more organizations subcontract the use of outside specialists, technologists, and services to carry out internal functions. For example, many productive organizations today subcontract the manufacture and assembly of parts for the products sold under their own labels. Even facilities, plants, equipment, and motor vehicles can be used on a lease-back arrangement rather than owned outright. Subcontracting and lease-back not only cut expenses but also open organizational boundaries so that it is increasingly unclear where one organization ends and another begins.

Considerable revisions will have to be made in the current views of employment turnover and seniority. At present, turnover is a costly process for other than seasonal industries; however, turnover may be valuable in the future because it permits the rapid reconstitution of an organization as its technology, products, and markets change. The use of subcontracted services allows an organization to change its labor force without having to consider seniority rights, fringe benefits, and other impediments to rapid employment change. Retirement, health, and welfare benefits will be vested in the individual so that he suffers no loss as he moves among organizations.

Open boundaries of modern work organizations have significant implications for the worker. The organization that pays the worker's wage or salary may not be the organization where he works. The worker may then give his loyalty only to the organization paying his wages rather than to his immediate employer. The inevitable competition for loyalty, commitment, and attachment will add to the burdens of supervision, and perhaps new styles of worker supervision will emerge. Mobility across organizational boundaries enhances the worker's sense of autonomy and provides variety in his work. Simply by changing offices regularly, the Kelly Girl stenographer or typist may have significant job variety although her work functions remain essentially unchanged. Similarly, the aeronautical engineer employed by an engineering subcontractor may move throughout the industry, adding variety to his job even though his specific engineering contributions may be highly specialized and esoteric wherever he works.

Eliminating the permanent attachment of an employee to one company will generate an even greater emphasis on technical competence and skill. Organizations will become more willing to hire a young man directly from college to fill an important position rather than offering the post as a reward to an employee with 20 years seniority even though his skills may be obsolete. The English have used the term *meritocracy* to describe the general trend of making the technical performance and competence of an employee the main basis for judging him. The future labor market is likely to adopt this criterion for hiring and retaining employees.

Since the employment contract of the future will cover only one aspect of the individual—his technical work performance—and since work will no longer dominate the worker's life, the concept of the loyal, lifetime organization man will disappear. Because of the continuing segregation of the work institutions from other institutions, the individual will have little need to bend his behavior and personality to the organizational demands and needs. Employment forms and preemployment investigations will no longer be concerned with the individual's behavior in nonwork institutions.

The need for rapid changes in the technological competence of the labor force will require industry and commerce to provide incentives designed to motivate workers to continue to learn new skills. An organization that promises that none of its employees will be doing the same thing five years from now will offer a significant opportunity for those who respond to an incentive of work variety. The cost to the employing organization for providing such an incentive will be the investment in employee training and reeducation, but the benefits of rapid changes in technology, materials, or markets will more than offset the cost.

New work incentives will probably be immediate and shortrun. Many welfare functions—retirement benefits, for example—now attached to the work organization will be specialized in a welfare institution and separated from the productive organization. Thus, the retirement program of a specific organization will not be a concrete inducement for work. The opportunity for the worker to vary the length of his work day or to choose his weekly work schedule could provide considerable incentive for working.

Work organizations will have to apply far greater imagination than they have in the past to provide conditions that will continue to make productive work acceptable in the society. The opportunity to use slave labor, as in early cultures or in recent totalitarian states and the imperative to work will no longer insure an adequate labor supply.

The productive institution will remain coordinate with other institutions, but within it will have to develop new ways of organizing work to make it palatable and sometimes even attractive.

Change, Time, and History

Because it is part of a social system of multi-equal, functionally specialized, independent institutions, any institution can change. Furthermore, because no single institution is bound to a set of values shared with all other institutions, the direction and extent of its change is unlimited. What, then, prevents bizarre or runaway change in an institution that could disrupt a whole society? When change does occur, why is the rate of change slower than what is theoretically possible? W. F. Ogburn (1922) long ago pointed out the phenomenon of cultural lag. He observed that change in some institutions does not immediately affect coordinate changes in interconnected institutions. According to Ogburn, the lag in response creates institutional imbalance and generates social problems.

Cultural lag can also be viewed as the time delay between a functional change in one institution and the establishment of a new set of links with other functionally interdependent institutions. Thus, social inertia emerges from the need to keep functional balance among institutions, and the rate of institutional change is slowed during the period of redistribution of institutional functions.

On the other hand, within any single institution there are wide opportunities for initiating changes that are not constrained by a value system shared by all institutions. In particular, the production institution has initiated rapid changes in technology and organizational form. These changes deal with producing goods and providing services; they have little effect on the values of other institutions or the society as a whole. For example, there are greater similarities between the production institutions in capitalist and advanced socialist societies than there are between the values of the production institution and other institutions within each kind of society.

By the year 2001, one generation from now, we will see vast transformations in the institutions of society. Major internal changes within each institution will ultimately require a balancing response from other institutions. Thus, the two sources of general social change will be the innovations in single institutions and the adjustment of functional balance among interdependent institutions. The production institution will be a major arena for social innovation.

SUMMARY

Traditional social analyses are based on the concept of the focal institution, such as the family, that dominates all other institutional spheres. Work, like all social behavior, derives its nature from the codes and rules of the focal institution. Social unity is maintained through mechanical solidarity—the broad consensus about the dominant values of society as witnessed within the focal institution.

Some contend that the focal institution in modern society is the production institution, the so-called military-industrial complex. However, this theory fails to recognize that, in our present complex society, several other institutions or trends, such as consumerism and humanism are competing for precedence. A more viable social concept is thus one of multi-equal institutions, separated in time and space, with highly specialized functions (such as education or incarceration of criminals) within specific organizational entities (such as universities or prisons). Institutions interact and compete for resources, including human resources. They differ in their values, and they demand different behaviors of their members. In the multi-equal institutional society, social unity is maintained through organic solidarity—a kind of institutional interdependence. Changes in one institution induce changes in others until functional balance is regained.

What implications do these concepts have for work in the future? First, when the production institution was focal and dominant, individual social status, worth, and rewards were defined by a person's contribution to the enterprise of production. Now, as other institutions move into positions of competing dominance, individual status and worth are defined less easily and with much greater ambiguity. In affluent societies, consumerism is increasingly valued, and good citizenship is, by implication, good consumerhood. The concept of man as a worker and a producer is being replaced by other concepts that reflect new directions in education, personal values, and patterns of work and nonwork in the individual's life cycle. The distinction between work and nonwork is blurring even more as we move from a production-dominated society to a multi-equal institutional society.

Second, work structure and organization will change greatly as institutional diversity and segregation increase. Continuing technological advances and the increasing demands of institutional accommodation will lead to increasingly permeable boundaries between work organizations, more rapid job obsolescence, and greater geographic mobility. Both individuals and organizations will need to adapt. Work organizations will need to design improved incentive systems to attract a labor force and to be ready and able to train and retrain employees. Employees, in turn, must be alert to opportunities for variety and change, and recognize the need for constant growth and development.

There will be many benefits for both individuals and work organizations in the future. Widespread retraining and development, interorganizational task forces, and improved incentive and reward systems will make the individual's work more interesting. For the work organization, greater flexibility in the work force will allow quicker and more efficient adaptation to the demands of technological and social changes.

REFERENCES

Bellamy, E. *Looking backward, 2000–1887.* Boston: Houghton Mifflin, 1898.
Boulding, K. *The organizational revolution.* New York: Harper & Row, 1953.
Durkheim, E. *On the division of labor in society.* New York: Macmillan, 1933.
Galbraith, J. K. *The new industrial state.* Boston: Houghton Mifflin, 1967.
Howard, J. *Please touch: A guided tour of the human potential movement.* New York: McGraw-Hill, 1970.
Jones, P. d'A. *The consumer society.* Baltimore: Penguin, 1965.
Keynes, J. M. *The general theory of employment, interest and money.* New York: Harcourt, Brace & World, 1936.
Lundberg, F. *America's 60 families.* New York: The Citadel Press, 1960.
Ogburn, W. F. *Social change.* New York: Viking, 1922.
Reich, C. A. *The greening of America.* New York: Random House, 1970.
Tawney, R. H. *Religion and the rise of capitalism.* Baltimore: Penguin, 1926.
Veblen, T. *Theory of the leisure class.* New York: Huebsh, 1918.
Weber, M. *Theory of social and economic organization.* New York: Oxford, 1947.

SUGGESTED READING

Argyris, C. *Personality and organization.* New York: Harper & Row, 1957.
Galbraith, J. K. *The affluent society.* Boston: Houghton Mifflin, 1958.
Huizinga, J. *Homo ludens: A study of the play element in culture.* Boston: The Beacon Press, 1955.
Tilgher, A. *Work: What it has meant to men through the ages.* New York: Harcourt, Brace & World, 1930.

Whyte, W. H., Jr. *The organization man.* New York: Simon & Schuster, 1956.

Young, M. D. *The rise of meritocracy: 1870–2033: An essay of education and equality.* London: Thames & Hudson, 1958.

CHAPTER 5

Work and Nonwork: Perspectives in the Context of Change

Edward C. Ryterband
Edward N. Hay Associates

Bernard M. Bass
The University of Rochester

Social, economic, and technological changes will continue to affect work in our society. For example, our persistent drives for more efficient ways of doing work and our expanding technological capabilities have led to automation, which has, in time, altered the nature of work. Fewer workers process and produce goods; more work in service occupations. Many other trends, now underway, will significantly affect the world of work. The most important include population growth, continuing technological change, a revolution of rising expectations, a continuation of the so-called generation gap, changing popular culture, and death and/or decline of traditional institutions. Each of these trends point to changes in the nature, meaning, and institutions of work.

POPULATION GROWTH AND CHANGE IN ITS COMPOSITION

The world's population has grown exponentially during the last 30 years and will probably continue to do so during the next 30. By the year 2001 there will be more than three and one-half times as many people as there were in 1930, and far more of them will be living in urban centers where more types of work will be available.

Unfortunately, world population growth will be unevenly distributed. Industrialized societies are more likely to effect a decrease in their population growth rate through contraception, liberalized attitudes toward nonprocreative sex, and abortion. Contraception and abortion are generally not so prevalent in or acceptable to developing countries, nor do these countries have the technical capacities in urban planning and agriculture to accommodate population growth.

Along with the general growth in population in the United States, there will be corresponding increases in the work force: the growth of the work force will in turn bring further changes in its composition. More old people, more young people, more women, more highly educated people—thus more professionals, technicians, managers, officials, and proprietors—are likely to be in the American work force of tomorrow. For instance, in 1960 in the United States there were approximately 10.5 million people between the ages of 18 and 24 in the American labor force; it is estimated that by 1975 there will be 18 million people of that age group in the labor force (*Fortune*, 1969). This figure does not include the increasing numbers of those who enter college or graduate school and who thus are not considered part of the full-time work force. If the trends for the period 1947–1962 persist—and there is evidence that they will—the work force of the next two decades will include more white-collar workers. For example, in 1967 there were 1,200,000 new white-collar jobs but only 300,000 new blue-collar jobs.

A number of consequences of these demographic changes in the work force are already apparent. People will have a longer working life; many will go on to second careers as they retire from or become obsolete in their first careers. The possibility of the second career exists today in such professions as the military, where retirements at ages 45-50 frequently signal the beginning of another job only remotely related to the first. Also, the appearance of more young people in the work force is pressing management to be better prepared to deal with younger, better educated employees who bring with them more personalistic values and a militant, impatient posture toward achieving their goals. Finally, population growth will force either the expansion of existing organizations or the creation of large numbers of new organizations to provide new job opportunities.

THE TECHNOLOGICAL IMPERATIVE

The Pace of Change

The growth of scientific knowledge, like that of the world's population, continues on an exponential curve. Man is likely to learn more in the next 30 years than he did in the past 100. The accelerating pace alone will make its mark. Rapid change, itself, perhaps the most obvious feature of contemporary society, may become even more symptomatic of society during the next two decades. For example, today's 40-year-old American has witnessed since he was born nearly a two-fold increase in the real Gross National Product accompanied by a 150 percent decline in the value of the dollar. The role of the government in the economy has shifted from 5.9 percent of the GNP in 1931 to 22.9 percent in 1969—a 288 percent increase. Moreover, this rise in earnings, productivity, and government spending has been accompanied by a smaller (36 percent) increase in the total work force.

As technological innovation expands and the pace of change increases, the expectation of change will rise as well. Awareness of change is further enhanced by the mass media, which diligently report new innovations like the supersonic transport and heart transplants. As people become increasingly aware of the temporary nature of things, they feel their own transience more acutely and turn more urgently to the present and its possibilities. With change the accepted norm, traditional values appear to lose relevance, fads come and go, the gap between generations widens, and the individual's place in society seems insecure.

Causes for rapid change: The science revolution and the knowledge explosion. There were an estimated two million scientists, engineers, and technicians in the United States in 1960; during the following decade, it is estimated that the number of scientists, engineers, and technicians increased to four million. The most likely result of similar increases expected for the 1970s and 1980s will be the invention of an even greater number of new products and services available for business, government, and educational organizations. Technological innovations of the next 30 years will probably include the increased use of laser and maser beams for sensing, measuring, communicating, cutting, heating, and welding. New sources of power for ground transportation will make mass and rapid transit more economically feasible. Mechanical aids or substitutes for human organs, senses, and limbs will become widely available. Devices to induce controlled and effective relaxation, new and more reliable educational techniques for assisting public and private learning, permanent manned satellites for interplanetary travel, permanent manned underseas stations, memory and learning pills, pills to control senility and mental illness, small computers for communications in home management—all seem possible by the end of the twentieth century.

In addition to these new products of science, the structures of science will have to change. As our capabilities for producing knowledge increase, so must our efforts at systematically organizing and distributing that knowledge. The number of specialists—systems analysts, computer programmers, microfilm technicians—who become experts in a restricted knowledge area continues to multiply; efforts at organizing this knowledge industry are just beginning, however. Scientists rely more than ever on computers to facilitate their research, but the dissemination of their findings is still jammed at the bottleneck of overcrowded professional journals.

Fully automated knowledge and energy distribution systems, with computer monitoring and information processing as their distinctive work, will be the industries of the future. With the increasing use of electronic data devices for data processing, information processing, decision making, and production automation, people both in and out of industry will know more faster and will thus be able to put it to more uses faster.

The rate of technological development will be limited only by the amount of funds society allocates for research. The current physical and social environments in the United States and in other societies suggest which technological thrusts are most likely to receive heavy financial support in the next 30 years. Science and technology will be asked to solve the problems of air and water pollution; to provide mass and rapid transit systems, adequate housing, and high-protein foods at low cost; to improve educational procedures and law enforcement; and to produce more social and educational innovations such as planned communities and neighborhood control, not city control, of schools.

Rapid change and the working man. It becomes increasingly impractical for a student to prepare for a specific lifetime occupation. Education should emphasize learning how to learn and how to avoid obsolescence in one's occupational specialty. Yet broad academic preparation fundamentally conflicts with the increasing specialization of work. Workers need to have a special skill as well as an opportunity to learn of new developments in their broad fields of interest; thus when the need for a particular specialty no longer exists, a worker can easily move to a new one within his general area of knowledge. The auto carburetor specialist of today has to be ready to become the electric-steam turbine expert of tomorrow. To accommodate environmental change, many work organizations will continue the current trend now found in the advanced technology industries. Internal organization will be more flexible, structured around temporary task project teams rather than fixed departments. The personnel of such departments will participate in long-range planning (a necessity, since total reliance on electronic data-processed planning causes costly errors), create and test new ideas, and develop strategies for routinizing rapid adaptation to changing production needs.

In the future, more managers will find themselves supervising scientists, engineers, and technical specialists. Thus, the managers themselves will need a broad technical background in order to be able to supervise the specialists. Experts and expert teams will make more decisions as no one manager will have access to all the necessary decision-making information. At the same time, opportunities for semi-skilled jobs, such as technical assistants, will continue to grow in number and importance. For example, one professional dentist and a staff of dental mechanics, hygenists, and technicians can care for an impressively larger number of patients than could one dentist by himself.

Organizational responses to the pace of change. Organizations will seek ways to reduce the uncertainties associated with change. First, they may institute organizational buffers to absorb the wide swings of change occurring in the external environment and to insure the stability of the inner organizational core. Specifically, large firms may create separate departments to research and test new developments in technology and the marketplace. Second, although business firms often are interested in promoting change in the marketplace to stimulate sales, organizations may try to control and prevent changes in the environment or channel them into a desired direction. Even now, owners of movie theaters campaign to arouse the public against pay television, rifle manufacturers lobby against gun licensing, and auto manufacturers fight against safety legislation. Third, organizations may cope with change by assimilating the bases for change within their own boundaries. To offset the shortage of trained automobile mechanics, the manufacturer sets up its own special training schools; the Tennessee Valley Authority cannot keep up with the increasing demand for electric power from its flood-controlling dams, so it builds steam plants to generate power; the American firm fears nationalization of its foreign holdings, so it brings into its management large numbers of foreign nationals to develop its identity as an international firm, or it joins forces with local government and business to establish mutual interest in the well-being of the enterprise (see also Thompson, 1967).

Finally, as government and the public interest become increasingly important in the total economy, more professionals and management personnel will work as liaisons between industry and government and between industry and public service. The private and public sectors of the economy will blur, and more personnel will transfer from one to the other sector.

Depersonalization

With the emergence of automation, our products and houses have increasingly become mass produced. Mass production, conformity, and urban crowding will continue to characterize life in the future. People today fear the increasing depersonalization of life in a highly automated, crowded society. Even though some experts insist that the fear of automation itself is not founded in fact and will soon dissipate, it cannot be denied that automation has brought enormous changes to our life style.

One side effect of increasing depersonalization is the loneliness of people crowded together in the cities of industrialized societies. Crowding does not produce intimacy, but leads instead to enhanced irritability. Crowding and conformity, as well as the pressure for greater rationality and productivity, may cause an increase in suicide. New quasi-religions that allow an individual to become close to others through spiritual nonrational experiences will become more popular. Unstructured meetings, the T-group phenomenon, and communal living are all counteractive moves against the depersonalization of a highly automated society. There will continue to be a need for more professional and semi-professional social and psychiatric workers skilled in group work that combats alienation.

Beyond these obvious concerns are still others that automation will continue to produce. Electronic data processing (EDP) probably epitomizes the Protestant work ethic: it is rational, it achieves, it does not complain, and, furthermore, it can be errorless. A society based on these values created EDP, and the success of EDP reinforces these same values. Increasingly, automation will be regarded as a potentially depersonalizing force that will conflict with the individual's desire for self-actualization and autonomy. Machine pacing, mass production, and the increased size of automating enterprises are all potential sources of conflict with the individual's search for identity through work. Many fear, as does psychology-oriented theologian Harvey Cox, that the nonrational components of man's nature are jeopardized in a depersonalized world because society's institutions have little time for nonrational demands and place little value on them. Thus, to be festive, to revel in awe, to celebrate is fine only if done in spare time to restore one's energy for the tasks of life. But the person who emphasizes, reveres, or indulges in emotion without apology will probably increasingly be branded as idiosyncratic. Hippies or yippies may continue to be a part of society in the future, but a large and influential component of our society will continue to react against nonachieving, nonrational people.

THE REVOLUTION OF RISING EXPECTATIONS

Abundance and the Consumer Society

In a setting of unprecedented material abundance, expectations rise. People expect more material goods as they are able to have more. Growth in personal income is likely to continue. Though much of this growth represents inflation, advertising, the availability of goods, the ease of credit, and the opportunities to spend will continue to increase during the next two decades. The mass media—television, magazines, newspapers, outdoor billboards—daily assault our senses with appeals to spend money. Yesterday's luxuries become today's necessities. Subtle and pervasive shifts in the nature of advertising have occurred, enhancing the status and sexual value of a broad range of consumer products. Spend now, pay later, you owe it to yourself, your family deserves the best that money can buy, consolidate your loans, instant credit—these are today's slogans.

Mass advertising has modified consumer attitudes. Self-seeking and self-indulgence may be harsh descriptions for today's and tomorrow's consumer; however, leisure-time expenditures in 1968 in the United States amounted to $150 billion. This estimate does not include expenditures for such items as second cars, second radios, or second television sets owned by many Americans today.

Generally, our social and consumer behavior emphasizes immediate rewards. Obviously, industry has capitalized on increased consumer demand, but a consumer-oriented society may have other, more subtle effects on work organizations. As the concept of delayed gratification disappears, industry may have to institute plans to recognize achievement earlier and closer to the successful completion of work assignments rather than at the end of a fixed period of time. As their patience diminishes and their perspectives narrow, people will seek short-range career goals. It will become increasingly difficult for industry to develop and maintain the supply of technicians in jobs that require long training periods. Substitutes for highly trained human skills such as job and training aids will become even more necessary. More training will take place on the job to allow workers the opportunity to earn full salaries while in training. Self-maintaining machinery and equipment and the use of computer diagnosis and repair will become more common.

Changes in Basic Values

Change will be such a norm that it may become an important value itself—that is, people will value change, newness, immediacy, variety, and novelty for their own sakes. Furthermore, the concept of inalienable rights will extend to material comforts in the future, and the government will probably play an increasingly active role in attempting to fulfill the rising expectations of most people. These changes in attitudes may be, as McLuhan and Packard and others suggest, a function of the new influences of mass media and advertising. On the other hand, they may be a function of changes in the values of hard work and affluence—changes that are a logical consequence of the technological revolutions that have occurred during the last 100 years. Our society's basic values of democracy, equality, and worth of the individual do not seem to have disappeared, and it would seem unwise to speculate whether they are of lesser or greater importance today than they have been in our past. New values, however, emphasize the importance of progress for the sake of progress.

Progress, efficiency, world competition, science, and rationality grow in importance from year to year. This state of flux implies society's willingness to change values rather than its desire to maintain, relatively permanently, one particular set of values. New attitudes toward morals, education, sex, social mobility, competence, and personal responsibility are emerging. Upward mobility, skill in one's trade or profession, and a man's responsibility for himself and family are traditional values of American middle-class society, but the importance of such values is diminishing. It is very difficult to perceive what values a majority of Americans support today or will support in the next two decades. American society is still largely a creature of the Protestant work ethic, but how much so? For how much longer?

The expectation and enhanced value of change will promote job rotation within the factory and office. Just as employees have to be ready to move from one job to another because of changes in the marketplace or in technology, so employers have to be ready to provide job changes for employees who grow to expect such opportunities for new experiences. Organizations of the future will have to consider multiple careers for employees, institute some minimum degree of job rotation where it does not already exist, and establish other opportunities for change such as sabbaticals for its employees to return to school or simply to take long leaves of absence.

THE GENERATION GAP

The young in any society question values, priorities, and prerogatives. Their questions help the structure of society to change, slowly but surely, and thus improve itself in time. The problem today and possibly for the coming decades is that the value of an established structure itself is in question. Increasingly, the questions are not, "What do I want to do with myself in society as it is?" but instead, "Do I want society as it is?" One young man spoke for many when he said that he was fed up with the traditional values of American society. When questioned which values, he responded, "The lot. Work hard. Get along in a corporation. Keep your nose clean and maybe you'll get a home in the suburbs, a key to the executive washroom, and two cars."

The turmoil on our college campuses that began in the mid-1960s is further evidence of a widening generation gap. The increasing use of hallucinogenic drugs on college campuses—and even in high schools and some elementary schools—is yet another symptom. What these events seem to say is that in addition to preferring to live in a world of their own (as youth have always more or less done), an increasing number of young people in our society are living in an anti-world, one whose very existence challenges the legitimacy of the adult world. During the past several centuries, the young have always desired to live in a world better than the one in which they began; what is different today is that some youth are engaging in and, indeed, feel they can properly engage in, a serious power struggle against their elders. Such a struggle is logical in an age when challenge and change have become normative values. The generation gap will not necessarily grow any wider in the 1970s and 1980s, but it will probably become an accepted part of our social fabric.

The gap is greatest between college youth and their elders. According to numerous surveys, noncollege youth seem much more willing to accept the values of their parents. But it is the college-trained youth who form the elite, who shape and lead our meritocratic society and whose new ideologies require new responses from organizations that need such youth as workers and managers. Thus contemporary organizations, earmarked for the most part by their faith in bureaucratic formalism, may have to reconsider the viability of their formalistic ways in the light of the demands and values of youth. Many young, bright college students will extend their highly personalized life style to their job situations. Organizations will have to adapt and change also if they are to attract and keep this highly individualistic but capable labor force. This group may compel management to redesign many jobs and working conditions to conform to the needs and desires of the current generation.

CHANGES IN POPULAR CULTURE

Growing Artistic Freedom

Traditionally, artists and writers have served as social critics. To a large extent they have represented a voice that was contemptuous of bourgeois American society, its capitalism, liberalism, materialism, and organized religion. *Tobacco Road, The Death of a Salesman, The Grapes of Wrath* are three examples from an earlier era of this largely critical, elite cultural heritage. Though now considered classics of American literature, at the time they were written they were less familiar to the general public than *Portnoy's Complaint* and *Hair,* two recent pokes at contemporary American society.

Until recently, the ethics and values of former decades dictated or implied quite strongly that artists and writers should recognize the limitations of propriety, dignity, and the law. The audiences were smaller, and rich patrons could exert influence over artists. In the past decade, however, a climate of change, intense questioning, and greater affluence has permitted works that are increasingly daring, works that in the past would have been labeled subversive or pornographic. For example, prior to the 1960s, movies such as *Bonnie and Clyde* or *The Graduate* and books such as *Portnoy's Complaint* could never have been published and widely distributed. Whether in ideas, words, or visual images, the artist in the last decade has gained unprecedented freedom.

Whether this trend will continue into the coming decades is not known. It will probably continue until there are no legal restrictions, and the responsibility for judging a piece of art will reside only in the individual. Nevertheless, today's artistic freedom reflects a redevotion to the value of personal freedom, which will affect all who share the artist's society. A new candor has emerged, a candor that employees are asking more frequently of their organizations. Such candor and freedom will no longer be the privileges of a cultural or managerial elite but the prerogatives of everyone.

Mass Culture

Traditionally, America's formal art and literature have been aimed at a restricted audience, an avant-garde elite. This elite bought the paintings, saw the expensive plays, and read the books that were produced by the nation's artists and writers. Today, however, the hard-cover book has been subverted by the paperback, the theatre by television, the concert by records and tapes, and paintings are copied cheaply by oil reproduction or other methods. In addition, personal income has risen so that people have more to spend for leisure and thus for participation in cultural activities. The trend makers now more frequently emerge from the masses, not the elite. The antiestablishment sets the pace; what is popular is good.

In response to this mass culture, artists have changed the thrust of their ideas. They are more experimental; they can find some audience for whatever they try or dare to say. As social critics, they are more strident. In a mass-oriented culture, however, much of the thrust of artistic activity lies outside the domain of social criticism. Concepts of art and fashion seem to be changing at an ever increasing rate; an expanding definition of culture now includes clothing fashion, inflatable plastic furniture, and indeed, even comic books. There seem to have been three major movements in fine art in the last decade alone: pop art, op or optical art, and kinetic art. New songs are popular only for a few days or weeks and then are replaced by others. This turnover is in contrast to the longer lasting trends of pre-1900 culture. The impressionists of an earlier day, after being rejected as ludicrous by French neo-classicists, became and continued to be a viable force in art for nearly 30 years. The symphonies of Haydn, the tone poems of Liszt, and the songs of Strauss remained with the classes for whom they were written for many generations. The increasing changeability in the arts seems to reflect growing desire to experiment in art form and content and to change merely for the sake of change. And if trends do last, they may only be the plastic creations of a promoter's ingenuity, such as the Golden Oldies and Flash Gordon revivals in popular records and movies. Artists, of course, are in a somewhat precarious position: the artist who is "in" today may be "out" tomorrow. Indeed, fad and whimsey both seem to be increasingly symptomatic of society today. The hula hoop, Batman, and left-bank existentialism all had a popularity in the 1960s that has since subsided.

Relevant to future work is the extent to which popular culture is producing a larger number of people who are quite sophisticated in a broad variety of political, social, and ethical issues, and who also value self-expression, emotion, originality, and freedom from traditional social constraints. Such sophistication has been associated with an increasing tendency, in the young particularly, to devote themselves to a highly personalistic style of behaving where situation ethics, freedom, and expression are most valued. The young are also becoming harbingers of culture and bringing their influence to organizations. Thus, indirectly, the popular dissemination of the ideas of the artist freed from public censure may forebode pending difficulties for bureaucratic models of organizing. People in work organizations, particularly managers, have reported self-actualization and autonomy to be important to them, and yet these values are the ones that are least satisfied in their jobs. In a culture that shares these values, the need for organizations to allow individuals the means of self-actualization becomes even more imperative. Moreover, the current group-oriented humanism may be irritating to an ethos that enhances individual liberty and expression. And as self-expression becomes more widely accepted, what will it imply for the average worker? He, too, is likely to want more personal liberty, more dignity, variability, and meaning in his working life. He sees that technology can solve the problems of mass transit and space travel; why can it not relieve the indignities of working conditions as well?

THE DECLINE OF TRADITIONAL INSTITUTIONS

The Decline of Formal Religion

In the past, the traditional institutions of religion, family, and the educational system have provided a stable base for society. Individuals knew and accepted their roles as defined by the stable institutional structure. Religion, for example, has traditionally tried to provide guidelines for coping with the pains and stresses of daily living as well as giving hope for a better future. Today, however, many feel that the guidelines have lost their validity and utility, and concern for the future has been submerged under the weight of the greater need for a new ethic to justify the present. Situation ethics increasingly is characteristic of theological thinking today. For some, the new theology gives new answers to old questions; for others, it reflects increasing skepticism about the value of traditional religious institutions. In either case, it criticizes, and calls for change in, religion's traditional stance on moral questions and demands that religious institutions develop new positions on social and political issues such as the population explosion and civil rights. Questioning the role of the church is likely to intensify in coming years. Results of surveys taken in the late 1960s strongly point to a marked reduction from the late 1950s in how positively the young feel toward the utility and importance of formalized religion. On the other hand, evangelism has recently been revived by youth—by the Jesus freaks, Athletes for Christ, and others. This growing, world-wide movement may be explained as either a faddish reaction to the overwhelming change in religion's place in modern society, as a last desperate attempt to hang on to traditional religion, or as the final death-throes of religion.

The implications for the future world of work are twofold. First, the Protestant Reformation provided a religious base for the Industrial Revolution. Calvin emphasized hard work as a means of salvation and material success as an indication of righteousness. This Protestant ethic enlarged upon earlier religious beliefs that sanctified work and condemned idleness. These beliefs provided a code that gave followers a sense of order, individual identity, and purpose at work. In an increasingly secular world, however, religion focuses more on this life than on the next, and material success does not necessarily indicate piety. Thus as secularism replaces salvation, work will no longer be a religiously supported virtue.

Second, the church has traditionally been a source of authority and propriety that may well be the model for the centralized authority and conservative manner typical of business organizations. But as traditional religion declines, personal responsibility and situation ethics emerge as new models. Such new models of responsibility and ethics will require organizations to reexamine their authority structures and perhaps to allow employees to take more personal responsibility for their tasks.

The Changing Community

Urban communities are growing. By the year 2001, perhaps 80 percent of the population of this country will be living in cities. The biggest cities will continue to spread until they merge with other cities to form vast, sprawling megalopolises. Indeed, three such megalopolises seem to be forming already. One on the East Coast includes Boston, Washington, D. C., New York, Philadelphia, Baltimore, and other cities in Connecticut and New Jersey. The second spreads from Chicago to Pittsburgh and includes the northern Indiana and Ohio cities of Gary, Fort Wayne, Akron, Toledo, and Cleveland. The third seems to be forming on the West Coast, beginning in the south at San Diego, spreading to Los Angeles and on to Santa Barbara, and perhaps eventually reaching as far north as the San Francisco Bay area.

Social structures within cities have already changed. Movement from rural areas to cities and, indeed, from city to city has become more common. For example, in the recent decades, the massive migration of blacks from the rural South to the cities of the North has enlarged the population of many northern cities. The entrance into the cities of a large number of unskilled workers, in addition to the prevailing prejudicial attitudes of Northern whites already occupying the cities, has created vast urban slums and ghettos. Suburbs swell as more people move out of the innercity ghettos; suburbs are likely to continue to grow in the coming decades.

Industry must increasingly consider the well-being of people as well as geography and the economy. The availability of talent, transportation facilities, housing, and the needs of minority groups are now important factors in decisions to locate a plant in the suburbs, in the central city, or in certain areas of the country. The innercity riots of the 1960s were in large part due to frustrations stemming from severe inequalities in the quality of life for which both the private and public sectors of society must share responsibility. In addition, organizations may have to consider community service as a corporate objective, sharing the responsibility for fighting air and water pollution and for revitalizing the cities as a place to live and work for the added millions who must, or choose to, inhabit them.

The Changing Family

The role and composition of the family are changing. Until the late 1940s, the family typically included the immediate family and relatives. The members of the extended family lived in geographic proximity to one another. Roles within the family were prescribed, understood, and accepted: father was the breadwinner and mother was housewife and homemaker. The parents were always present and child-rearing practices were unchallenged. Permissiveness was not widely practiced in the 1940s, and the current, more extended role of women unheard of. The family was the focus of social life. In addition, the community surroundings of the family were familiar and homogeneous; more people lived in small towns populated by citizens who were ethnically and attitudinally similar. Reactions against this authoritarianism led to a search for democracy but resulted instead in widespread laissez-faire permissiveness.

Today's city family is different. It is no longer an extended, geographically proximal family. It is now a nuclear family, including only parents and their children. In addition, the members of the nuclear family are often geographically separated. The young remain in prolonged adolescence (absence from the labor market) through extended periods of formal education. Increasingly, the children bring new ideas and practices into the family from sources other than their parents. For example, many youth hold different attitudes toward sex than their parents do.

The children of our increasingly permissive society expect to fill self-defined roles, not roles prescribed for them by parents or other external authorities (including work organizations). Today's youth, like their parents, know more, spend more, and thus expect more—including more personal freedom. A growing number of diverse personal contacts at school and exposure to television and other forms of mass media reinforce their expectations.

In the less isolated setting of urban America, they meet and learn from more people of varied ethnic, occupational, and attitudinal backgrounds than did their parents. As this urban trend continues, social contacts between different groups are likely also to increase, and, as people become aware of the great variety of family practices, the anti-traditionalist trend in family structure and roles is also likely to continue into the coming decades.

One possible effect of the shift from extended to nuclear families is that the work organization will assume the role of the extended family. Organizations have already begun to assume a larger social role in Japan. Company employees and their families develop friendships and loyalties through their ties to the company. As employees change jobs within the same company but make and break friendships by moving from one city to another their new company ties become stronger than new friendships with neighbors in the community.

Changes in Education

Changes in educational institutions are likely to continue through the coming decades. New developments in curricula have already become evident in the elementary and secondary schools. For example, new math and the teaching of foreign languages are present at the elementary school level. Special programs for the gifted and slow students have become more and more common.

In higher education, increasing numbers of students are populating liberal arts colleges, universities, and advanced technical schools.

Students who have emerged from changing and more fluid families have brought to higher education an increasing anti-traditionalist spirit. They are able and willing to question the relevance of higher education. They question not only the value of academic curricula but also the university's entire relationship to them and to the larger society. They question the morality of nuclear testing, the arms race, and America's role in the world. Today's questions may be outdated by 1975, but the process of questioning, rather than the content of the questions, is the important ingredient in the students' new posture.

Current changes in education hold ironic implications for work in the coming decades. Increased enrollment, better teaching methods, and broader curricula will provide work organizations with a larger supply of workers who will be better prepared in sophisticated, technical specialities. On the other hand, this new talent pool is becoming increasingly independent and individualistic and will be less likely to fit into present organizational frameworks of authority and rewards.

The Government

Government and law are another socializing force along with the family, educational systems, and religion. Society increasingly questions the relevance of existing laws at either the federal or state level. Civil rights is today's emphatic issue. In the past 15 years, a variety of new laws governing the civil liberties of minorities have been passed. In addition, the right of government, or any of its agencies, to invade the privacy of individuals is in question; electronic eavesdropping and procedures for arrest are criticized. Most important, there has been in the last decade a documented change not only in the willingness of private citizens to seek government reform but in the method of seeking reform as well. In the past, the vote seemed to be sufficient; today, however, community action groups, combined with traditional lobbies, exert considerably more pressure on legislators to pass or oppose laws. Much of the pressure to end our military involvement in Vietnam has come from both traditional lobby groups like the church and new aggregations of private citizens, especially college youth. On many issues—civil rights, poverty, and peace—organized protests in the form of peaceful demonstrations, passive resistance, and violent protests are becoming increasingly commonplace. Nevertheless, in spite of the growing number of protests and other forms of requests for expanding individual liberty, government's influence on the individual will increase in the coming decades.

Many predict that the welfare economy that began in the 1930s and the regulated capitalism that began even earlier in the United States are likely to continue to expand in definition and influence during the 1970s and 1980s. In the 1960s the government regulated prime lending rates, gun control, steel prices, and civil disobedience; today, government protects the consumer, regulates the speculator, and provides marginal support and subsidies to some degree for almost all segments of society. Tomorrow's business firms will be forced to consider the health and welfare of society: they will be more cautious about expansion, especially when it causes inflationary pressure; they will pay more attention to the recruiting, hiring, and firing practices that are now prescribed by federal law; they will support more federally sponsored welfare programs, participate in more compensatory education programs for the underprivileged and technologically displaced employee, and perhaps contribute to guaranteed minimum annual wages.

Government will probably have some influence in all areas of all types of organizations. Advertising, pricing, and recruiting practices have all come under scrutiny. Television networks have been limited in the amount of prime-time programming placed in affiliated local stations. Cigarette advertising has been curtailed. It would be shortsighted, however, to argue that the government's involvement is only a restraining force; greater aid to small businesses, investment tax credits, reduced stock purchase margins, and the like are all positive, encouraging forces.

Most obvious today are major efforts to provide equal employment opportunity. Civil rights legislation has already forced many firms to be more critical of their own recruitment, selection, and career-development efforts with minority groups. Less obvious influences exist also. For example, government health restrictions on the tobacco industry have encouraged many tobacco companies to diversify their product line in order to survive. In fact, government efforts have forced many firms to change practices quickly (for example, handling masses of recalled cars or investing in new anti-pollution equipment). Making these changes has in turn probably increased those firms' sensitivity to conditions requiring change.

Many trends—in government, in the attitudes of youth, and in technology—point to change in the future. Examination of the future world leaves us with a feeling of enormous fluidity. It is, perhaps, merely avoiding the issue to predict change without specifying in more detail the nature of life in the future. However, reason overcomes the seductiveness of speculation and calls for focusing more on the process of the emerging world of the 1970s and beyond, and less on its contents. It is the change process that already is calling on organizations to be more aware of their own structures and the relevance of their responses to society's changing values and demands.

SUMMARY

Many of the social, economic, and technological forces that have influenced today's world of work will continue to shape the nature of work in the future. The most important of these trends include population growth, technological change, rising personal expectations, the generation gap, changing popular culture, and the demise or decline of traditional institutions. The earth's population is growing exponentially but is unevenly distributed throughout the world. In the United States, a larger population will mean more people in the labor force—including more elderly people, more women, and more highly educated people—and workers will probably remain in the labor force for longer periods of time.

Man's knowledge also is expanding exponentially as a result of the science revolution. Rapid change is a fact of life and will continue to affect people throughout their lives and in all aspects of their lives. A special problem for individuals is the sense of increasing depersonalization, alienation, and loneliness, wrought by massive and rapid changes in population and technology. In his continuing search for identity and self-actualization, man has developed counter-movements such as sensitivity training and new forms of religion.

Accepting constant change as a norm means that basic values must change. What is good, accepted, or popular today will probably not be so tomorrow. Traditional institutions, such as formal religion, educational establishments, the community, the family, and the government, which previously have played important roles in socializing individuals, are either declining in importance or changing in the nature of their influence.

Artists and writers are more actively criticizing the present structures of society and of work. Their practices are in accord with tradition; but, today, they enjoy increasing freedom and latitude of artistic expression, and their criticisms are being heeded by more and more people. Young people today are questioning the established structure and challenging the legitimacy of adult patterns of living. Today's students are more active, individualistic, and insistent in their demands that work be meaningful as well as productive. Self-actualization and personal freedom are of greater importance. If organizations are to attract many of the bright young people of today, they will have to accept, allow, and plan highly individual and personalized life styles for these new members of the labor force.

REFERENCES

Fortune. A special issue on American youth. January 1969, **79**(1), 66–187.
Thompson, J. D. *Organization in action.* New York: McGraw-Hill, 1967.

SUGGESTED READING

Bauer, R. A., & Bauer, A. H. America, mass society and mass media: V. Mass society reevaluated. *Journal of Social Issues,* 1960, **16**(3), 56–66.
Bier, T. E. Contemporary youth: Implications of the personalistic life style

for organizations. Unpublished doctoral dissertation, Case Western Reserve University, 1967.

Boneau, A. The educational base: Supply for demand. *American Psychologist,* 1968, **23**(5), 308–312.

Churchman, C. W. Information retrieval and EDP in the year 2000. In L. A. Appley & A. W. Angrist (Eds.), *Management 2000.* Hamilton, N. Y.: American Foundation for Management Research, 1968.

Drucker, P. F. A conversation with Peter Drucker on the psychology of managing management. *Psychology Today,* March 1968, **1**(10), 21–25.

Drucker, P. F. *The Age of Discontinuity.* New York: Simon & Schuster, 1969.

Fromm, E. *Escape from freedom.* New York: Holt, Rinehart & Winston, 1961.

Gilman, G. The computer revisited. *Business Horizons,* 1966, **9**(4), 77–89.

Gist, N. P., & Fava, S. F. *Urban Society.* (5th ed.) New York: Thomas Y. Crowell, 1964.

Haas, J. A. Middle manager's expectations of the future world of work: Implications for management development. Unpublished doctoral dissertation, University of Pittsburgh, 1969.

Hartman, R. I. Some managerial implications of the cybernation revolution. *Personnel Journal,* 1969, **48**(1), 42–48.

Kahn, H. *The year 2000: A framework for speculation of the next 33 years.* New York: Macmillan, 1967.

Kenniston, K. You have to grow up in Scarsdale to know how bad things really are. *New York Times Magazine,* April 27, 1969, 27+.

Kerr, C. A conversation with Clark Kerr. *Psychology Today,* October 1967, **1**(6), 25.

Kristol, I. Report from the United States. *Fortune,* July 1968, **78**(1), 41–42.

Lipstreau, O. The automation syndrome: Symptoms and treatment. *Management of Personnel Quarterly,* Spring 1966, **5**(1), 31–35.

Main, J. Reinforcements for reform: A special report on youth. *Fortune,* June 1969, **68**(7), 73–74.

Mann, F. C., & Neff, F. W. *Managing Major Change in Organizations.* Ann Arbor, Mich.: Foundation for Research on Human Behavior, 1961.

McLuhan, M. *The medium is the massage.* New York: Random House, 1967.

Michener, J. A. The revolution in middle-class values. *New York Times Magazine,* August 18, 1968, 20.

Murphy, G. Psychology of 1975: An extrapolation. *American Psychologist,* 1963, **18**, 689–695.

Newsweek. Black mood on campus. February 10, 1969, **73**(6), 53–60.

Newsweek. Special report: Sex and the arts. April 14, 1969, **73**(15), 67–74.

Newsweek. Special report: The drug generation grows younger. April 21, 1969, **73**(16), 107–110.

Newsweek. Special report: The class of '69. June 23, 1969, **73**(25).

Packard, V. *The Hidden Persuaders.* New York: David McKay, 1955.

Porter, J. The future of upward mobility. *American Sociological Review,* 1968, **33**(1), 5–19.

Simon, H. A. The corporation: Will it be managed by machines. In H. J. Leavitt & L. R. Pondy (Eds.), *Readings in Managerial Psychology.* Chicago: University of Chicago Press, 1964.

Squibb, A. J. The year 2000. *The Pittsburgh Press,* January 15, 1968, 21.
Staats, E. Government and the manager in the year 2000. In L. A. Appley & A. W. Angrist (Eds.), *Management 2000.* Hamilton, N. Y.: American Foundation for Management Research, 1968.
Wolff, K. (Ed. and tr.) *The Sociology of Georg Simmel.* Glencoe, Ill.: The Free Press, 1950.

CHAPTER 6

Work and Nonwork: Merging Human and Societal Needs

Marvin D. Dunnette
Leaetta Hough
University of Minnesota

Henry Rosett
Emily Mumford
City University of New York

Sidney A. Fine
The Upjohn Institute for Employment Research

MERGING WORK AND NONWORK

Is it too much to expect that in the future man's capacity for work will be fully integrated with his capacity for pleasure? This chapter traces the meager beginnings, the feeble first steps man has

We wish to thank Ruth Bass of the University of Rochester for permission to use portions of her unpublished paper, "Present and Future Societal Needs for Which New Jobs Are Required," and Jean Barsaloux of the University of Minnesota for permission to use portions of her unpublished paper, "Winning Battles and Losing Wars: The New Careers Program." Esther Wattenberg, Director of the Office of Career taken toward that goal and offers some thoughts on further actions to speed the process.

Perhaps in the year 2001 we will no longer suffer from alienation and apathy; quality of life rather than a sense of needing to belong will provide unity of purpose, and we will have learned to build constructively on our differences rather than waste our efforts in group conflict. Human values and organizational goals in the world of tomorrow will stress autonomy, diversity, and acceptance. Achievement, though still important, no longer will be Western man's central aim. Production of goods and services will be planned toward the broad goal of providing pleasure and improving the quality of each person's life. The worlds of work and nonwork will have merged. Man's capacity for joy and his search for self-actualization will find easy and open expression.

A big order? Yes. Even so, its realization seems within reach, though far from easy to attain. So far, society's maladaptive use of its human and natural resources has been counter to the hope of providing a better life for all. Future efforts to improve the physical and environmental well-being of people, however, will yield millions of new job opportunities—new careers to use fully the human resources available in society.

A RESOURCE CONSERVATION INDUSTRY

Technology. In the broadest sense, the age of technology has generated new needs, needs so great and so important that already a new industry—the resource conservation industry—is developing to meet them. Consider, for example, the needs created by just one segment of technology, the invention and mass production of the automobile. Vast numbers of cars and drivers have led to new jobs in driver education, automobile inspection, traffic control, building and maintenance of roads, air pollution control, noise pollution control, recycling junked automoblies, and so on. Other areas affected by the technological revolution are education, urban and rural development,

Development at the University of Minnesota, generously provided detailed information about the New Careers Program for Barsaloux's paper. Statistical data for it came largely from two papers: "Down the Up Staircase," by P. Larson, M. Bible, and R. Falk (Minneapolis: University of Minnesota, May 1969); and "The Ability of Professionals to Supervise Paraprofessional Personnel in Human Service Agencies," by R. Falk (Minneapolis: University of Minnesota, June 1969).

recreation, community services, health care, and pollution control. Needs for improving the quality of our environment and the quality of life create countless new job opportunities.

Education. Only 50 percent of American high schools today provide professional counseling and vocational guidance to students. Increasing the number of counselors—through para-professional training, which will provide new careers—can result in bringing re source conservation job opportunities to the attention of more high school students, encouraging them to enter this field. Better utilization of human resources requires such earlier and greater emphasis on how those resources may be best utilized and directed in the world of tomorrow.

Urban and rural development. Urban-development legislation has a long history; yet, it is estimated that over eight million substandard housing units still exist in the United States. These must be replaced or rehabilitated at prices people can afford. Such work will help to provide jobs and incomes for the unemployed and may also serve as excellent training for such skilled trades as carpentry, plastering, painting, papering, masonry, and glazing.

Rural America also faces the severe problems of low income, few jobs, and substandard education. Extension agents who understand both administrative problems and agricultural development and marketing must train local people. Experts in technical and leadership training could begin to develop the resources of particular rural areas, and trained aides could make significant strides toward improving rural educational systems.

Recreation. Recreational services provide stimulating activities in all phases of human living—educational, social, cultural, and physical—and many new jobs in recreation are created each year. Total employment in the management of public and private recreation areas is expected to reach 1.4 million by 1980. For young people in rural areas, the creation of recreational services provides job opportunities in their own communities.

Within both urban and rural communities, there is already a demand for recreation workers who can perform in many capacities. More personnel are needed to organize and supervise individual and group activities and to direct physical, social, and cultural programs for all ages at hospitals, community centers, and playgrounds. Paraprofessionals can easily supervise special activities such as tennis, basketball, and even arts and crafts. Many recreational workers today are para-professionals who assist social workers in correctional and welfare institutions as well as in schools and hospitals. Opportunities exist also in industrial settings where recreational activities are provided for company employees. There are shortages of trained recreation workers in hospitals, local government projects, and youth organizations throughout the country. Employment opportunities in these fields grow each year.

Community services. Modern cities demand broader and more comprehensive community services, including law enforcement, day care centers, employment services, and family guidance and counseling services. For example, in the United States today, nearly 400,000 children under 12 are unsupervised during their working mothers' absence from their homes. As more women move into the labor force in the years ahead, these numbers will increase. The establishment of day-care centers will create new jobs as well as answer the direct need for child supervision. The personnel working in these centers may also be able to teach children about such things as home management, nutrition, textiles, clothing, furnishings, buying goods and services, use of leisure time, and economic responsibility.

Health. Cities and rural areas are in serious need of trained medical personnel. Many people do not go to clinics or hospitals for care because of family responsibilities, the lack of accessible facilities, or simply fear of institutional complexities. Para-professional medical workers are needed to teach out patients to recognize symptoms of common disorders, do follow-up studies on patients, provide transportation to and from clinics, care for children and older people, allay patients' anxieties, and to listen to complaints. And these medical workers need to be in accessible locations. Hospitals, also, need more personnel to orient and interview incoming patients and, in general, to give patients more attention.

Pollution control and conservation. Nearly every major river system is polluted. Air in urban areas is contaminated. Man's natural environment needs immediate attention to remain habitable.

Yet pollution is as complex as it is widespread. Smog and soot make our cities dirty but also irritate our eyes, injure our lungs, and affect paint, metals, and even the stone of our buildings. Insecticides and fungicides can contaminate both crops and soils and, eventually, the waterways. The environmental crisis demands intensive efforts to combat and control pollution; thousands of workers are needed to help reverse the ecocidal process. For example, sanitation and health workers, testers, inspectors, environmental educators, research personnel, demonstration agents, and people who function as agents for change are desperately needed.

NEW CAREERS FOR THE POOR

Clearly, society's needs dictate an increase in job and career opportunities in education, health care, environmental renewal, personal services, and recreational activities. These new careers can provide greater personal fulfillment for the nearly 21 million poor people in the United States while also leading to improvement in the overall quality of life for everyone. In a word, wisdom in using the forces and innovations of technology to create a resource conservation industry should reduce the waste and destructive exploitation of human and natural resources.

Job training programs have been tried in the past, but unfortunately they have not been uniformly successful. Two case histories may help us to understand what has gone wrong.

NEW CAREERS IN COMMUNITY SERVICES

In July 1967, an ambitious two-year program was undertaken in a large Midwestern city to train and place nearly 300 unemployed or underemployed persons in new jobs. The federal Office of Mobilization of Economic Resources provided funds for the project, and 15 user-agencies, such as the public school system, the police department, and family and children's services, cooperated in the program. These agencies worked with the central new careers office in developing and designing such jobs as teacher aide, correction aide, counselor aide, and social worker aide. Although the jobs varied, most emphasized the abilities of the new careerists to represent the community, to act as cultural translators between agency and community, to recognize the community's problems, and to suggest ways of improving communications between community residents and the agency.

To qualify, applicants for training had to be 22 years old and either unemployed or underemployed, and there were health requirements for some positions (for example, teacher aides could not have any illness that might harm children). After this preliminary screening, heads of households, members of minority groups, ex-convicts, and the undereducated received priority. In short, the program dealt with people who, because of their economic, racial, or educational backgrounds, had previously been unable to gain access to stable jobs and adequate education. Of 900 who applied for the program, 270 were selected to participate. The central office staff met with these 270 new careerists to discuss details about jobs, salaries, and training. Careerists then selected the positions in which they were interested; the central office then referred them to the agencies offering the positions.

New careerists worked 20 hours a week at the user-agencies and devoted another 20 hours to educational upgrading. On-the-job training was provided by supervisors at the agencies (for example, a teacher trained the teacher aide in the classroom). In addition, most agencies provided someone who periodically checked with new careerists and their immediate supervisors and reported the trainee's progress to the center.

While training in special skills needed for particular duties was provided by the user-agencies, a nearby university developed a curriculum to provide knowledge basic to human service jobs. Course prerequisites were waived, and by granting two credits per academic quarter for on-the-job training and by setting up a counseling service for careerists, the university not only provided, but encouraged, educational upgrading. In addition to the university's program, the public school system conducted classes and administered high school equivalency tests to careerists who wanted high school diplomas. Thus new careerists were given the educational base for career advancement and job mobility.

Training results. At the end of the first year, half the men and a third of the women had left the program. It should be noted, however, that many of these people dropped out almost immediately and never were deeply involved in the program. Of 104 dropouts, no information was available for most about their reasons for quitting. Some said they did not like the work they were given; others had been jailed or were having other problems with the law; and some had simply never completed the recruitment and placement phase of the program.

At the end of the second year, 55 more had dropped out, but 111 were successfully placed in permanent para-professional positions. A few of the new careerists had taken good jobs at agencies other than the ones originally contracted to place careerists. Of the 111 careerists employed in permanent positions at contracted user-agencies, 91 were employed as teacher aides, counselor aides, and social worker aides in the school system. Unfortunately, most user-agencies—other than the schools—simply did not provide permanent job opportunities for careerists. One agency, for example, had serious financial and contractual complications that caused the employment termination of all but two of the 54 careerists with whom it had initially contracted. Had it not been for the public schools, almost none of the new careerists would have been employed successfully in the agencies to which they were assigned.

Educational upgrading was generally successful. After two years, 3 had received bachelor's degrees, 23 had earned two-year associate of arts degrees, 103 had completed 45 credits and received certificates, and 26 had successfully passed high school equivalency exams.

Problems. A variety of difficulties and problems weakened the overall success of the program. Problems ranged from such mundane matters as scheduling and coordination of activities to fundamental ideological differences about educational philosophy or the so-called proper roles for new careerists to fill. Most agencies seriously failed to do a systematic job of planning on-the-job experiences for new careerists. Professionals did not know how to subdivide their jobs so as to sort out the parts most adaptable to and meaningful for new career training. Some professionals seemed to guard their knowledge jealously in an apparent concern that the new careerists might seek to replace them on the job market at lower pay rates. Supervisors and new careerists held sharply differing views of the careerists' responsibilities. Many supervisors saw the trainees merely as an extra pair of hands, someone to perform the menial, uninteresting, and onerous tasks. Trainees, in contrast, believed what the recruiting brochures had announced. They expected to be trained and to have opportunities to do important tasks and to improve their knowledge and skills. Dropouts reported that their expectations were not fulfilled. Moreover, the varied natures of the training organizations—that is, the university and the user-agencies—presented a conflict for the para-professionals: were they students or employees? The occasional scheduling of classes during working hours, or vice versa, placed conflicting and impossible demands on the para-professionals.

Role conflict and role ambiguity. Many of the hardcore unemployed probably experienced role conflict between what they had perceived themselves to be before entering the program and what they believed they were obliged to become according to the ambiguous, poorly defined expectations of people running the program. It is also likely that attitudes required for long-term employment were in conflict with their own previous attitudes and those of their friends. Different individuals react to the tension induced by role conflict in different ways. One way, in this program, was to try to get those who were running the program to modify their demands or, at least, to clarify them. Another way was to escape the tension by leaving the program.

Role ambiguity took the form of uncertainty about job responsibilities and about how trainees were to meet expectations. A lack of communication among individuals in the program was probably the source of the problem. The trainees were uncertain how their supervisors were evaluating them, and they worried about job security and opportunities for advancement. In addition, the organizational structure itself contributed to role ambiguity because lines of authority were not defined; it was not always clear over whom a trainee had authority, or who had authority over him.

NEW CAREERS IN HEALTH SERVICES: THE LINCOLN HOSPITAL PROJECT

During the 1940s and 1950s physicians became increasingly convinced of the benefits of treating the mentally ill in their own communities rather than isolating them in remote hospitals. President Kennedy's call for a "bold new approach" in mental health care resulted in the Community Mental Health Centers Act of 1963. Two thousand centers were envisioned throughout the nation, 51 in New York City alone. One of the first and largest programs developed was the Lincoln Hospital Mental Health Service, sponsored by the Albert Einstein College of Medicine of Yeshiva University (see Hallowitz & Riessman, 1967.) Its target was the Southeast Bronx, a congested and impoverished section of New York City, with a predominantly Puerto Rican and black population. The area has high rates of male unemployment, narcotic addiction, and admission to state mental hospitals.

Strategy included opening neighborhood service centers. These storefront offices were to be staffed by 5 to 10 neighborhood mental health aides under the supervision of two professionals. The rationale for using people from the local community was that nonprofessional helpers closely identified with the patient and his situation should be able to reach those who would otherwise be inaccessible. Also, the introduction of indigenous workers into the new jobs was a means of providing meaningful and socially rewarding jobs for them.

Three centers were opened, each serving a five-block radius. These psychosocial first aid stations were to provide a place where anyone could walk in and immediately receive some degree of assistance for any of a wide range of problems. In addition to working with individuals, the stations organized such community action programs as tenants' councils and welfare rights demonstrations.

After three and a half years, 50 nonprofessionals had been trained. Of these, 60 percent were women between 20 and 72 years of age. Seventy-five percent had completed high school. Initial reports were ambitious, enthusiastic, and optimistic. Training and administrative problems were acknowledged, but the positive aspects were said to outweigh the difficulties.

In 1968, the project received the American Psychiatric Association's Silver Award for innovation in mental health. However, in a candid paper presented in May 1968, Emanuel Hallowitz, the director of the Neighborhood Service Center program, described role conflicts and other problems in the project. In summarizing the Lincoln Hospital Project experience, he wrote that the poor do not necessarily have more special knowledge, insight, or intuition than more affluent people, nor are the poor necessarily more sympathetic to others in the same plight. Hallowitz stressed the need to decide whether the goals of a program are the rehabilitation of the employee or the delivery of service to others. Actions designed to help develop better knowledge for a new employee sometimes had to be made at the cost of efficiency in delivering service. It was difficult to maintain realistic standards of performance for new personnel, who often were inordinately afraid of being fired.

The project's difficulties, accurately described by Hallowitz, exploded into open conflict 10 months later. A community mental health worker, who was also a leader of a black militant faction, designated himself the new director. Two-thirds of the staff members occupied the administration building and locked out nonsupporters. The activists were not representative of the community, which was 70 percent Puerto Rican. As one community organizer remarked, "Baby this is some people's revolution. You got white shrinks from Westchester, the VC flag, posters of Che and Malcolm, but there ain't a Puerto Rican button in sight" (Roman, 1971).

One year after the revolution the program still had not regained momentum. A series of acting directors failed to establish stable working relationships with the local community. Many professionals left for positions that promised less conflict. Mental health aides had less mobility than the professionals and most remained, but it is certain that many clients were deprived of services desperately needed, and quite often such neglect led to further deterioration in the patients' conditions.

The very urgency of problems in the Southeast Bronx and the demands for immediate action undermined the effectiveness of the program. The budget expansion from one million to four and a half million dollars occurred faster than the university and medical school bureaucracy were able to accommodate it. The physical distance between those legally responsible for controlling funds and the community workers compounded budgetary inefficiency. Frequent delays and errors in pay checks created great hardship on poor workers with little or no cash reserves and were interpreted by militant critics as exploitation by the white establishment. The Health Policy Advisory Center and dissident workers charged maximum feasible malfeasance and manipulation.

There was agreement that the voice of the local community should be heard but disagreement over answers to the key questions, "Which community?" and "Who is its spokesman?" The program became the focus of competitive action by black and Puerto Rican groups vying for control in the mental health center. The demand for community control was the breaking point of the program.

Problems. Group pressures, power plays, and political maneuvering plagued the Lincoln Hospital Project. In responding to the needs of the community for new services, the program often conflicted with existing value systems, political interests, economic interests, and institutions. In this setting of conflict, the primary goals of creating new careers and of improving mental health services fell by the wayside.

Many problems of the Lincoln Hospital Project relate to the long tradition of professionalism in the field of medicine. Though highlighted more distinctly in the medical area, this conflict between professional control and outside community control is also inherent in most new career programs. It is common for professions to set standards and seek to control members while they exclude the layman from supervision of professional work. The layman is assumed to be too uninformed or too emotionally involved for adequate evaluation.

The protectionism of the medical practitioners in the Lincoln Hospital Program was attacked in the *New Careers Bulletin* of New York University: "Professionalism is associated with credentialism and maintenance of the status quo, 'A largely white system serving ... and exploiting the monopolistic plantation system.' The New Ideology is highly critical of the professional: he doesn't understand the community; he is elitist and distant and not willing to accept accountability from consumers; he doesn't have the necessary skills; and finally, what he knows how to do, in many cases, should not be done—police functions, miseducation, checking on welfare clients, cooling people out, and so on."

In establishing new careers in a field, the issue of professionalization must receive considerable attention. Professionalism means that the worker does not identify primarily with his patient or client or with the local community; instead, he identifies with his colleagues and their work. In this case, spokesmen in the *New Careers Bulletin* and others pressed for identification with the community as opposed to professional identification. However, if professionalism in the training and work of new careerists is discouraged, several consequences may follow. When nonprofessionals are not imbued with attitudes of the professionals, there will be conflict. The more highly trained specialists will be accused of mistrusting the nonprofessionals and exploiting them.

Both these case studies show how poor planning, faulty coordination, politics, role definition problems, and special interest groups can hamper attempts at innovation in the development of stable new career programs. Expectations are raised and new demands are made. Political forces are unleashed. New careers cannot reasonably be expected to fit neatly into existing structure; redistribution of functions necessitates power shifts that cause conflict, which in turn leads to pressure for political intervention. New careers programs need protection against precipitous change—protection that is not available in programs dependent upon election returns.

Manpower Training and Development Programs

New careers have not been the only area where results have been less than fully successful. Manpower training and development programs designed to prepare disadvantaged persons for existing jobs also have a poor record. To be sure, such programs have succeeded in imparting requisite skills and knowledge for all sorts of jobs—welding, food service, auto mechanics, tailoring, clerical work—but few trainees have actually been employed in the jobs they have been trained to do. For example, a project set up to train hard-core unemployed to become truck drivers had practically no success. Nine out of 10 trainees successfully passed the state driving test at the end of their instruction; of 32 interviewed, nearly all were placed on jobs by the New York City trucking authority, but a few months later only 4 were still on the job. Lorton Reformatory in Washington, D. C., experienced a similar outcome following placement of over 50 of the graduates from its intensive vocational training program. Six months after placement few were still employed. Follow-up interviews with employers to determine the cause of employment instability yielded, among others, this observation: "Before you trained them they were just sons of bitches. After you trained them they were skilled sons of bitches." Interviews with the workers themselves revealed deep-felt patterns of exploitation (low pay, long hours), poor working conditions, limited career growth opportunities, fear that previous arrest records would be used against them, and resentment toward the insensitivity of supervisors to severe personal problems such as unattended young children at home and long distances to travel (Fine, 1969).

It is possible that new career and manpower training programs have typically taken far too narrow a view of human performance. Past failures attest to the simple fact that the mere lack of functional capacities and abilities is far from the major problem of training the hard-core unemployed or of developing new career opportunities. If this were the central problem, it would have long since been solved. Unfortunately, the problem goes much deeper and extends much more broadly (see Technical Addendum at end of this chapter).

A competent work performance is the result not only of the acquisition of knowledge and skills needed for a specific job, but also the product of many other skills acquired not only in work but also in nonwork situations. The total person comes to work, and it is this totality that is usually evaluated rather than just the person's actual task performance. Other attributes such as attitudes significantly affect the overall judgment of a person's work performance. For example, regularity, dependability, initiative, and resourcefulness are factors affecting both quantity and quality of work. Moreover, workers vary greatly in steadiness. Why are some so much more steady than others? Why do some accept time demands and constraints or relate to supervisors so much better than others—better, that is, in terms of getting along, productivity, and growth?

To be productive, an individual must internalize a wide range of middle-class culture values. His entire history of socialization is a key to understanding his present work behavior; the whole person is involved in work, not just that part that appears to be work-relevant. To understand the nature of work performance, analyses of far more than the mere functional and specific job skill requirements are needed. It has been proposed that an understanding of human work performance must take account of three major types of skills: adaptive, functional, and specific content.

Adaptive skills are those that enable an individual to meet the demands for conformity and change made by the physical, interpersonal, and organizational arrangements and conditions of a job. Specifically, adaptive skills include management of oneself in relation to authority; ability to move toward, away from, or against others; adjusting to space and time (direction, self-routing, self-pacing, punctuality); adaptations to dress codes (style and grooming); caring for property; and controlling impulses. These skills, rooted in temperament, are normally acquired in the early developmental years, primarily in the family situation and among one's peers, and reinforced in the school situation.

Functional skills are those that enable individuals to function in relation to things, data, and people with some degree of complexity appropriate to their abilities. For example, functional skills include tending or operating machines; comparing, compiling, or analyzing data; and exchanging information with, consulting with, and supervising people. These skills, rooted in aptitudes, are normally acquired in educational, job training, and avocational experiences, and are reinforced and amplified in specific job situations.

Specific content skills are those that enable an individual to perform a specific job according to the specifications and conditions of a particular employer and according to the standards required to satisfy the consumer of that employer's products or services. These skills, rooted in personal experience and preference, are normally acquired either in a specialized technical training school or institute, or on the job. The specific skills are as numerous as specific products, services, and employers who establish the standards and conditions under which those products and services are produced.

The concepts of functional and specific content skills roughly parallel earlier concept formulations bearing on such basic skills as reading, writing, and arithmetic, and the specific application of these skills in particular situations. Recognition that adaptive skills are also essential to job success is a much more recent formulation, however. The problems of adaptation pointed out in the two projects described above indicate a failure to recognize the importance of adaptive skills. That is, the individuals involved in new career or manpower training programs are probably adequately trained in functional and specific skills, but their adaptive skills training rarely receives sufficient attention. Generally the trainees lack the adaptive skills needed to cope with the unfamiliar stresses and strains of the work setting as well as those needed for coping with the role conflicts and ambiguities usually encountered during the training period. However, it is not just the individual that must adapt; organizations must also be alert to and accommodate the specific needs of these new workers.

MAN-JOB ADAPTATION: ORGANIZATIONAL ACCOMMODATION

To make good use of his functional skills in meeting the specific demands of any job, adaptation and accommodation must take place between an individual and the work organization. An individual's functional skills will ordinarily be most efficiently applied and utilized when his adaptive skills are closely attuned to specific organizational conditions and requirements; they will be least effective when his adaptive skills are incompatible with specific organizational demands. Hence effective worker performance and good job training and career development demand an alert organizational system sensitive to the adaptive as well as functional and specific content skills of employees and, most important, a readiness to accommodate its own nature and functioning to the adaptive capabilities and/or potentials of its employees.

Sociologists, child development specialists, and educators have studied the influence of family, social class, and early childhood experiences in school on the acquisition of adaptive skills. Findings from research in all of these areas indicate that differential socialization yields differential adaptive skills, or that differential adaptive skills are a result of the social class, and early childhood and family experiences of individuals.

Successful adaptation seems to require not only conformity to, or the acceptance of, societal norms but also positive and flexible interaction with the environment. Moreover, successful adaptation implies responsiveness not only to society's expectations and rules but also to its novel demands. A person may fit into a particular environment—that is, conform—but when he moves to a different environment, his previously adaptive behaviors may be maladaptive. Consequently, successful adaptation demands behavioral change even though the new behavior is contrary to previous values and attitudes.

Difficulties encountered by most new careers programs flow directly from their unfortunate attachment to bureaucracies. Complex bureaucracies have usually been rigid rather than accommodative, and they have demanded of target participants behaviors that ignore the participants' generally very limited adaptive skills. Program courses have been designed to teach mainly functional skills and impart information about things, data, people, and information processing. Even the on-the-job training and apprenticeships have dealt mainly with specific content. Stresses induced by adaptive breakdowns are regarded frequently as sources of personal and value conflict, not as stimuli for creating adaptive skill training procedures. Program directors are not entirely at fault; their negligence is due in part to the absence of available adaptive skills training methods.

Considerations for Teaching Adaptive Skills

Adaptive skills training is likely to be complex and costly; it cannot be implemented successfully in a series of one- or two-week orientation programs. If adaptive skills are to be learned by adults whose present skills are maladaptive to technological situations, the problem will require nothing less than a total approach. In a sense, society must be willing to make the effort similar to that used in some institutions with persons with mental and emotional problems who are dealt with intensively in a program combining hospitalization and treatment in a normal environment setting.

First, new methods must be developed to assess systematically the level of a person's adaptive skills and, in particular, the relevance of those skills to different job or career assignments. Second, current training and development programs, such as the Job Corps and residential halfway houses, should be evaluated to ascertain what conditions are more or less suitable for different types of persons. Learning conditions simulating early childhood, family, and peer group situations may prove most effective for altering adaptive skill levels to fit specific social and technological conditions. Third, it will be necessary to learn the best way for reinforcing positive adaptive skills in young adults. Can adaptive skills be taught apart from functional and specific content work skills? What is the proper mix and/or emphasis in a work situation? If adaptive skills training is to lead to competence in specific content skills, specific skill training probably should be integrated from the beginning with the more basic skills training.

The emphasis in vocational training should be shifted from teaching a specific skill to teaching functional abilities useful in a variety of settings. Learners should be exposed to a variety of contexts in which they can try out their newly acquired skills and knowledges. This can be done by providing relevant shop or laboratory work situations supplemented by field trips and demonstrations. Company training should, of course, not be the only agency for imparting adaptive skills; schools should continue as important training sites. Curricula should focus not only on subject matter and work-relevant knowledge and skills but also on such adaptive dimensions as attitudes, values, and work habits. Teaching methods should include field trips to places of work, films depicting work and nonwork activities, visits, talks, demonstrations, and role playing. Such activities would allow the students to explore different styles of successful work adaptation. Both teachers and vocational counselors need to be aware of and reinforce a variety of adaptive behavior and attitudes that will be needed in work situations.

Costs of adaptive skills training programs will often exceed the costs of broad content-oriented educational programs. Nonetheless, it is crucial to undertake such training if we are to follow the technological imperative for improving the quality of life through broadening the scope of job and career possibilities. On the other hand, the costs of neglecting such teaching programs would certainly be very high if measured in terms of continued financial dependency, delinquency, criminality, and similar social upheaval for increasing segments of our society.

PROGNOSIS AND HOPE

Highly efficient and accurate communication between individuals and organizations will be the critical glue in the merged worlds of work and nonwork in the year 2001. Through better communication, adaptation and accommodation will be assured and sustained, and the role conflict and role ambiguity so prevalent in current job training and career programming will have long since disappeared. Ambiguity and conflict in work settings have inevitably led to emotional tension, anxiety, fear, anger, hostility, and finally apathy. But the emergence of new careers is now fully conceded to be a complex social process involving massive change in social arrangements and redefinitions of existing occupations. Creating each new job category means an emergence of a new group, shifts in relationships between colleagues, patterns of economic rewards, and redistribution of autonomy, power, and prestige. It is our hope that the adaptive skills of our present industrial and educational institutions are sufficient to allow them to move flexibly and creatively toward the adaptive skill training programs such as we have discussed above. Only then can the development of a great new industry—a resource conservation industry devoted to giving men and women full opportunities for pleasurable self expression in the world of tomorrow—be certain.

SUMMARY

It may be hoped that, by the year 2001, the desire for a better quality of life will have inspired the elimination of conflict and exploitation. But the need to cure the social and environmental ills of today demands the creation of a vast array of new jobs. These new jobs can provide opportunities for improving both the quality of the environment and the lives of individuals. Technological advances have generated so many needs that a resource conservation industry is developing. New jobs in this industry will fill needs in education, urban and rural development, recreation, community services, health, pollution control, and conservation. Careers in these areas represent an opportunity for providing personal fulfillment for the poor, the unemployed, and the underemployed.

Unfortunately, job and new careers training programs have not been uniformly successful. For example, a new careers program in community services was undertaken in a large Midwestern city. Both educational upgrading and on-the-job training were provided; yet, after two years, only 41 percent of the new careerists were successfully placed. Problems in this program included poor scheduling, unfulfilled expectations, role conflict, and role ambiguity. Another new careers program, the Lincoln Hospital Project in New York City, also was unsuccessful in meeting its double objective of providing both new jobs and improved health services for the poor. The program faltered in the midst of bureaucratic inertia, and group conflicts, power plays, political maneuvering, and protectionistic professionalism continued to undermine it. In both these projects poor planning, inadequate role definitions leading to role conflict and role ambiguity, difficulties of reallocating decision-making power in the hierarchical structure, and unfulfilled expectations hampered the development of stable new careers.

Similarly, industrial manpower training and development programs have often been unsuccessful in preparing individuals for stable employment. Though these programs have probably trained the individuals to perform adequately specific job skills, other factors, such as attitude, have often been neglected or improperly dealt with during the training period. Skill, in effect, is far more than specific job skills or general mechanical ability. It has been proposed that the skills associated with successful employment are of three types: (1) adaptive skills—the ability to conform and change; (2) functional skills—aptitudes and abilities to deal with things, data, or people; and (3) specific content skills—specialized skills necessary for specific tasks. Many training programs for the disadvantaged and underemployed have failed to deal effectively with adaptive skills. Successful new adaptive skills training must begin with the assessment of each individual's adaptive needs so that individualized educational programs or working conditions may be tailored to each person's requirements.

Adaptation and accommodation must occur between each individual and his work organization. Individuals must acquire adaptive skills, and organizations must be sufficiently flexible to respond to individual needs. Most difficulties encountered by new careers and manpower development training programs are related to rigid bureaucratization and insufficient organizational accommodation to individual needs. Organizational flexibility is necessary for the fulfillment of both human and societal needs.

TECHNICAL ADDENDUM: NEW APPROACHES FOR NEW CAREERS—STRATEGIC AND TECHNICAL CONSIDERATIONS[1]

How have poor planning, faulty coordination, and role definition problems affected most new career program efforts? An examination of the basic conditions of difficulty is essential if society is to move beyond the present shambles by the year 2001. Broadly speaking, there are two points of view—strategic and technical.

From a strategic point of view, it must first be ascertained how new careers can fit into existing personnel structures. Such structures

[1]This Technical Addendum was written by Sidney A. Fine.

are arenas of individual aggrandizement for status, power, or careerism. These structures do, therefore, reflect the basic needs of people for recognition, response, and self-realization, as well as their ability, or inability, to exercise good will and good intentions.

Most present career employees have, over the course of time, worked out personal strategies for getting ahead. They are obviously not willing to step aside for incoming new careerists who operate under different sets of rules. If new rules are indeed more advantageous, they should be administered for the existing work force either before or at least at the same time as their introduction for new careerists. For example, if performance standards are going to be changed for new careerists, they should also be changed for present career employees. If new careerists are to receive transportation assistance, special training courses, or other support services, these same benefits should accrue to present employees, too. Although the need for such equal treatment may seem obvious, it has been, surprisingly, widely ignored.

On the technical level, the implementation of new policies must be examined. In general, persons in charge of public service agencies, especially those agencies concerned with human services, are ignorant of specific role requirements. They know little of how an employee's actions may or may not contribute to specific goals, or how to achieve certain standards of performance; they know little of the technology of the work or how the work should be supervised. Managers at all levels, from the lowest to the highest, must thus learn to define their job goals. Though under constant review, the goals at any time must be firm and explicit. They must, of course, reflect the values and beliefs of the organization but state them explicitly in terms of time, cost, manpower, location, and user (consumer or client). This explicitness is essential for assessing work performance, especially in human service organizations, where bureaucracies tend to shift their focus to record keeping and maintenance activities and away from their essential service roles. Employees can easily outguess the bureaucratic mechanism to learn exactly how to beat the system—to catch on to where the payoff is and then respond accordingly.

Second, task behaviors must accomplish the objectives of the organization. Each employee must know exactly how his contribution relates to overall objectives. In addition, specific job behavior must be explicitly defined; words such as "assists," "prepares," "develops," and "directs" are too general to have effective operational meaning. Job descriptions must outline in specific detail the sources of information, nature of instruction, tools, equipment, methods, and guidelines so that for any job one can draw reliable inferences about the degree of complexity of the task, its relation to things, data, and people, the relevant performance standards, and the general education and specific training required to perform according to standard. Not until these conditions, attainable through existing knowledge, are implemented can an effective personnel management base be laid for the year 2001.

What will happen if these conditions for improving job analyses and job descriptions are met? Four valuable outcomes are likely: accountability, self-selection, team identification, and payment according to achievement and usefulness to the team. All four outcomes have favorable implications for both productivity and personal growth.

Accountability means that every task performance will be capable of evaluation, both intrinsically, according to an employee's behavior, and organizationally, according to the relative contribution toward achieving objectives. Both descriptive standards for the whole performance and numerical standards for specific service or behavioral output will be useful. Given the setting, organization, and resource limitations, it will be possible to trace failure in achieving objectives back to the constituent tasks themselves; thus it can be determined whether failure is due to the objectives set, the methods available, the state of the art, the skills and training applied, or to some combination of these.

Self-selection may be the most important and powerful force in bringing worker and work together. It is certainly the most widely ignored and distrusted, but need it be? Is it possible that self-selection hasn't worked only because of inadequate and imprecise job information, as described above? For example, it has been my experience in the recruitment and promotion situations where task information, delineated in terms of the dimensions described above, was presented to potential candidates, that most of them eliminated themselves for one reason or another. When adaptive skill requirements were also provided, further self-selection took place. Why not learn to control the process of self-selection, a process that passes the option to the workers and makes self-selection part of their own growth? It should be emphasized that every aspect of self-selection as described here is job related.

Team identification is an alternative to job identification. Instead of filling job slots, people would participate in fulfilling overall organizational objectives. Objectives would be the responsibility of teams of workers. A team leader would fulfill several managerial functions such as serving as a channel of communications between team members and higher levels of management for routine organizational information, providing training support for new team members, and acting as a major source of technological and methodological information relevant to objectives and an arbiter in coordinating assignments to team members.

Workers would enter the team largely through self-selection and team acceptance and be taught the more elementary tasks by team members. Workers could progress at their own speed and in accordance with the availability of other team members to train and give support for more and more difficult tasks. They could choose to specialize in some tasks, share obligations for others, or learn all the tasks necessary to achieve the objective. Teams would rotate tasks, including technical and janitorial maintenance. With the learning of each task, the worker would grow in flexibility and in functional capability. Training support would take place both on and off the job. Two observations are in order: (a) much work is now done this way, but not properly acknowledged and rewarded as such, and (b) teamwork is not appropriate for really creative (not innovative) work, nor are really creative individuals usually good team members.

Although lip service is often given to the idea that pay scales are based on merit, they rarely are. For the most part, people are paid on the bases of formally negotiated or informal arrangements (collective bargaining, salary surveys, labor market agreements), seniority, status, and monopolistic practices. Even within a single labor market area, there exist wide pay discrepancies for any given job. Collective agreements tend to establish employment uniformity for those workers included in the agreements, but, even when quality of performance is accounted for, there is still considerable discrepancy between workers inside and those outside the agreement. Too often, workers must bargain for salaries on the basis of their position in the organization or their title, rather than on the basis of job performance. A homemaker is one of the most notorious examples of unfair practices. Well-organized assembly line workers and semi-automatic machine workers performing work that could easily and possibly be performed better (as the work is designed) by a robot are paid three or four times as much as the workers to whom they entrust the care and well-being of their children and who must exercise considerably more discretion and perform a much greater variety of tasks.

Workers employed in the year 2001 would be paid a basic rate for performing a basic core of entry tasks. Then, following a reasonable period of probation, they would receive additional increments

From the start, they would be assigned to a team and allowed to learn additional tasks as they became ready for them until they had learned all the tasks relating to the objectives of the team. They would then earn a team rate. They would carry no job titles, but would be identified with the team and the particular job to be done. There would be no specific educational requirements for achieving pay rates, although functional and specific training would be available and encouraged to enhance the worker's ability. There would be additional increments within pay rates for achieving higher standards. Team leaders and team members would determine who deserved such special merit increases on the basis of task performance standards. However, special merit increases should be quite exceptional, since team participation would recognize a wide range of effective performance.

REFERENCES

Fine, S. A. *Guidelines for the employment of the culturally disadvantaged.* Washington, D. C.: The Upjohn Institute for Employment Research, September 1969.

Hallowitz, E., & Riessman, F. The role of the indigenous nonprofessional in a community mental health neighborhood service center program. *American Journal of Orthopsychiatry,* 1967, **37**, 766–788.

Roman, M. Community control and the community mental health center: A view from Lincoln Bridge. In *Community Control: Realities and Possibilities.* New Haven: Yale University Press, 1971.

SUGGESTED READING

Amram, F. New careers employment stability. General College and Minnesota Center for Sociological Research, University of Minnesota, June 1970.

Bowman, Garda W., & Klopf, G. J. *New Careers and Roles in the American School.* New York: Bank Street College of Education, December 1968.

Bruner, J. Skills relevance and the relevance of skills. *The Saturday Review,* April 18, 1970, **LIII**(14), 66–68.

Craig, P. G. Socioeconomic change and managing tomorrow's work force. *Personnel Journal,* August 1969, **XLVIII**(8), 628–633.

Falk, F. The ability of professionals to supervise paraprofessional personnel in human service agencies. General College and Minnesota Center for Sociological Research, University of Minnesota, June 1969.

Federal programs for the development of human resources. . . . A compilation of replies from departments and agencies of the U. S. Government to a questionnaire formulated by the Subcommittee of Economic Progress, Joint Economic Committee, Congress of the United States, 89th Congress, 2nd Session, Joint Committee Print, December 1966. 3 vols.

Fine, S. A. *The 1965 third edition of the dictionary of occupational titles—Content, contrasts, and critique.* Washington, D. C.: The Upjohn Institute for Employment Research, December, 1968.

Fine, S. A. *Guidelines for the employment of the culturally disadvantaged.* Washington, D. C.: The Upjohn Institute for Employment Research, 1969.

Goldenberg, I. Halfway houses give hope to retarded. *Washington Post,* March 31, 1967.

Harrington, M. *The other America.* New York: Macmillan, 1962.

Hoff, W. Training the disadvantaged as home health aides. *United States Public Health Reports,* July 1969, **LXXX**(7), 617–623.

Kahn, H., & Weiner, A. J. *The year 2000.* New York: Macmillan, 1967.

Kahn, R. L., Wolfe, D. M., & Quinn, R. P. *Organization stress: Studies in role conflict and ambiguity.* New York: Wiley, 1964.

Kimball, T. L. Wilderness and public lands. *The Living Wilderness,* Winter 1966–1967, **XXX**(95), 14–17.

Larson, P., Belding, N., & Falk, F. A critique of agencies in the Minneapolis New Careers Program. General College and Minnesota Center for Sociological Research, University of Minnesota, September 1968.

Larson, P., Bible, M., & Falk, F. Down the up staircase: A study of new careers dropouts. General College and Minnesota Center for Sociological Research, University of Minnesota, May 1969.

McCollum, W. J. Employment outlook for recreation workers. *Occupational Outlook Quarterly,* U. S. Department of Labor, May 1965.

Miller, S. M. Breaking the credentials barrier. *New Careers Perspectives,* August 1969.

Outdoor recreation for America. A report to the President and to the Congress by the Outdoor Recreation Resources Review Commission, January 1962.

Phillips, L. *Human adaptation and its failures.* New York: Academic Press, 1968.

Shomon, J. J. Wake up foresters, you're needed! *American Forests,* May 1967, **LXXIII**(5), 12–15+.

Somers, G. G. (Ed.) Retraining and upgrading of disadvantaged workers. Industrial Relations Research Association, proceedings of the Twenty-first Annual Winter Meeting, Madison, Wisconsin: University of Wisconsin, December 1968.

United States Public Health Reports. Health services for the poor. March 1969, **LXXXIV**(3), 192–198.

Walther, R. H. A study of Negro male high school dropouts who are not reached by federal work-training programs. Washington, D. C.: Social Research Group, George Washington University.

CHAPTER 7

Turning Work into Nonwork: The Rewarding Environment

Lyman W. Porter
University of California, Irvine

In the future, organizations can assume a much more vigorous and imaginative role than they have in the past in motivating employees. Organizations can provide work incentives that will make the work situation both more rewarding and more satisfying for individuals as well as more helpful to organizational goal attainment. They can motivate employees by actively structuring reward environments.

In order to undertake this more energetic role in influencing employee behavior, organizations must act on two assumptions: (1) individual behavior can be modified; (2) the work environment can be modified. Most organizations implicitly believe that individual behavior can be modified, and yet they fail miserably to act on that assumption. At best, they adopt some sort of formalized training program designed to convert a recruit into a minimally qualified employee. Most training focuses on limited objectives and fails to take into account motivation and behavior change. Furthermore, much of the training is concentrated in an extremely short segment of time during the initial few days or weeks of employment and produces nothing in the way of behavioral effects beyond that period. It is as if the organization does not expect the individual to change from that time on.

At worst, some organizations, particularly smaller ones, have no formal training program. They simply show the individual how to do a certain job, give him a copy of company rules, and put him to work, usually telling him he will learn the ropes as he goes along. These organizations ignore the possibilities of even a limited amount of behavior change. Satisfactory work performance depends on the adequacy of employee selection, and, since hiring is often haphazard in such firms, a match between organizational needs and employee behavior occurs often only by chance.

Organizations do not hesitate to make technological changes—that is, to substitute a more efficient machine for a less efficient one or to change the routing of marketing data in response to a formal systems analysis; to that extent, they act on the assumption that the work environment can be modified. However, when it comes to changing or modifying employee behavior, opportunities are overlooked entirely, met with passive indifference, or else actively resisted. Somehow, work organizations have come to believe that compensation, work and nonwork schedules, performance feedback, and other, similar elements of the work environment are sacred cows that must not be disturbed lest changes create worse problems than they were designed to solve. It is doubtful that organizations, and indeed the national economy, would have developed at all had this conservative attitude toward the work environment been applied to technological innovation.

Both human behavior and work environments are more adaptable than is commonly recognized. How, then, can the organization in the future influence human behavior? One method is to make the work environment more rewarding. Organizations will need to understand and apply the concept of reward contingencies—that is, to relate rewards to specific work behavior. Organizations use reward systems at the present time, but their methods are imprecise and often ineffectual. Using reward contingencies more effectively will not be easy, but the results can justify the effort.

Motivating marginal members of the work force currently presents one of the biggest challenges to organizations. If progress can be effected with the marginally employed, it should be even more feasible to bring about changes in regular, or nonmarginal employees. The following sections of this chapter examine the case of the marginal work force member, extend the analysis to the broader employment scene, and finally, offer a few speculations about possible implications for the year 2001.

THE USE OF REWARDS IN MOTIVATING MARGINAL WORKERS

Recent social developments in this country have focused attention on marginal members of the employed work force. Marginal workers are individuals who in the past have not held positions of employment on a regular basis, yet who are presumed to be capable of developing into at least minimally adequate workers. In order for such individuals to become minimally adequate performers, effort on the part of government, work organizations, and individuals will be required on a number of fronts: recruitment, skill training, and motivation.

This discussion is limited to on-the-job motivation—specifically, the use of rewards—and, drawing on existing literature in general psychology, social psychology, and organizational psychology, develops some potentially applicable reward systems for motivating marginal work force members.[1] Practical considerations of cost, feasibility, and difficulties are relegated to secondary importance; the primary aim is to highlight and stress what is psychologically possible.

Definitions of Terms

Marginal worker. A marginal worker (MW) is an individual who has failed to demonstrate consistent work attendance or has failed to meet organizationally defined standards of adequate performance, or has failed to do both. Marginal worker is a somewhat broader term than hardcore unemployed. The latter term usually implies a record of little, if any, steady employment, thereby stressing attendance. The term marginal worker includes not only the hardcore unemployed but also those who may have had relatively steady employment but who are chronically on the borderline of, or below, the level of adequate performance as defined by the organization. Obviously, if the marginal worker's performance is consistently and decisively inadequate, he will be fired. If the same pattern of inadequate work performance followed by employment termination develops in a successive number of jobs, the worker becomes a member of the hardcore unemployed. There are, however, some individuals who can manage to stay employed more or less consistently but whose performance is so close to inadequate that they must be classified as MWs.

---

[1] The author wishes to acknowledge the valuable assistance of Michael Harrington in collecting basic source material for this section of the paper.

This definition of MW also stresses two distinct aspects of work behavior that must be considered in any discussion of the effects of rewards on motivation: attendance and performance. These two aspects of work behavior frequently are not highly correlated with each other (March & Simon, 1958). While some rewards and reward situations affect both types of behavior, other rewards and methods of administering rewards may have an effect on one but not on the other.

Motivating. Motivating means bringing about the desire on the part of the individual to meet organizational requirements for attendance (that is, low rates of job turnover, absenteeism, and tardiness) and performance (for example, output). A motivated worker exerts effort, mental and physical, to attend regularly and on time, and to perform at an adequate level of output.

Rewards. Rewards are positively valued (desired) goal objects. Such goal objects reinforce behavior to the extent that they increase the frequency of the responses they follow. Whether rewards in fact serve as reinforcers depends on the manner in which they are administered as well as on the extent to which they are desired.

Types and Sources of Possible Rewards

The methods of administering rewards deserve as much attention as the specific types of rewards that can be offered, particularly in motivating marginal workers. Nevertheless, before the administration of rewards can be discussed, it is necessary to specify the standard types of rewards that are possible and appropriate for MWs and also to indicate the major sources of these rewards (see Table 1). The following discussion examines the probable role of ten specific types of rewards in motivating the MW (see also Vroom, 1964).

1. *Financial: Wages.* Opsahl and Dunnette state that "although it is generally agreed that money is the major mechanism for rewarding and modifying behavior in industry, . . . very little is known about how it works [1966, p. 114]." They further point out that "the principal research problem is to discover in what way money motivates employees and how this, in turn, affects their behavior." In a statement particularly applicable to the question of the motivation of MWs, they stress that "money's incentive character, to be fully understood, must also take account of the perceptions of money by the recipient [1966, p. 114]."

Table 1. Types and Sources of Possible Work Rewards

Type	Source			
	Organization	Supervisor	Work group	Individual
I. *Financial*				
1. Wages	X			
2. Fringe benefits	X			
II. *Interpersonal*				
3. Status	X	X	X	
4. Recognition (praise)	X	X	X	
5. Friendship		X	X	
III. *Intrinsic to work*				
6. Completion	(X)	(X)		X
7. Achievement	(X)	(X)		X
8. Energy expenditure	(X)	(X)		X
IV. *Developmental*				
9. Skill acquisition	(X)	(X)		X
10. Personal growth	(X)	(X)		X

X = Direct source
(X) = Indirect source

Since money can be used as a means of satisfying many needs, particularly those associated with (but not limited to) basic necessities of life, wages would seem to be an obvious and potentially powerful reward in motivating the MW. However, it would appear that several conditions need to exist before the MW would see a given wage as a motivator. First, the reward would have to exceed the amount of money he can currently gain from other sources (for example, welfare, gifts, nonlegitimate activities). Second, the MW would have to see some connection between an action on his part (for example, coming to work on a regular basis) and wages. The less precise this connection (such as the payment of wages even when attendance or promptness is irregular, or the separation in time between the payment and the behavior), the weaker the effect on motivation. MWs, in particular—because of their current environment and past experiences—tend not to see connections between their own behavior and wages. Finally, money must have some value for the individual. To the extent that the individual feels that he will not be able to use money to obtain other things that he wants, he is not likely to be motivated by wages. For example, some MWs, in some circumstances, desire to obtain from others certain kinds of interpersonal responses that have little if anything to do with the amount of money earned.

2. *Financial: Fringe benefits.* Although fringe benefits are not exclusively financial (as, for example, company-sponsored athletic teams), they tend to have strong financial implications. As with wages, the source of fringe benefits is the formal organization.

Perhaps the major fringe benefit in most organizations is the company-financed (often including contributions from the employee) pension or retirement plan. For the typical middle-class employee, the opportunity to participate in this plan is likely to be a key factor in rates of attendance and turnover. For the MW, however, the reward —income after retirement—is so far removed from current behavior that it is unlikely to have much impact. Distance in time is a factor also—though to a lesser extent—in the effectiveness of other fringe benefits such as vacations and hospitalization. Furthermore, fringe benefits are seldom contingent on the quantity or quality of performance; instead, they are based on seniority or continued attendance. Thus, at best, fringe benefits could contribute to the solution of only one part of the problem of motivating the MWs of the organization.

3. *Interpersonal: Social status.* The social status of an MW includes his status in the organization and his status off the job. His status in the organization can stem from the organization's formal actions, from his immediate supervisor's actions, and from the actions and reactions of his fellow workers. His status off the job will often be affected by his status on the job, but there is no necessary correlation between the two (for example, as when a newly employed MW receives a modicum of status in the new work situation but is scorned by some of his friends who themselves are not employed).

The organization has some, but still limited, power to administer the reward of status. By its methods of assigning individuals to jobs, the organization can attempt to confer a formal type of status on the individual. If other workers, however, do not believe an individual merits a particular position, it is not likely that the individual will receive indications from his coworkers that he has status. Therefore, he is not likely to see the organization's action as rewarding. For many, if not most MWs, the organization will not be able to assign high-status positions until the worker is well along in the organization in both job tenure and performance, and hence no longer a MW.

The supervisor and work peer group, separately or together, have the power to confer status upon the individual even if the organization does not or cannot. Again, however, in many job situations the supervisor or the work peer group will not confer status on the MW until he has earned it. This may take quite some time for the initially marginal employee, and long before he has earned it he will have departed the scene.

Even if the MW achieves some minimal status within his work organization, his status outside the organization may continue to be low. To the extent that he associates with others who do not value regular employment, he is likely to be accorded low status off the job. Thus, organizational and supervisory efforts in this area of rewards are frequently attenuated by outside influences beyond the organization's control.

4. *Interpersonal: Recognition.* Much of what was said above for status applies to recognition, since the two rewards are often linked together in practice. Recognition, as used here, is the explicit acknowledgment of achievement that may or may not result in a change in social status. Such recognition, including praise and expressions of approval, can come from the formal organization, from the supervisor, or from the work peer group.

The extent to which recognition is motivating depends, as do other rewards, on its perceived value and on the connection the individual sees between it and his own behavior. In work situations, recognition from one source frequently is accompanied by disinterest or disdain from other sources, and hence the total value for the individual is often less than those giving recognition realize. In the case of MWs, attempts by the organization or the supervisor to confer recognition may be undercut by the actions and expressed attitudes of non-MWs if they feel the recognition is unwarranted.

In the past, MWs probably have received little if any explicit recognition from either organizations or peers. The reason, of course, is that in most instances MWs very early failed to meet organizational standards of attendance and performance, and therefore the organization, or the immediate supervisor, did not find it possible or appropriate to give recognition.

5. *Interpersonal: Friendship.* There are two notable features of this reward—namely, that the organization per se has only an indirect and relatively small role in providing friendship, and that the reinforcing effects of friendship are related almost exclusively to attendance rather than performance.

The major question for the MW is whether he will encounter a net gain or a net loss in friendship by taking and staying with a job. He must decide whether the job is worth the partial loss of friendship contacts from his nonwork peers. His decision depends mainly on how quickly his supervisor and members of his work peer group can provide new friendships to supplant that loss. Often it takes the new organization member (either MW or non-MW) some time to learn whether and to what extent others feel friendly toward him. Furthermore, the cues may be indistinct and indirect. Thus friendship is a relatively weak reward in the early phases of an MW's affiliation with an organization unless some explicit indications of friendship are provided.

6. *Work intrinsic: Completion.* There is considerable evidence that many individuals will make strong efforts to complete tasks that they have begun and that the act of completion provides a rather strong reinforcing experience. Obviously, satisfaction in task completion is a self-administered reward; even though others may believe, and communicate their belief, that an individual has completed a task, the sense of completion stems from within the individual. The organization and the supervisor, however, can play a major role in facilitating this reward by creating conditions in which the individual is able to experience a sense of completion.

MWs, at least initially, may have relatively weak drives to complete tasks. Their past experiences have tended to deprive them of many opportunities for task completion that are typical in the prework history of the non-MW. And, if they have not actually completed many tasks, they are unlikely to have been reinforced regularly for task completion. Thus, organizations, especially in the person of the immediate supervisor, should not assume that the MW will exert any extra effort to complete a task.

7. *Work intrinsic: Achievement.* Achievement is a self-administered reward similar to completion but defined more broadly. It is the feeling associated with attaining or reaching a difficult or meritorious goal.

McClelland (1961) has found that there is considerable variation in the extent to which individuals will strive for achievement. His findings indicate that experiences associated with attainment of difficult goals are quite rewarding for some workers but not others. McClelland's data also suggest, however, that certain types of training can increase an individual's motivation (desire) for achievement.

The above characteristics of the "sense of achievement" reward would seem to have some obvious implications in motivating the MW. A high percentage of MWs, because of past experiences, are likely to enter the work force with relatively little desire for achievement. Thus, offering difficult or tough goals to them early in their work career is likely to have very little impact. It is possible that achievement opportunities encountered later in the work experience will be perceived as more rewarding.

8. *Work intrinsic: Energy expenditure.* Although the expenditure of energy is often regarded as dissatisfying rather than satisfying, there is, as Vroom (1964) points out, evidence to indicate that the opportunity to expend energy (presumably in reasonable amounts) can be rewarding. That is, activity is often preferred to inactivity.

In considering opportunity for activity as a possible reward for MWs, it must not be assumed that, because they have shown relatively little desire for steady, adequately performed work, MWs regard energy expenditure as inherently distasteful. That is, the observation that an individual seldom works, or seldom performs adequately when he does work, is not sufficient evidence to determine that he does not like to expend energy. Instead, the reasons for poor performance may lie in a previous pattern of reinforcements for energy expenditure. The MW probably has received little if any reinforcement for merely being active. Neither the organization nor the supervisor can guarantee that an expenditure of energy will be a rewarding experience. All that they can do is provide the opportunity for an individual to expend a reasonable amount of energy on his job. Whether the expenditure of energy is then rewarding depends upon how the individual experiences it. Presumably, however, jobs at the extreme ends of the continuum—those requiring very little energy expenditure or those requiring great energy expenditure—are less likely to yield rewarding experiences than jobs requiring moderate energy expenditure.

9. *Developmental: Skill acquisition.* The opportunity to learn new skills is a reward that is often offered to the average or above-average member of the work force. Other than the initial training necessary to place him in his first job, the opportunity to learn new skills is probably infrequently offered to the MW. Yet, if the amount and timing of this reward were adjusted to the MW's gradually developing work behavior and expectations, it might become an influential

reinforcer. At the present time, however, there has been little research in the use of skill acquisition as an incentive.

10. *Developmental: Personal growth.* Skill acquisition means learning specific skills, but another developmental reward is the opportunity for personal growth in the larger sense. Personal growth is an individual experience and cannot be conferred by the organization or supervisor. But, just as in several of the preceding rewards, organizations and supervisors have an important role to play by the way in which they enlarge (or decrease) the individual's opportunities to experience personal growth. Where these opportunities are present and the individual experiences the sense of growth, the results may be beneficial to both attendance and performance. The difficulty is that the MW may be unable to recognize the opportunity for personal growth because he has for so long not seen the work situation as in any way connected with his own self-development. Thus, for personal growth to be rewarding for the MW, the organization will need to help the individual to see himself as capable of growth and to see the work situation as a source of explicit opportunities for personal growth.

Methods of Administration of Rewards

How should rewards be administered? As indicated above, the methods of administering and dispensing rewards are often as crucial to their motivational effectiveness as the specific nature of the rewards themselves.

There are three major approaches to reward administration: (1) operant conditioning, (2) modeling and social imitation, and (3) expectancy theory. Each has certain ties to the other two approaches. We shall point out some of these interrelationships as we proceed, but no attempt will be made to supply an exhaustive cataloging of such relationships.

Operant conditioning. Shaping—the selective or differential reinforcement of already existing responses in the individual's repertoire—is the basic process in operant conditioning that is used to elicit desired behavior. Essentially, shaping rewards the individual in such a manner that he makes successive approximations of the desired behavior. Initially, almost any response is rewarded, thereby increasing the general response activity of the individual. Shaping then progresses as the individual is required to exhibit certain approximations of the end behavior before he receives the reward. The proper response becomes more specific as the individual is required to demonstrate behaviors that are successively closer approximations to the designated correct behavior.

In situations involving MWs, many organizations and supervisors have not followed reinforcement policies implied by the principle of shaping. That is, newly hired employees are allowed relatively short periods of time to produce exactly the desired work behavior. Very little reward is given when any part of the required behavior (that is, both consistent attendance and performance at or above some standard) is not exhibited, whereas full reward is given if the exact required behavior is exhibited. It is highly unlikely that many MWs can produce the required behavior in the time allowed the new employee to reach a satisfactory level of performance under ordinary working conditions. Thus many MWs, because they fail to exhibit the required attendance and performance behavior, will fail to receive any rewards. And, failure to receive any reinforcement is likely to drive the MW back to his nonwork status and to confirm his belief that the work situation offers him nothing.

Occasionally, in their desire to be of assistance to MWs (especially when such assistance is part of the organization's policy of community or social service), some supervisors and organizations will adopt still another policy. This policy, which is just as nonshaping as the one described above, is the unconditional reinforcement of all behavior. That is, the MW is rewarded both for behavior that is quite divergent from the desired responses and for behavior that approximates the desired. Thus unconditional reinforcement does not teach the individual to discriminate between acceptable and unacceptable behavior, and it is unlikely to be helpful in advancing the MW toward non-MW status.

The principles of shaping, when employed by individuals who are particularly influential to the MW, can be powerful tools to help the MW transform his actions into normally acceptable employment behavior. Shaping is equally applicable to raising both attendance and performance levels. For example, rewards initially could be given for simply showing up for work, regardless of whether the MW was tardy or had been absent the day before. As time goes on and as the MW has had the opportunity to experience some rewards, the basis for rewarding the MW could shift to regular attendance with minimal tardiness. The appropriate rates of change in shifting reward contingency to closer and closer approximations of the final desired behavior on the part of MWs have yet to be established. Also, unspecified in the principle of shaping is the designation of which types of rewards will or can be used. Because they can be dispensed relatively quickly and often, wage payments, recognition and approval, and opportunities for task completion would be among the most appropriate rewards.

While shaping is a useful method of aiding an individual to learn a desired behavior, other operant methods, particularly reward scheduling, must be employed to help the individual maintain desired behavior. Reward schedules are of five basic types: (1) continuous (reinforcement for every correct response or set of desired behaviors); (2) fixed-ratio (the reinforcement of every n^{th} response); (3) fixed-interval (reinforcement after regular intervals of time); (4) variable-ratio (the ratio of reinforcements varies around some mean value); and (5) variable-interval (reinforcements are given at time intervals that vary around some mean value).

In laboratory situations, each of the five schedules has been shown to produce a different rate of response and different resistances of the responses to extinction (Reynolds, 1968; Bandura & Walters, 1963). But have employing organizations adequately explored the possible consequences of different types of reward schedules for either regular employees or MWs? No. It is not known, for example, whether various ratio or mixed ratio-interval schedules of reinforcements would work better than the current universally used fixed-interval schedules. There are indications that they would.

One possibility in adapting reward schedules to the needs and development of MWs is to pay wages at the end of each day for at least the first several weeks or months on the job. Such a reward schedule would be cumbersome and unnecessary for non-MWs, but it might very well be a useful method with some MWs. Another possible reinforcement schedule is to pay the MW a bonus for regular attendance—for example, a bonus at the end of the week for appearing for work on at least four days out of five, or a bonus on a fixed-ratio schedule for every n^{th} day of attendance (see Lawler & Hackman, 1969). There is no reason, however, to confine the use of reinforcement schedules to monetary rewards. It is apparent, though, that reinforcement schedules are most feasible for specific, frequent rewards that are directly contingent on certain minimal behavior requirements.

There are other methods of operant conditioning that could be useful in helping develop strong motivation in the MW. These methods include counterconditioning, to reduce the MW's fears or anxieties caused by specific aspects of the work situation; extinction, to reduce or eliminate undesired behaviors; and discrimination learning, to assist in the acquisition of skills. In short, operant techniques offer many possibilities for application to the work setting.

Modeling and social imitation. A second approach to modifying behavior through the use of rewards is modeling or social imitation, whereby the target person (the MW in this case) observes the actions of another person (the model) and, particularly, observes the consequences of that other person's behavior. As Bandura and Walters (1963) point out, the key feature of modeling is the vicarious reinforcement that the individual receives by observing the actions of the model. Thus if positive work motivation is to be developed in the MW, the MW must observe models receiving reinforcements that he considers highly desirable.

Modeling can have, presumably, three somewhat different effects. First, the target person may acquire responses that are relatively or completely new to him. Second, modeling may strengthen or weaken those inhibitory responses that already are a learned part of the target person's behavior. If the model is not punished for an ordinarily inhibited response but is rewarded, this event presumably may weaken the observer's inhibitory tendencies for the same response; likewise, the target person's inhibition of a nonuseful response could be strengthened by observing the model receiving unfavorable consequences for making a similar nonuseful response. Third, modeling can sometimes simply serve as a cue to elicit previously learned but now forgotten (not inhibited) responses that the observer is already capable of making.

Much of the research on social imitation has been carried out with children, juvenile delinquents, and adults in psychotherapy, but there seems to be no reason why modeling could not be used with MWs in the work situation. Organizations would, of course, have to determine appropriate conditions for effective modeling—that is, the type and position of the individuals who serve as models, the specific context in which the modeling takes place, the nature of the immediately prior events, the nature of the responses to be modeled, and so forth.

Expectancy theory. Expectancy theory is the general motivation theory developed and elaborated by Atkinson (1964), Peak (1955), Vroom (1964), and Porter and Lawler (1968), among others. It sometimes is called a path-goal approach to motivation and states that the effort a person expends to perform some task is a joint function of both the value the individual attaches to obtainable rewards and the expectation (or perceived probability) that a certain amount of energy expenditure will result in an obtained reward. Holding ability constant, the knowledge of these two variables should enable one to predict the level of individual performance. More important, expectancy theory specifies two key conditions that must be influenced if effort is to be increased: (1) the value the individual puts on certain rewards; (2) his expectations of obtaining them by effort.

In applying the path-goal approach to reward systems designed to motivate MWs, organizations must ascertain what kinds of rewards the MW desires and attempt to generate increased desire for some of the rewards (such as a sense of achievement or friendship) that are available in the present work situation. Organizations and supervisors commonly treat the MW as if he puts roughly the same value on various rewards as does the typical non-MW. Because the MW is likely to have had previous life and work experiences rather different from those of the non-MW, the assumption that his reward values are the same as those of non-MWs is probably in error. At any rate, the first step is finding out what the MW's values are. A second step might be to provide MWs with information that would serve to increase the desirability of some of the values.

The organization must then consider the MW's expectations or beliefs about the effect his actions will have on obtaining desired rewards. The MW's past experiences are likely to have trained him to be quite cynical, or to hold low expectations, about his chances of obtaining desired rewards from the organization, including his supervisors and work peers. Thus a major reason for an initial low-motivation level would be his extremely low expectations. Shaping, however, through differential reinforcement, can alter the individual's perceived probabilities. Of course, money or other tangible rewards can be accompanied by verbal reinforcement that stresses the connection between effort and rewards. Verbal rewards can often enhance other rewards.

APPLICABILITY OF WORK ENVIRONMENT STRUCTURING TO THE REGULAR EMPLOYEE

At best, MWs will still present difficulties for the organization. However, if some of the approaches discussed here prove effective with MWs, they should have even more potential for other members of the work force; this possibility will be discussed next.

In many respects, it should be easier to use reward contingencies with non-MWs than with MWs. The average non-MW typically exhibits work behavior that approaches acceptable if not outstanding levels of performance. The organization ordinarily does not have to wait a long time for an employee to exhibit desirable and necessary responses. Correct task behavior (following initial training) is already part of the non-MW's existing repertoire of actions, and there is only a small gap between the employee's actual performance and the ideal performance as defined by the organization. The regular employee is more likely also to respond to a wider variety of rewards. Furthermore, he will have some capacity to tolerate reward delays and will often be responsive to less tangible and more abstract rewards. Thus, in motivating the non-MW, the organization can be more flexible in structuring the work environment to provide rewards.

In other respects, however, the non-MW employee may present severe problems for the organization, especially if the non-MW is highly educated and he possesses high-level, widely transferrable, desirable skills. The highly skilled employee has greater opportunities for interorganization mobility and so will present a challenge to organizations that wish to obtain his loyalty and commitment. Present trends indicate that there will be an increasing percentage of this kind of knowledge worker in the future, but organizations will be hard pressed to retain the best of these individuals. Those organizations that are able to develop and implement imaginative reward contingencies for continued, committed service will have a distinct advantage over other organizations.

In order for organizations to implement a more effective reward policy, they must first ask these questions: What rewards will attract and keep the individual who easily could take his skills to another organization? What really happens to a person and a work group when they perform exceptionally well? Most organizations have given the standard reward packages administered in the standard fashion. They have structured their reward environments with little or no imagination. There needs to be much more variation in reward policies, practices, and scheduling than currently exists in present American business and public enterprises.

New Reward Systems

What is possible? What new kinds of rewards can be made contingent on continued commitment to the present organization or on especially meritorious performance? The discussion below examines only those rewards over which the organization will have more or less direct schedule control, including those rewards related to, or associated with, the immediate job in addition to those rewards related to activities outside the organization.[2]

1. Opportunity to schedule own hours of work. This reward would be granted to those individual employees or work groups who have a target date for the completion of work that can be performed at any hour of the day or night. For example, many computer programmers prefer to work from 10 P.M. to 6 A.M., or around the clock in work periods longer than eight hours. Obviously, employees on many types of jobs must synchronize their efforts with the work of other employees on other jobs, and thus it would not be practical to permit self-determination of work scheduling for everyone. However, scheduling one's own hours for work is feasible for workers other than computer programmers, and many individuals would desire this reward.

2. Redistribution of job duties. This reward would take the form of allowing the individual to allocate his time on the various tasks of his job according to his own desires as long as specified tasks were accomplished. Such a reward probably would be most effective with groups, wherein group members would be allowed to redistribute assigned tasks among themselves.

3. Opportunity to create new jobs. Individuals who reach especially high performance goals could be given time and perhaps other resources (such as the help of another employee) to invent new jobs in the organization that would not only contribute to the organization's overall progress but at the same time provide for the worker the chance to innovate.

4. Opportunity to participate in bonus drawings. This reward could take advantage of a variable ratio schedule. Employees performing above a set standard would have their names entered in a drawing. If their names were drawn, they would receive a bonus proportionate to the degree their performance exceeded the standard. Numerous variations of this reward could be adapted to the special circumstances of the organization.

[2] Ideas about several of the following rewards were stimulated by a paper prepared by Ray Olsen of TRW Systems. Specifically, rewards 2, 5, 8, and 9 are adapted from Olsen's paper.

5. Opportunity to choose any area of the organization in which to work for a limited period of time. The administration of this reward could be (but would not have to be) similar to that of the bonus drawing mentioned above. That is, all individuals who exceed set performance standards would participate in a drawing; the winners would then receive the opportunity to choose their work place in the organization for a period of time proportionate to the degree their performance exceeded the standards.

6. On-the-job nonwork activities. This reward is probably more appropriate for a work group than for an individual. The organization could give work groups that meet certain performance objectives by a specified time the opportunity to engage in various nonwork, social activities at the work site instead of work. Such activities could include parties, speaker forums, and other forms of recreation, such as playing bridge. Organizations already foster or sponsor many of these activities during nonwork hours. Except for the fact that this idea appears to violate canons of the Protestant ethic, would not the organization perhaps benefit by using nonwork activities as a reward during working hours?

7. New organization ventures. This reward would apply to work groups. In return for high production rates, groups would be eligible (again, selection could be made by lottery) to try to organize new ventures or tasks for the organization to undertake. Profit organizations could provide the capital to develop a new venture. Nonprofit organizations could provide time for the rewarded employees to conceive and design new ways the organization could contribute to society. Newly created ventures must, of course, be compatible with the already existing tasks of the organization; however, some new ventures could possibly become sources of organizational regeneration.

8. Accrual of time off. Under this reward system, a deserving employee would accrue time-off units, to be spent at his discretion but within some set of organizational constraints. Most organizations already use one form of this reward: employees accrue additional vacation time the longer they remain with the organization—that is, an employee receives 2 weeks per year up to 10 years, 3 weeks per year from 10 to 15 years, and so forth. However, few if any organizations make the accrual of time off contingent on performance levels. Most organizations administer this reward (for length of service) at fixed intervals rather than on a ratio schedule of reinforcement (for performance per unit of time), thereby overlooking its possible effect on employee performance.

Two possible variations of the time-off reward are as follows:

8a. Educational leave. As a reward for high-level performance, the employee could accrue time-off credits to be spent specifically for furthering his education. This reward could be administered on a ratio schedule of reinforcement.

8b. Civic activity leave. This reward is the accrual of time-off credits to be spent in civic or governmental activities.

9. Intercompany exchange of employees. For some individuals, the opportunity to spend time temporarily in some other organization could be an effective incentive. The length of time allotted to the individual for an intercompany sabbatical leave could be made proportionate to the degree of exceptional performance. The feasibility of this reward would depend on reciprocity agreements among cooperating organizations.

Conditions for Implementing New Reward Systems

Innovative restructuring of the reward environment requires the following:

1. Specification of performance objectives. Organizations, (even under most programs of management by objectives), will need to specify more precisely the objectives the organization and its component units want to accomplish. No fuzzy-minded "broad goals" will do if many of the new reward practices are to work.

2. Specification of methods of measurement of performance. The organization must distinguish incorrect from correct responses. That is, the criteria for reaching an objective must be determined explicitly and in advance so that the employee will know whether he is moving toward or away from the opportunity to receive a highly significant reinforcement.

3. Methods to insure an opportunity for receipt of rewards. Note that we are saying "opportunity for receipt" rather than receipt per se. This is because some of the kinds of rewards we have outlined utilize adaptations of a variable ratio reinforcement schedule in which the individual is guaranteed the chance to participate in the receipt of special types of rewards following a certain level of performance but is not necessarily guaranteed a reward every time he exceeds performance norms. The key point is that organizations must make sure that they do not fail to follow through on giving *some* rewards in accordance with the details of the nature of the reinforcement schedule. The individual's belief in the linkage between performance and rewards must be maintained and strengthened above all else. If this belief disappears, brilliantly-conceived reward strategies will come to naught.

TOWARD 2001

The problem of motivating the MW toward acceptable job attendance and adequate performance levels is already with us, but improved methods of solving this problem are certainly not far off. If some of the new approaches to worker motivation are successful, the problem may be greatly diminished if not wholly solved by the year 2001. What is not expected to diminish greatly within the next three decades is the challenge to the organization to use fully the human resources of workers. During the next 30 years, the composition of the work force will change. No longer will most organizations employ predominantly white adult males; the work force will become less homogenous with the inclusion of more women in supervisory roles, more minority groups of different cultures, and more youths with different value systems. Motivational and reward practices that have until now been effective will probably not be very effective in the future. Thus organizations will be forced to restructure their reward environments. Only those organizations that meet this challenge can look forward to a productive existence in the year 2001.

Whatever new systems are adopted by organizations, there is sure to be one prominent feature of the work environment in 2001: work and fun will be combined on the job. People will not have to go off the job to obtain real enjoyment. The merger of work and enjoyment will not, however, occur at the expense of organizational performance; through the effective restructuring of the reward environment, high levels of organizational performance can become the means for direct, personal gratification. Employees of progressive organizations of the future will be eager to perform.

SUMMARY

The restructuring of reward environments in work organizations may in the future actually blend work and enjoyable nonwork. Human resources today are seriously under-utilized. By applying incentives in more innovative ways, organizations will allow both the marginal worker and the effective worker to experience greater meaning, satisfaction, and usefulness in their lives. A wide variety of rewards is available in most present work situations: (1) financial rewards—wages and fringe benefits; (2) interpersonal rewards—social status, recognition, and friendship; (3) rewards intrinsic to work—task completion, sense of achievement, and energy expenditure; and (4) developmental rewards—skill acquisition and personal growth. The sources of these rewards vary. Some come from the organization, some from the supervisor, and others from the work group and from within the individual.

Though these rewards are readily available, their use at present is rarely effective. If tomorrow's work institutions are fully to develop human potential, they must employ greater innovation in the administration of available rewards. Possibilities include opportunities for the individual to determine his own working hours, to determine how to distribute his time among necessary tasks, to determine the area or department in which to work, and to participate in bonus drawings for special prizes. Not all individuals will find each type of reward equally desirable. The organization must not only determine exactly which rewards are appropriate for each individual but also learn the nature of each employee's expectations of what his own work effort may yield for him.

The timing of the distribution of rewards also is crucial. Each reinforcement schedule has a different effect on speed of skill acquisition and maintenance of work performance standards. Moreover, reinforcement schedules affect individuals differently. Today's organizations almost uniformly use a fixed-interval schedule of reinforcement. In the future the timing of the distribution of the rewards should be varied in order to assure a more rewarding and more motivating work environment for every worker.

Appropriate reward administration can successfully modify the behavior of the marginal worker. By changing the type of reward, his expectations of receiving the reward, and the schedule used for distribution of rewards, organizations will be able to integrate marginal workers into the mainstream of the work force. Operant conditioning, social modeling, and expectancy theory principles all can be applied toward the ultimate goal of merging the functions of work and of nonwork for each employee by the year 2001.

REFERENCES

Atkinson, J. W. *An introduction to motivation.* Princeton, N. J.: Van Nostrand, 1964.
Bandura, A., & Walters, R. H. *Social learning and personality development.* New York: Holt, Rinehart & Winston, 1963.
Lawler, E. E., & Hackman, J. R. Impact of employee participation in the development of pay incentive plans: A field experiment. *Journal of Applied Psychology,* 1969, **53,** 467–471.
March, J. G., & Simon, H. A. *Organizations.* New York: Wiley, 1958.
McClelland, D. C. *The achieving society.* Princeton, N. J.: D. Van Nostrand, 1961.
Opsahl, R. L., & Dunnette, M. D. The role of financial compensation in industrial motivation. *Psychological Bulletin,* 1966, **66,** 94–118.
Peak, H. Attitude and motivation. In M. R. Jones (Ed.), *Nebraska symposium on motivation.* Lincoln: University of Nebraska Press, 1955.
Porter, L. W., & Lawler E. E. *Managerial attitudes and performance.* Homewood, Ill.: Irwin, 1968.
Reynolds, G. S. *A primer of operant conditioning.* Chicago: Scott, Foresman, 1968.
Vroom, V. H. *Work and motivation.* New York: Wiley, 1964.

SUGGESTED READING

Galbraith, J., & Cummings, L. L. An empirical investigation of the motivational determinants of task performance: Interactive efforts between instrumentality-valence and motivation-ability. *Organizational Behavior and Human Performance,* 1967, **2,** 219–236.
Georgopoulos, B. S., Mahoney, G. M., & Jones, N. W. A path-goal approach to productivity. *Journal of Applied Psychology,* 1957, **41,** 345–353.
Hackman, J. R., & Porter, L. W. Expectancy theory predictions of work effectiveness. *Organizational Behavior and Human Performance,* in press.
Lawler, E. E., & Porter, L. W. Antecedent attitudes of effective managerial performance. *Organizational Behavior and Human Performance,* 1967, **2,** 122–142.
Skinner, B. F. *Science and human behavior.* New York: Free Press, 1967.

CHAPTER 8

Work and Organizational Life in 2001

Bernard M. Bass
The University of Rochester

Edward C. Ryterband
Edward N. Hay Associates

Boston, 2001 A.D. Work is equalized so that people who do the onerous, dirty work spend only a few hours per day at it, whereas white-collar and professional workers in desirable jobs work more hours. Self-actualization motivates most workers; extrinsic compensation is not as important as the reward of challenging work. Large businesses have replaced small businesses. Strikes are a thing of the past. Poverty and unemployment do not exist. Careers are self-chosen after intensive study of occupational information; the choice of a profession may be delayed until age 30. Career selection depends mainly on scholastic tests and performance. Service conveniences include open-stack libraries, supermarkets, and shoppers' orders filled from central warehouses. A system of socialized medicine maintains qualified medical schools and licenses physicians. Telephone cables pipe music into each home. Everyone uses international credit cards. Savings accounts are no longer used or needed. Records of individual merit are filed centrally. Workers are classified according to ability;

both promotion and the opportunity to undertake new careers are based on merit, and promotions are publicly announced. Paid vacations occur at regular intervals. Workers retire at age 45. Production and consumption are nationally planned. Women enjoy full equality with men in all types of occupations. Marriage is based on love, not on economic necessity. Society treats crime as a mental illness.

The Boston of 2001 A.D. is not much different from the Boston of today. However, in 1887, when it first appeared in Edward Bellamy's *Looking Backward,* this picture of the Boston of the future was a sensational prediction. For the public of 1887, Bellamy's vision was a radical, utopian departure from the realities of nineteenth-century life.

Despite the accuracy of many of his predictions, Bellamy did not foresee an increase in the rate of change. He imagined a static utopia. Except for the use of pneumatic tubes—already available in 1887—for delivery of written messages, he had little notion of mechanized information and service. He foresaw central laundries instead of home washing machines, and domestic servants instead of automated household equipment. Many of his prophecies have materialized in the countries behind the Iron Curtain rather than in the United States—for example, badges for meritorious work, severe punishment for deviation from the work norm, and using small panels of judges instead of trial by jury.

LOOKING BACKWARD

In the ironic tradition of Jonathan Swift, Bellamy created a fantasy world that had no further need of lawyers, legislators, or even politicians. He looked ahead to a time when the major problems of his day—private monopoly, class privilege, ruthless competition, the business cycle, economic dislocation and its consequential unemployment and distress—were solved. No doubt, like Bellamy, we will be victims of our limited vision and base our predictions of the future on the contemporary ideal rather than on current trends and countertrends. It may thus be instructive to look back to Bellamy's time, to the year 1887, to see what changes in work and organizational life in the United States have occurred since then.

In 1887, many of today's communication media and transportation services were in the planning stages. Telephone service and automobile transportation were about to begin; the first powered flight was 16 years away; the existence of radio waves had been mathematically deduced; radioactivity and X rays were soon to be discovered; the theory of relativity was less than a generation in the future; tests of individual differences were being developed; modern anthropology, psychology, and sociology were about to be born. "The war" was the Civil War. Steam locomotives set records that remain unbeaten; the Wollerith punched cards—basic to much of modern high-speed data processing—were soon to expedite the 1890 census.

Work in 1887 meant sweatshops, 12-hour days and 84-hour weeks. In Oregon, the widow of a fatally injured employee was sued by the company for damage to the equipment that occurred in the accident that killed the employee. The radical unionism of the IWW and the Grange was failing, but the rising trade unionism represented by the AF of L was to survive. Unions and child labor laws were the urban issues of the day. Most of America, however, was rural and agricultural, and, in many respects the United States was merely a developing country aided by French and English capital.

LOOKING FORWARD

What will work in the future be like? What will be the consequences of growing urbanization, the population explosion, the continued burgeoning of the electronic data processing industry, the growth of mass communications and the mass media, the civil rights revolution of the 1950s and 1960s, the expansion of business interests into overseas markets, changes in management philosophies, the growing number of corporate mergers, the expanding influence of the government on private industry, and changes in basic individual values? What will the individual in an organization of the year 2001 be like? What will be his motivations for working, the rewards he receives, and his attitudes toward work? What will interpersonal relationships be like in the organization of the future? Finally, what will it be like to manage a productive organization of the future? Will conflict, or the method of resolving conflict, be different from what it is now? How will organizations make decisions, and how will they approach the problems of growth, change, and management development?

INTERPERSONAL DYNAMICS IN THE FUTURE ORGANIZATION

Communications

Communications will play an important role in determining the general structure of future organizations. As organizations become more specialized, more complex, and larger in size, and as the number of resident specialists and the use of highly technical language increase, organizations will need faster, more effective methods for handling larger amounts of complex lateral and vertical communication. Sophisticated communications systems of the future will include the wider use of cable television, specialized closed-circuit transmitters, and teleconferences.

Cable television in the future will provide at least 80 different channels of two-way communication. The specialized closed-circuit transmission of computerized diagnosis, printed documents, data retrieval from data banks, news, training information, and the most recent data on inventory, prices, markets, and schedule changes will provide management personnel with immediate access to information about conditions and changes both inside and outside the organization. Conference telephone calls are already commonplace today, enabling managers in different cities to hold a group meeting without having to gather in one place. Currently available transceivers can distribute printed matter at such conferences. With the increasing availability of cable television channels, the audiovisual teleconference will become equally practicable and feasible, eliminating much of the current need for traveling to business meetings.

The decreasing need for face-to-face communications. Organizations will disperse their offices and factories throughout the country as the need declines for managers and representatives of different departments and organizations to gather in one place. Many firms will disperse geographically into smaller, more homogeneous groupings. By 2001, the most dramatic change in work life may be the marked reduction in commuting to work and traveling between cities for organizational business. In addition, more job-related activities could take place within the home, and those individuals physically isolated from co-workers would be free from traditional forms of supervision and thus more responsible for their own work. Evaluation of an individual's performance will be based on the achievement of previously set objectives. The socio-emotional side effects of fewer face-to-face contacts among organizational colleagues can only be surmised. Perhaps the sense of isolation and alienation from the community may be greater, and consequently, the need to interact with the family and friends will increase.

The computer's effects on communication. Computer technology will continue to shape the course of organizational communication processes and make possible the more efficient storage of more information. The amount of available information will continue to increase as information-storage methods continue to improve. By means of a variety of microstoring processes, the space required for a library of books can be reduced to one storage cabinet. Until recently, computer-stored information was kept on tapes that were stored until retrieved for a specific purpose. Modern computers, however, commonly provide random, immediate access to virtually unlimited amounts of data kept permanently in live-storage memory banks. In addition to retrieving information faster (within microseconds), such systems are able to respond almost simultaneously to a number of requests for unrelated information. This rapid retrieval system will continue to provide the basis for future developments in information systems.

The increase in available information made possible by rapid, accurate retrieval systems will in turn necessitate an increase in the number of knowledge workers. Furthermore, systems of information storage and retrieval will exert pressures on organizations to take advantage of new technological developments. Organizational decision making will thus become more rational as more decisions are based on surveys of well-estimated costs and gains.

Supervision

The same forces that propel enterprise toward greater economic efficiency also will encourage individuals to behave in an efficient and rational way. At the same time, however, there will be increasing psychological and social pressures within organizations to minimize loss of humanity, creativity, and morale. The manager of the future will have to reconcile the forces of economic efficiency and psychosocial pressures; he will have to be scientist, administrator, and humanist (see Kirkpatrick, 1968).

The supervisor's job. There are some who feel that supervision in the future will be the same as it is today; the supervisory process will still include innovation, planning, and nonprogrammed decision making. Others forecast changes in the supervisor's role. He will confront more complex technical and commercial problems, and thus will delegate more responsibility to good skilled men working for him. Because many specialists will serve under him, the supervisor will need to be a generalist, to receive openly and respond flexibly to the frequency of changes in information and the ideas of his subordinates and staff specialists. As his simpler tasks are increasingly performed by automated control, he will have to spend more time in creative thinking. Since logic and science will become the pervasive features (and values) in a future dominated by electronic data processing, his evaluation of subordinate skills will have to be more logical and scientific. Finally, the supervisor of the future will have to be better prepared to cope with heterogeneous teams of subordinates from various ethnic, racial, and socioeconomic backgrounds, as well as with mixed groups of men and women.

Supervision and the computer. Over a decade has passed since Leavitt and Whisler (1958) predicted that the use of electronic data processing for information gathering, storage, and retrieval and for decision making would make a substantial impact on organizations of the 1980s, especially on the supervisory process and management structure. Many of their predictions still seem viable. For example, top managers will take on increasingly creative functions. Middle management will be reorganized; much of it will become more structured as its functions become increasingly suited to the use of electronic data processing systems. The less talented managers will supervise the maintenance of equipment that handles routine functions; those with talent will move toward the creative jobs at top management levels. The line between top management and middle management will become more sharply drawn.

Leavitt and Whisler also predict that increasing numbers of information-processing specialists will create a widening rift between those who have information and use it to make decisions and those who are charged with merely carrying out those decisions. In an age of electronic data processing, planning will be the job of operations researchers and computer specialists. A computer-management elite, already present or developing in many organizations, will expand still more and will take on increased responsibilities and power because of its access to all information relevant to the organization's functioning.

Many writers have predicted that the composition of top management will be different in future organizations. Increasingly, experts in linear programming or in operations research will either comprise top management or will act as close advisors to top management. General management will also be affected by computer developments. For example, the development of real-time information processing will probably lead to better understanding of the relationship between a firm and its environment. A real-time information system receives information at any given point in time, processes the information, and returns the analysis or decision material through an output terminal almost instantaneously; "real time" simply means that management gets the information in time to use it.

Top management's most valuable use of real-time systems can be the simulation of long-range plans—that is, the computer can simulate and evaluate the effects of broad differences in company strategy over the long run without the organization's having to risk the possible damaging results in actual experimental changes in strategy. Simulations, based on comprehensive and accurate information, will be able to provide more accurate forecasts of what would happen if the company, for example, introduced a new package or new product, or changed its warehouse locations. The process is like "quickening" in the controlling of submarines and space vehicles: the computer displays for the operator the place where the vehicle will be in a few moments; the operator responds to this information. This computerized procedure has many implications for real as well as simulated time in various kinds of industrial operations; when human operators cannot react fast enough to present conditions, the near future can be displayed for them. For testing new packaging and sales strategies, the computer could simulate the decision process of consumers. The nonprogrammed decisions made in recruiting and hiring management personnel may be simulated and examined for better understanding. The effects of new production processes or materials mixing may likewise be tested in advance at markedly reduced costs. Such synthetic experimentation is an example of the more creative functions for which the computer will liberate the manager.

The computer will affect lower management, too. Early predictions generally forecast greater job routinization for these lower levels. Some observers now believe, however, that a computer-based information system can aid middle and lower managers to furnish detailed information to higher levels. Thus middle and lower management will spend less, not more, time in routinized activities.

Students today receive minimal instruction on computer use; tomorrow's students will probably be thoroughly indoctrinated in the uses and benefits of computers. The typical supervisor in the year 2001 is thus likely to use the computer as a tool to give him not only better and faster information but more time to concentrate on other aspects of his jobs, such as solving human relations problems.

The Future Work Group

Technology will play a major role in shaping the character of the future work group. Because of the need to increase knowledge sharing, organizations will rely increasingly on project task forces. A specific task force will operate as a unit for the duration of the project; at the completion of a given project, the task force will disband, and the individual members will be assigned to new task forces. At all organizational levels, individuals will probably belong to a number of different work groups, some to more than one group at the same time. Managers will work with teams whose purpose may be to administer or plan activities for other groups. They will also be members of task forces or committees whose purpose will be to carry out specific projects—for example, labor-management committees responsible for industrial relations. They will work with pressure groups, such as community agencies, from outside the organizations (Jenkins, 1966).

Membership in several task groups will create challenges and problems for managers as well as for other employees who also maintain multiple group membership. Conflicts of loyalty, conflicting demands on time, and confused perspective are possible problems. For instance, an engineer serving on a production team whose task is to reduce a product's production costs may also serve as an advisor to a marketing team working with that same product. Concessions to one team may be costs to the other. In addition, the nature of temporary project teams will probably enhance employees' feelings that they have many acquaintances but few friends or lasting relationships at work.

Still, job enlargement and job enrichment are the likely rewards of multiple group membership. Members of project teams will be part of small work groups and thus have a better opportunity to contribute. Though dependent on a central information source, they will have greater autonomy from central authority. A small work group with one project to master is more cohesive and thus more conducive to information sharing. In addition, work on projects may be the basis of compensation; workers would be paid as various phases of a project were completed rather than at regular time intervals. Similarly, peer assessments, along with supervisory evaluations, could form the basis of compensation that would be more directly related to individual contribution on the project.

Increasing numbers of highly educated people, especially scientists and technicians, suggest that in the future the work group composition and authority will be different. The permissive atmosphere and egalitarian authority structure of the research and development team will become commonplace, perhaps eventually replacing today's authority structure and its status symbols. Societal trends such as the accommodation of youth and the decline in traditional institutions indicate that informality will increase and that conformity to inflexible, unquestioned rules will probably diminish. These changes will reflect the growing desire for more meaningful personal relations and the greater emphasis on the individual's feelings.

Organizational Structure

In *The New Industrial State,* John Galbraith (1967) argued that continuing developments in technology will increase the cost of production because the global tasks or goals that organizations set for themselves will take longer to complete. (An increase in time and cost does not, however, apply to the production of a single unit, which will probably take less time because of the more sophisticated equipment.) As a result, the efficient operation of any given organization will require greater investments of time and money. The extensive investment of time and money will in turn necessitate greater commitment to and more precise planning of a project that is finally adopted by an organization.

The continuing technological advance seems likely to produce many other organizational changes during the coming decades. For example, organizations will probably rely more heavily on research and development to achieve competitive advantage in future markets. Boundary lines between the firm and its larger environment also will change. Relationships between government, distributors, consumers, shareholders, competitors, suppliers, employee sources (trade unions and groups within the firm) are and probably will continue to be very complex. These relationships will become even more intertwined as more components of the environment overlap. Within the constraints imposed by fixed investment in equipment, organizations will have to become more adaptive by depending mainly on rapidly changing, temporary systems that deal with different problems as they arise (Bennis, 1967).

Continuing new technological developments will thus dictate the decline of rigid bureaucracy, and, in an environment of change, the structural models of organizations may have to reflect a compromise between the control required by expensive capital investment in equipment and the more fluid adaptability offered by less rigidly structured models. In future organizations, bureaucratic or otherwise, changes are likely to occur in structural variables—that is, in centralization, size, complexity, staff and line demarcations, international character, and relation to the government.

Centralization versus decentralization. As a consequence of the increasing influence of electronic data processing on the future of organizational structure, some writers forecast that larger organizations will back away from the present trend to decentralize. The centralization of information processing, achieved by electronic data processing systems, should lead to comparable centralization of decision making, planning, and management control. But this view is challenged by those who see decentralization into profit centers as the principal trend in organizations of the future. A middle course seems most likely. One possibility is that future organizations will centralize certain functions while keeping other functions decentralized. For example, centralized control may exist only in planning, resource allocation, and reporting activities that depend on a centralized electronic data processing system to coordinate and process masses of information. Another possibility is the use of the computer to facilitate both centralization and decentralization; recently developed mathematical techniques can support a decentralized as well as a centralized authority structure. Of course there are many factors beyond electronic data processing that will determine the nature of a firm's structure; availability of labor, tax benefits, population shifts, and new markets will all play a part.

Organizational size. An increase in organizational mergers and the rising demand for goods and services suggest that future organizations will be larger than those of today. However, other signs indicate that organizations will not increase in size. For example, recent government pressures are likely to reduce the number of future mergers; businessmen are beginning to doubt the viability of the conglomerate model as a short cut to corporate success; the conglomerates created by merger actually operate as a complex of smaller, nearly autonomous corporate entities, and thus cannot be considered a completely homogeneous corporate form.

Staff and line functions. There will be a growing number of highly educated professionals, principally research and development specialists and computer-allied specialists, who will occupy organizational staff positions. Very possibly, their power will surpass that of the present-day staff advisor. Moreover, the complexity of future organizations will create a greater need for the coordinating specialist.

Organizational complexity. In some organizations the present hierarchical structures will undergo drastic changes. For example, as supervisors at first and second levels come to have more access to automatic information systems, they will be able to supervise more subordinates. The number of supervisory levels are thus likely to decrease as the lateral span of control broadens. The hierarchical structure of some jobs, especially the highly routinized, is likely to remain pyramidal in structure, but, for the increasing number of tasks that require innovative work, organizations will probably employ a flexible, less pyramidal design.

The multidimensional nature of future organizations also will affect hierarchical structures. The traditional organization chart outlines a pattern of accountability or authority. The charts of future organizations will indicate not only patterns of authority but also the patterns of organizational flow—that is, the routes of information and the patterns of decision making. The project team—a highly specialized, cohesive work force characterized by shared authority among team members, rapid and efficient information sharing, and internal interdependence—appears to meet the structural needs of future organizations for assuring explicit methods of information transmission.

Internationalism. Increasingly, American businesses have found lucrative markets and high growth rates overseas, particularly in Western Europe. Foreign firms are finding equally lucrative markets in the United States; the French or Japanese executive who resides in New York City is commonplace. Multinational corporations will become prevalent in the coming decades of the twentieth century, and their management also is likely to be multinational. As these firms engage in job-rotation practices, it will be increasingly common for a citizen of one country to live in another country and work for a corporation of a third country.

Multinational organizations will develop in a context of rising nationalism, especially in the third world of African, Asian, and South American nations where internal political struggles often lead to conflicts with foreign business interests. To reduce causes for resentment and hostility, the management and work force of typical divisions within international firms will be for the most part host nationals. Creating more jobs, however, will not be enough; firms will have to be more willing to assist in the development of their host countries.

There are also increasing numbers of government agencies with overseas responsibilities—for example, foreign trade missions and the Peace Corps, as well as multinational politico-economic alliances in Latin America and Asia similar to the European Economic Community (Common Market). The international expansion of both public and private organizations reflects the growing importance of the international community as a source of financial and social gain.

Internationalism will increase the exchange of business and personnel practices among different countries. The family allowance, granted to workers by some industries in Europe, will become more common in the United States. American industry's layoff practices will be accepted in Japan and Europe. Real income for workers doing the same type of job in different countries will grow more uniform as competition for workers transcends national boundaries and as managers in the employment of the same firm rotate from country to country. Rising expectations of and greater opportunities for workers and managers in countries where income is still depressed will not only increase pressures to raise compensation for management and professionals in countries that are presently oversupplied with such personnel, but will also increase the danger of brain drain from those countries that lack management and professional resources.

Government and organizations. Government and private organizations will have more influence on each other in the coming decades. As a regulator of business activities and as a consumer of business products and services, the federal government is and will continue to be an important influence. Congressional regulatory legislation will probably become more restrictive, and new, powerful pressure groups will also constrain business freedom. The new consumer advocates, led by Ralph Nader, crusaded in the mid-1960s for auto safety, and their efforts led to some regulatory legislation. Public alarm about air and water pollution will probably lead to stronger legislation to combat industrial pollution.

If the United States follows a course similar to that of Western Europe, we are likely to move farther away from a capitalist economy and closer to a mixed economy. Public nonprofit corporations, such as the Tennessee Valley Authority, will meet national and local needs that private enterprise alone cannot or will not meet. Services such as the mail system, now operated as a government agency, have already been modified into autonomous, nonprofit corporations; private railroads may reorganize into public corporations.

The structure of future organizations will have to change for a variety of reasons. The population explosion, the advancement of science and technology, the increasing interdependence of the public and private sectors—all point to modifications in organizational structures. The nature of new structures may vary and may not even be foreseen at this time, but the forces present today will be sources of change in organizational complexity, size, structure, and management.

MANAGING FUTURE ORGANIZATIONS

Managing Conflict

If the labor history of Western Europe is indicative and if present trends continue, organized labor will become less militant. Organized labor in the United States is now part of the establishment. There is, however, potential for intense conflict among the many diverse working and management groups. Behind these conflicts seems to be a rapidly changing social fabric. During periods of rapid change, the frustrations of adapting are greater than during quieter or more stable times. Research findings indicate that one reaction to accumulated frustration is aggression.

Although the intensity of conflict may grow, the composition of the conflicting groups will have changed. Even more than today, union organizations in the future will be fewer, larger, more highly centralized, and more broadly based over a number of industries and occupational groups. The membership of the typical multi-industrial union of the future will include clerical, professional, and technical employees as well as those in production. Professional staffs will plan and negotiate at national levels. Professional bargainers will face professional bargainers. Local unions will be concerned with social and educational, rather than economic, issues. Local leaders will be primarily information transmitters.

The militant—that is, actively protesting—and disgruntled segment of the labor force will in the future include agricultural workers, white-collar professionals, police, and teachers rather than blue-collar workers. The power of the new militant groups, however, will be centered in their ability to affect the public immediately. For example, the 1960s' strikes by garbage collectors, hospital workers, and teachers all had enormous and unsettling impacts on the affected cities, and bore far more immediate consequences than a walkout by steel or auto workers does.

Finally, blue-collar labor and organizational management seem to be consolidating against society's newest militants: students and blacks. Educated blacks and young educated whites are also likely to unite in the future to confront (for very different reasons) both labor and management. Thus industry will be forced to cope with a rising tide of disturbances in the community, in the innercity, and in the educational institutions.

Management and labor will no doubt still argue over wage and price spirals in the year 2001. Retirement plans will be different in the future, however; if workers change jobs before retirement age, their pensions will go with them. Moreover, workers displaced by automation will receive large severance pay. Since the Industrial Revolution, technological improvements in the work process have met opposition from workers whose jobs were threatened by machines. Although national growth has made possible the retraining and absorption of many displaced workers, automation has accelerated the pace of change in jobs. The computer affects many occupations and organizations; its appearance often leads to conflict. Even in those organizations where technological displacement has not occurred, many officials and lower-level employees express concern about their future roles in a changing organization.

Although there are no prevailing styles of conflict management today, researchers are studying the mediation process and conflict resolution. As more people become aware of the causes and consequences of intergroup and interpersonal conflict, and as they learn to manage conflict by means of sensitivity training and other social, psychological, and educational programs of the future, more conflicts will be resolved constructively.

Managing Decision Making—
The Computer's Effects

The computer will exert greater influence on organizational decision making in the future. Computer analysis will replace human analysis and decision making as computer specialists become more capable of specifying parameters and input data in ways the computer understands. The computer's ability to make decisions is already being applied with increasing effectiveness. Electronic data processing will give rise to new technologies that further affect the manner of displaying and analyzing information.

Management Development

The importance of management development. Management development will take a more prominent place in future organizations for a number of reasons. As computers take over routine decision making, tomorrow's manager will have more time to devote to unprogrammed activities such as solving human relations problems and developing subordinates. Managers will need training to be effective in all areas, and there will be a proliferation of new concepts and techniques that both new and incumbent managers must learn. For example, a manager in the future will need greater knowledge of computer uses in addition to skills in quantitative analysis and decision theory. As knowledge and technology advance, management development and retraining will be the only effective means to avoid individual managerial obsolescence. Still another reason for the emerging importance of management development is the threatened shortage of future qualified professionals and managers; future organizational growth will call for more managers.

The growing need of management development will lead to changes in the way development programs are designed. For example, a number of authors stress self-development as an important part of management development (see Argyris, 1967; Levinson, 1962; Likert, 1967; and Schein, 1966–1967). Thus many current forms of management development may in the future reflect this new emphasis on self-development.

Management training techniques in the future. Management development will continue to depend heavily on the university for training programs ranging from one-day courses to broad programs leading to a degree in business administration. One well-known university extension service already offers as many as 250 such programs a year. University faculty also may be invited to conduct special in-company programs. The universities will continue to be the sources of fundamental technical knowledge, new information relative to managerial jobs, skills in decision making and human relations, and broader perspectives concerning functions other than managerial. Because of the specially tailored nondegree programs, the distinction will not be so great between university- and nonuniversity-educated managers. Participation in career-growth programs will be as important as a college degree.

The future will bring a greater use of new training techniques, such as computer-assisted instruction, audio-visual tapes (and videotape replay systems), simulators, and laboratory techniques using nonverbal as well as verbal group experiences. Efforts will also focus on methods of shaping specific behavior—for instance, on how to convert win-lose negotiations into problem-solving meetings. Other, totally new techniques are also likely to appear in the coming years.

SUMMARY

In the year 2001 A.D., some of us will work even harder and in more complex and challenging jobs than we face today. But gratifications from creative success experiences at work also will be greater. The boundaries between work and play for the creative elite will be less distinct than they are today. At the same time, those who do not find work satisfying will have minimally secure, guaranteed incomes and more opportunities for leisure and play.

The technological imperative will have tremendous impact upon the organization and the individual. Growth and change will be goals in and of themselves rather than mere events. The complexity and capabilities of computers and communication systems—cable television, specialized closed-circuit transmitters, teleconferences, and elaborate computerized information processing systems—will reduce the need for face-to-face communication, increase the accessibility of information, and, thereby, improve the quality of decision making. In short, technological advances in communications and computers will have far reaching effects upon the individual, the work group, supervision, and the organizational structure.

Temporary task forces, comprised of highly educated and specialized workers, will be formed. For individuals, these temporary task forces may lead to conflict of loyalty, conflicting demands upon time, confusion of perspectives, and few lasting friendships at work. But the rewards will be job enlargement, job enrichment, and much greater opportunity for individual contribution. The internal composition of these task forces will require different kinds of management or supervision. Task force members will demand permissive environments and egalitarian structures. High-level supervisors and managers will delegate more responsibility; they will emphasize greater coordination among specialists, more creative thinking and planning, and more attention to interpersonal needs and human relations. Organizations will have to direct special efforts toward developing those managerial skills required for resolving conflict, for computer-assisted decision making, and for the development of self and subordinates.

The organizational structure will be far more flexible in the future than it is today in order to accommodate and promote changes in the individual, the work group, and supervisory and managerial functions.

REFERENCES

Argyris, C. How tomorrow's executive will make decisions. *Think,* 1967, **33** (6), 18–23.
Bellamy, E. *Looking backward, 2000–1887.* Cambridge, Mass.: Harvard University Press (Belknap Press), 1967.
Bennis, W. Organizations of the future. *Personnel Administration,* 1967, **30** (5), 6–19.
Galbraith, J. K. *The new industrial state.* Boston: Houghton Mifflin, 1967.
Jenkins, R. L. The supervisor of the future. *Training and Development Journal,* 1966, **20**(8), 28–30, 32–36.
Kirkpatrick, F. H. Implications of the behavioral sciences on management practices in the year 2000. In L. A. Appley & A. W. Angrist (Eds.), *Management 2000.* Hamilton, N. Y.: American Foundation for Management Research, 1968.
Leavitt, H. J., & Whisler, T. L. Management in the 1980s. *Harvard Business Review,* 1958, **36,** 41–48.
Levinson, H. A. A psychologist looks at executive development. *Harvard Business Review,* 1962, **40**(5), 69–75.
Likert, R. *The human organization: Its management and value.* New York: McGraw-Hill, 1967.
Schein, E. H. Attitude change during management education. *Administrative Science Quarterly,* 1966–1967, **11,** 601–607, 614–628.

SUGGESTED READING

Anshen, M. The manager and the black box. *Harvard Business Review,* November-December 1960, 85–92.
Anshen, M. Managerial decisions. In J. T. Dunlop (Ed.), *Automation and technological change.* Englewood Cliffs, N. J.: Prentice-Hall, 1962.
Barnett, V. M. The impact of higher education upon the management environment in the year 2000. In L. A. Appley & A. W. Angrist (Eds.),

Management 2000. Hamilton, N. Y.: American Foundation for Management Research, 1968.

Bass, B. M. *Leadership, psychology and organizational behavior.* New York: Harper & Row, 1960.

Bass, B. M. Implications of the behavioral sciences on management practices in the year 2000. In L. A. Appley & A. W. Angrist (Eds.), *Management 2000.* Hamilton, N. Y.: American Foundation for Management Research, 1968.

Bennis, W. Organizational developments and the fate of bureaucracy. *Industrial Management Review,* 1966, **7,** 41–55.

Berkowitz, L. *Aggression: A social-psychological analysis.* New York: McGraw-Hill, 1962.

Bryson, B., Cirino-Gerena, G., Frey, D., & Thomas, E. A model for constructing a test of leisure interest. Unpublished manuscript, Purdue University, 1967.

Consortium for the Negro MBA. University of Rochester, 1968.

Davis, K. Individual needs and automation. *Academy of Management Journal,* 1967, **6**(4), 278–283.

Drucker, P. F. A conversation with Peter Drucker on the psychology of managing management. *Psychology Today,* March 1968, **1**(10), 21–25.

Drucker, P. F. *The age of discontinuity.* New York: Simon & Schuster, 1969.

Edgerton, H. A. *World of work interest group conference, September 1967,* San Francisco.

Fisch, G. G. Line staff is obsolete. *Harvard Business Review,* 1961, **39**(5), 67–79.

Frederick, W. C. The next development in management science: A general theory. *Academy of Management Journal,* 1963, **6**(3), 212–219.

Gilman, G. The computer revisited. *Business Horizons,* 1966, **9**(4), 77–89.

Haas, J. A. Middle manager's expectations of the future world of work: Implications for management development. Unpublished doctoral dissertation, University of Pittsburgh, 1969.

Hartman, R. I. Some managerial implications of the cybernation revolution. *Personnel Journal,* 1969, **48**(1), 42–48.

Henry, E. R. Implications of the behavioral sciences on management practices in the year 2000. In L. A. Appley & A. W. Angrist (Eds.), *Management 2000.* Hamilton, N. Y.: American Foundation for Management Research, 1968.

Hurd, C. C. Automation and management. *Advanced Management Journal,* 1964, **29**(2), 7–11.

Katz, R. L., Knight, K. E., & Massey, W. F. The computer in your future. *Stanford Graduate School of Business Bulletin,* 1965, **33,** 2–9.

Koontz, H. Management and challenges of the future. *Advanced Management Journal,* 1968, **33**(1), 21–30.

Linden, J. Leisure time in the coming decades. Unpublished manuscript, Purdue University, 1967.

Lipstreau, O., & Reed, K. A. A new look at the organizational implications of automation. *Academy of Management Journal,* 1965, **8**(1), 24–31.

Mann, F. C., & Neff, F. W. *Managing major change in organizations.* Ann Arbor, Mich.: Foundation for Research on Human Behavior, 1961.

McCallum, L. F. Challenging horizons for creative managers. *Advanced Management Journal,* 1967, **32**(8), 3–8.

McClelland, D. C. *The achieving society*. Princeton, N. J.: D. Van Nostrand, 1961.

Michael, D. N. Some long-range implications of computer technology for human behavior in organizations. *The American Behavioral Scientist*, 1966, **9**(8), 29–35.

Miller, N. E. Liberalization of basic S-R concepts: Extensions to conflict behavior, motivation and social learning. In S. Koch (Ed.), *Psychology: A study of a science*. Vol. 2. New York: McGraw-Hill, 1959.

Murray, T. J. Management problems of tomorrow. *Dunn's Review*, February 1967, 24–26.

Odiorne, G. S. *Management by objectives: A system of managerial leadership*. New York: Pitman, 1967.

Porat, A. The decision to automate a small commercial book. A behavioral approach to the analysis of decision-making processes. (Tech. Rep. No. 19) Contract NONR 624 (14), 1968.

Porter, J. The future of upward mobility. *American Sociological Review*, 1968, **33**(1), 5–19.

Ramo, S. The impact of scientific and technological advances on tomorrow's managers. In S. Ramo, M. W. Gross, J. W. Hull, & L. A. Appley (Eds.), *Meeting today's responsibilities for tomorrow's managers*. Pasadena, Calif.: Industrial Relations Center, California Institute of Technology, 1964.

Ream, N. J. The state of information retrieval and data processing in the year 2000 and its implications for management. In L. A. Appley & A. W. Angrist (Eds.), *Management 2000*. Hamilton, N. Y.: American Foundation for Management Research, 1968.

Roszak, T. *The making of a counterculture*. New York: Doubleday, 1968.

Schein, E. H. Attitude change during management education. *Administrative Science Quarterly*, 1966–1967, **11**, 601–607, 614–628.

Secord, P. F., & Backman, C. W. *Social psychology*. New York: McGraw-Hill, 1964.

Simon, H. A. *The new science of management decision*. New York: Harper & Row, 1960.

Simon, H. A. The corporation: Will it be managed by machines? In H. J. Leavitt & L. R. Pondy (Eds.), *Readings in managerial psychology*. Chicago: University of Chicago Press, 1964.

Stewart, B., Gorman, B., Morris, K., & Sellman, S. A leisure-time interest inventory. Unpublished manuscript, Purdue University, 1967.

Straus, M. A., & Houghton, L. J. Achievement, affiliation, and cooperation values as clues to trends in American rural society, 1924–1968. *Rural Sociology*, 1960, **25**, 394–403.

Whisler, T. L., & Schultz, G. P. Automation and the management process. In M. S. Wadia (Ed.), *The nature and scope of management*. Chicago: Scott, Foresman, 1966.

Williams, R. M. Individual and group values. *Annals of the American Academy of Political and Social Science*, 1967, **371**, 20–37.

CHAPTER 9

Auditing Change: Human Resource Accounting

John Grant Rhode
University of Washington

Edward E. Lawler, III
University of Michigan

A favorite cliche for the president's letter in corporate annual reports is "Our employees are our most important—our most valuable asset." Turning away from the president's letter and looking to the remainder of the report, one might ask, "where is the human asset on these statements that serve as reports on the firm's resources and earnings?" What is the value of this "most important" or "most valuable" asset? Is it increasing, decreasing, or remaining unchanged? What return, if any, is the firm earning on its human assets? Is the firm allocating its human assets in the most profitable way? No answers are to be found [Brummet, Flamholtz, & Pyle, 1968].

Corporation presidents are not alone in stressing that employees are the most important asset many organizations have. During the last 20 years, behavioral scientists have repeatedly pointed out the value of human resources. However, the balance sheets and profit-and-loss statements that comprise the typical corporation's annual report contain no information on the cost or value of the organization's human resources.

Low- and middle-level managers are often told by their superiors that people are the key to the organization's success. Managers are encouraged to train their people and help them develop, yet no data are ever gathered on how effectively they use these resources or on whether human assets are increasing or decreasing in value. The management information system reports data on only the profits, sales, and physical assets of the organization. Thus in the absence of human resource accounting, many managers are more concerned with the physical assets of the organization than with the human assets.

The exclusion of human asset data from annual reports and internal management information systems would seem to be a very serious omission, particularly for those organizations that provide only knowledge, research, services, or entertainment. Computer software companies, certified public accounting and architectural firms, legal and medical practices, advertising agencies, research and development companies, government agencies, universities, talent agencies, movie studios, opera companies, television and radio stations—all have human assets that are much more important than their physical or monetary assets. The increasing number of service organizations should create a growing demand for the measurement and disclosure of their human assets. Indeed, the idea of placing economic value on an organization's human assets already has received attention from many different quarters—Hekimian and Jones (1967) in management, Bakke (1961) in labor management, Likert and Seashore (1963) in organizational psychology, Schultz (1961) in economics, and Hermanson (1964) and Brummet, Flamholtz, and Pyle (1968, 1969a, 1969b) in accounting.

Will human resource accounting be a common practice in the year 2001? If so, how will organizations measure the value of their human assets? Before these questions can be answered, serious consideration must be given to determining the uses to which human asset data can be put and to solving the problem of measuring human resource values.

EXTERNAL REPORTING

A strong case can be made for requiring corporations to report to the public the value of their human assets. In order to make an informed investment decision, the investor needs to know more than just the value of a company's physical assets (Pyle, 1970). He needs to know the competence and motivation commitment of the employees and the likelihood that they can function together as an effective work group. He needs to know whether an organization is building up its human assets or liquidating them (in order to generate short-term profits), and whether an organization is fat—that is, overstaffed with high-salaried, under-used employees. Human resource accounting systems potentially provide this kind of information. Unfortunately, there has been no systematic research on how knowledge of human asset data would affect investor behavior; there is, however, one case history that suggests it might have quite an impact.

On August 8, 1968, C. Lester Hogan, executive vice-president and general manager of Motorola's semi-conductor division, resigned his position and took seven of his division's top executives with him to Fairchild, where he became president and chief executive officer. Investor reaction was immediate. During the 24 hours following Hogan's resignation, the price of Fairchild's stock rose from $59 to $67 per share, and Motorola's stock dropped from $138 to $130 per share. The market value attached to the personnel changes may be estimated by multiplying the price change per share by the company's average number of common stock shares outstanding. Fairchild's 1968 average of 4,327,578 shares outstanding times $8 per share reveals an increase in market value of $34,620,624. Motorola's 1968 average of 6,133,470 shares outstanding times an $8 per share decrease indicates a market devaluation of $49,067,760. Within a short period, the shareholders of Fairchild and Motorola demonstrated their ability to assess the value of human resources. While common stock prices change for a variety of reasons, the primary cause is the investors discounting the organization's future earnings flows. Other, unknown factors may have influenced the stock price changes in the Motorola-Fairchild case, but price movements for both companies were relatively stable before and after the day of announced personnel changes.

Unfortunately, the opportunity to measure human resources is seldom available in as objective a form as the change in market value for the Fairchild and Motorola common stock. Historically, accountants have relied on the entity and proprietary theories, whereby either the business organization or its owners both own and control an organization's assets. Hermanson (1964) notes that, following the abolition of slavery, labor resources lost their status as assets when it became not only immoral but illegal to own laborers. (The one exception is professional sports teams, which are able to buy and sell exclusive rights to the athletic services of employees.) Consequently, unowned assets such as human resources were noticeably absent from balance sheets until 1970, when the R. G. Barry Corporation issued its "Total Concept Pro Forma Financial and Human Resource Accounting Statements."

Barry considers human resource accounting an attempt to identify, quantify, and report an organization's resource investments that currently are not included in traditional accounting methods (Barry Corporation, 1970). Barry's effort is based on the work of a University of Michigan research team that was created to develop and implement human resource accounting in industry. According to this group, human resource accounting is a process whereby effective measurement within an organization is accomplished through the identification and measurement of, and communication of information about, the organization's human resources (Brummet, Flamholtz, & Pyle, 1969b). The human asset data reported by Barry is unaudited, and the public is informed that the information is to be used only by internal management.

When accounting reports are prepared for circulation outside the organization, certain reporting criteria determined by the Securities and Exchange Commission (SEC), the American Institute of Certified Public Accountants' Accounting Principles Board, and the newly established Financial Accounting Standards Board must be met before the organization's stock can be listed for public trading. Generally accepted accounting practice requires stating assets at historical cost—the amount a business organization paid for its inventory or manufacturing plant. Because the difference between original cost of assets and the current value of those assets may be considerable, financial statements based on historical cost often provide only limited information for investment purposes. Regardless of such possible discrepancies, however, business entities currently receive certified appraisals of their assets only if those assets are stated on a historical-cost basis. (For a list of generally accepted principles of accounting on a historical-cost basis, see Grady, 1965). Presumably, human resources would also have to be accounted for on the basis of cost rather than value if they are to be listed for audit certification. The external reporting of human resource value is thus limited to the total cost of recruiting, acquiring, training, familiarizing, and developing personnel. This method of human resource accounting suffers from a number of obvious inadequacies that are discussed below.

TAX CONSIDERATIONS

Human assets could be listed and depreciated by corporations on their federal income tax returns. In the *Federal Tax Course* (1973), the Internal Revenue Service (IRS) provides a guideline to determine the useful life of business assets in order to assist organizations in calculating depreciation expenses, but the guideline does not include human resources. Thus if human resources are to be accounted for no differently from physical and monetary assets, current tax practices, aside from determining useful lives for depreciation expenses, offer an interesting economic problem. Under existing tax laws, a business organized for profit can legitimately deduct expenditures made for recruiting, acquiring, training, familiarizing, and developing personnel in the year the expenditures are made. If organizations defer their entitled deduction of these expenditures and list the cash outlays as assets, the professional accounting and SEC requirement of recording assets at historical cost is met, but the tax result for the organization is economically dysfunctional.

Assume that a business elects to list $2,000,000 of its expenditures on recruiting and training personnel as its investment in human resources rather than immediately deducting the costs. Further assume that the organization writes off its human resources over a ten-year life at a rate of $200,000 per year. The added income tax of $936,000 ($1,976,000 minus $1,040,000) for reporting human resources under existing accounting principles is an unnecessary cash drain on the organization (see Table 1). During a period of high prime

Table 1. Comparative Income Statements: Human Resources Accounting and Traditional Historic Cost Financial Accounting

	Human Resource Accounting	Traditional Financial Accounting
Net Sales	$25,000,000	$25,000,000
Less: Cost of Sales	(16,000,000)	(16,000,000)
Selling, general, and administrative expenses*	(5,200,000)	(7,000,000)
Income before federal income taxes	3,800,000	2,000,000
Federal income tax (52 percent rate)	1,976,000	1,040,000
Net income	1,824,000	960,000

*Expenditures on recruiting and training total $2,000,000. All other selling, general, and administrative expenditures total $5,000,000.

interest rates, there is an advantage to deducting the entire $2,000,000 of recruiting and training costs rather than listing these amounts as assets and deducting only $200,000. The added $936,000 paid in income tax represents an immediate additional cash outlay that would not have been necessary to pay under conventional tax regulations, but an organization solely concerned with improving its short-term earnings may wish to list its human assets as investments rather than to deduct the entire amount. It is also possible that corporations would have to pay property taxes on their human assets if they decide to list them. Most organizations would, of course, find this added tax undesirable.

A likely solution to the problem of reporting the tax effects of human resource accounting would be the issuance of separate financial statements for reports to the public and reports to the IRS—a practice followed by most of the largest corporations.

INTERNAL REPORTING

According to Horngren (1972), internal financial reporting, or managerial accounting, provides information for planning and controlling operations and for formulating major plans and policies. Managerial accounting reports are not circulated outside the organization because of the danger of disclosing financial details to competitors. And, in contrast to external accounting, internal financial reports are unaudited and outside the surveillance of governmental regulatory agencies like the SEC and the IRS. According to the researchers who first developed the concept at Barry, human resource accounting is intended only to assist management, not for use in financial statements, and thus should not be constrained by legal restrictions, accounting convention, or tax laws. Human resource data are included in managerial accounting reports so that managerial responsibility may be extended to evaluating human assets as well as physical (inventory, plant, machinery, delivery equipment) and monetary (cash, accounts receivable, investment securities) assets.

Human resource accounting probably has more use within, rather than outside, the firm; there are a number of ways it can contribute to better decision making. However, a human resource accounting system logically could be developed for inclusion in the external reporting system, and it would be a mistake to assume at this early date that human resource data should be excluded from external reporting.

Behavioral scientists have for years argued that corporations do a poor job of evaluating employee performance. Evaluation criteria tend to be too subjective or not inclusive enough; the supervisor's rating is still the most commonly used measure. Lawler (1971) indicates that, because employees often view such ratings as arbitrary, capricious, and ineffective, they do not accept them as valid measures of their performance. The organization then has difficulty motivating employees and designing valid manpower plans. Management information systems are relatively objective, but they are often insufficient. Reports include the sales, production, and profit of a part of the organization over a given period of time but do not indicate how effectively the human assets of the organization are being managed. Changes in human assets and the organization's ability to function as an effective human system tend to affect sales and profits only at a later time, perhaps not for several years. Thus a manager can mismanage the human assets he has and still look good over the short term. In one case, for example, a bright, authoritarian manager took a plant out of the red while at the same time liquidating the organization's human assets (that is, reducing training, giving no pay increases, dismissing highly paid, talented people, enforcing tight budgetary controls that lead to turnover) and decreasing the ability of the organization to function effectively without him. The effects of his actions did not show until several years after he had left the plant (Argyris, 1953).

The failure of the organization to evaluate human assets can cause particularly severe problems in those organizations that rotate their managers every few years. Such failure to evaluate makes it possible for a manager to liquidate human assets and thus achieve a high rating on such measures as return on investment (ROI) and profits before he is transferred and before the effects of his poor judgment begin to show up in the traditional financial measures. His successor, however, inherits a deteriorating situation and thus achieves poor results. The organization can react in one of two ways: either to blame the departed manager for the poor results or blame the present manager. At a higher level, an entire organization can achieve rapid gains by liquidating human assets, and the results of such a company-wide policy will not show up for several years in the external financial reports of the company. The investor has no way of knowing whether the ROI from improved profits represent a long-term gain or a short-term upswing reflecting only the liquidation of the company's human assets.

Human resource accounting can contribute to better performance evaluation by including human asset data that are not included in financial information systems (see Brummet, Flamholtz, & Pyle, 1969a, 1969b; Likert, 1967). An organization could then measure immediately and directly an individual manager's use of the human assets for which he is responsible. Since managers tend to perform well in those tasks for which they are rated, knowing they will be evaluated should encourage them to put more effort into human-asset management, team-building activities, and the development of people. Human resource accounting should also give organizations valuable information for making decisions in manpower planning.

PROBLEMS ASSOCIATED WITH HUMAN RESOURCE ACCOUNTING

Organizations will never be able fully to implement human resource accounting until several difficult problems are solved. Perhaps the biggest obstacle is developing an adequate means of measuring the value of human resources. The historical and replacement cost of recruiting and training employees has thus far been espoused as the valuation base. But why is employee value equated with recruiting and training? The answer may be the professional accounting constraint of assessment by historical cost. Consider, however, some of the difficulties of calculating the value of human resources at the historical cost of training:

1. Because people, unlike machines, can continue to add to their skills, an individual's value can increase beyond that of his training cost.

2. An individual may raise his skill level through personal experience—at home or while on vacation—independent of their work place and at no cost to the employer.

3. Two individuals who receive the same training may demonstrate different abilities in implementing their training. One individual may be able immediately and favorably to affect his subordinates as a result of his training, but the other person may demonstrate only partial use of his training. Should the historical cost of training then serve as the valuation base for these two human resources?

Valuing human resources at the historical cost of training also fails to account for individual technical contributions or personal breakdown. An individual may develop for the organization a patent or process worth considerably more than the cost of his training and recruiting. Or, an employee may become so disturbed and imbalanced as a result of his participation in particularly intense sensitivity-training sessions that his behavior becomes erratic and destructive. The historical cost of his training may be far less than the ultimate loss to the organization.

Another measurement problem is determining how an individual's asset value should be written off the accounting records. Physically and mentally, individuals grow and deteriorate at different rates in their personal and working environments. Some develop as a result of their work experience, others do not; some leave the organization after a few days, others stay for years. In addition, skill requirements are always changing, and today's valuable employee may be obsolete tomorrow. Developing a way to write off an individual's value, given the difficulty of predicting changes in his ability to contribute effectively to the business organization, seems to present an overwhelming problem. Woodruff and Whitman (1970) state that the Barry Corporation writes off the cost of employee obsolescence and impaired health, but do not explain Barry's procedure.

The problem of measuring human resources is similar in difficulty to the search for the so-called ultimate criterion mentioned years ago by Thorndike (1949). Thorndike argued that a person's job contribution should be measured against an abstract ultimate, defined as the total overall goal of a given organization. Obviously, such a goal is never attainable; even worse, it is rarely even definable. Guion (1965), for example, observed that such amorphous and meaningless phrases as "all things considered" and "overall contribution" have frequently been used in efforts to define Thorndike's ultimate criterion. Attaching a dollar value to these phrases would probably provide a serviceable measurement of human resource value, but the difficulty of determining an individual's overall contribution and then measuring his contribution in dollars still remains the most critical problem associated with human resource accounting.

Other measurement problems are likely to appear as organizations increasingly turn to human resource accounting. It is important to note, however, that there are many similar measurement problems in evaluating physical assets, but valuation still takes place, even if sometimes unsatisfactorily. It may be unfair to ask human resource accounting to solve problems that have not yet been solved by traditional accounting practice.

Assuming for the moment that proper valuation can be made, disclosure of individual resource value could cause additional problems—for example, in pay administration. Adams (1963) has stated that pay satisfaction is a function of the ratio between inputs and outcomes. Employees compare their input-outcome ratio to the input-outcome ratio of similar others; when the ratios are equal, they feel satisfied with their pay. However, when the ratios are unequal in their favor, they feel overpaid, and when their input-outcome ratios are larger than those of others, they feel underpaid and dissatisfied (Adams, 1963). Pay dissatisfaction tends to lead to, among other things, turnover, absenteeism, and strikes, but feelings of overpayment have few significant consequences. Most organizations make an effort to see that as few employees as possible are overpaid or experience pay dissatisfaction. But since there is no accepted measure of employee input, employees often value their inputs more highly than their organization does. If employees question pay administration practices, the organization has to admit that it uses subjective procedures such as job evaluation and superior's ratings. Thus human resource accounting could aid salary administrators by providing them with the kind of data they have long needed in order to measure employee input and administer salaries more objectively. If, however, the organization decides to ignore the available human asset data, it will risk even greater employee dissatisfaction. An employee will have "proof" of pay inequities when he knows that he is valued at x but paid y while his comparison other is valued at $x - a$ but paid $y + b$.

Disclosure of individual asset value could also affect employee bargaining power both inside and outside the company. Armed with current salary information and individual value ratings, employees could go to other department managers, or to the employment office of a rival firm, and bargain for better positions. At present, the value of employees is not obvious to people outside the organization, and it is difficult for organizations to recruit from their competitors and for employees to demonstrate their value to other companies. This is not true in all professions. In professional sports, an athlete's ability and his value to his organization are subjected to public display and assessment week after week and year after year. Similarly in the academic job market, the relative merit of a professor's research and scholarly contributions is highly visible. Interestingly, in both areas barriers have frequently been developed by organizations to prevent the free movement of people: universities adopt standard recruiting agreements, sometimes extending so far as to consist of "no raid" policies; professional sports organizations literally own their players. It is likely, therefore, that if companies were to publish human resource data, this would dramatically change the nature of the job market and significantly alter recruiting practices among industrial organizations. At first, job mobility and turnover might increase sharply, only to be followed by organizational constraints and agreements designed to "protect" a company's human resource investments.

Publication of human asset data could also have a negative effect on the motivation of some employees, particularly those whose asset value is declining. A loss of self-esteem might significantly and adversely affect a worker's motivations. Regardless of age or salary, if a worker knows that the organization has assigned him a decreasing asset value, he is likely to perceive himself as less adequate. Furthermore, Festinger (1954) has pointed out that people evaluate themselves according to how they perform in comparison with others, and an individual's self-esteem could suffer from a comparison of his asset value with the higher value of others. Thus awareness of a low human asset value could have a negative effect on the employee.

On the other hand, his awareness of an increasing human asset value could raise the individual's self-esteem and motivation. Knowing his asset value could encourage him to plan his career more carefully and raise questions about how he is used by the organization and his opportunities for development.

One way of preventing possible negative consequences of human asset data would be to keep this information secret. At present, many organizations do not reveal managerial salaries. However, the salary information still leaks out, often in a distorted form, and false information can have a more damaging effect than accurate data (Lawler, 1971). An informational leak leading to a distorted picture of employee asset values could also be dangerous.

A further danger of human resource accounting may arise from the manager's knowledge of his subordinate's asset values. Presumably, the organization will evaluate a manager on his use of physical, monetary, and human assets. Managers who are judged on the basis of return on investment may find it in their self-interest to fire or transfer high-value human assets to indicate a high short-term rate of return on a year-end comparison of profit to human asset total. Because of their inherent mobility, human resources can be moved about more easily than fixed material resources such as heavy machinery or manufacturing plants. A manager may have much more discretion and control over the human assets than the physical assets for which he is responsible. Accordingly, human resources are more subject to managerial malpractice than material resources. Such managerial misuse of human assets may severely hurt the organization in the long run.

Preventing the managers from knowing the personal asset totals of their subordinates offers a partial solution to the problem of unwise liquidation of human assets, but managers could then object to being evaluated on the basis of what to them are unknown criteria. A more reasonable solution would be to educate managers to perceive human asset data as different from physical asset data. Organizations could, for example, reward managers for increasing the human asset value of their subordinates, or allow managers to "sell" their assets to other parts of the organization and realize a "profit." Further, the replacement cost of an employee who quits could be charged immediately as an expense. Yet the mere reporting of value for human resources does not mean that such value will ever be realized by the organization. Reporting human asset values to a manager could, under the right conditions, motivate him to manage his assets and better provide him with performance feedback that is at present unavailable. As Vroom (1964) has pointed out, accurate feedback can be a significant source of motivation.

Many managers could possibly resist the collection of human asset data. Argyris (1971) has pointed out that managers resist the implementation of sophisticated management information systems because such systems produce data that limit their managerial freedom. The introduction of new management information systems particularly threatens the manager who is suddenly held accountable for his performance in an increasing number of new areas that have never before been measured, especially if he has been achieving good results only by sacrificing in those areas that will be measured under the new system. The addition of human resource accounting could have a similar effect: managers could be evaluated on an additional set of measures that limit their freedom to achieve good results on the more traditional measurements of sales and profits.

THE R. G. BARRY CORPORATION EXPERIMENT

The discussion of human resource accounting has thus far been highly speculative because at present very little research has been done on human resource accounting. At the moment only the R. G. Barry Corporation experiment, initiated in 1966, has made its way to the prominent published literature. The Barry system purports to measure investments in management personnel on the basis of both historical and replacement costs (see Figure 1). Barry has designed instruments to measure investments in individual managers for each of the functional areas and to record these costs (see Woodruff & Whitman, 1970).

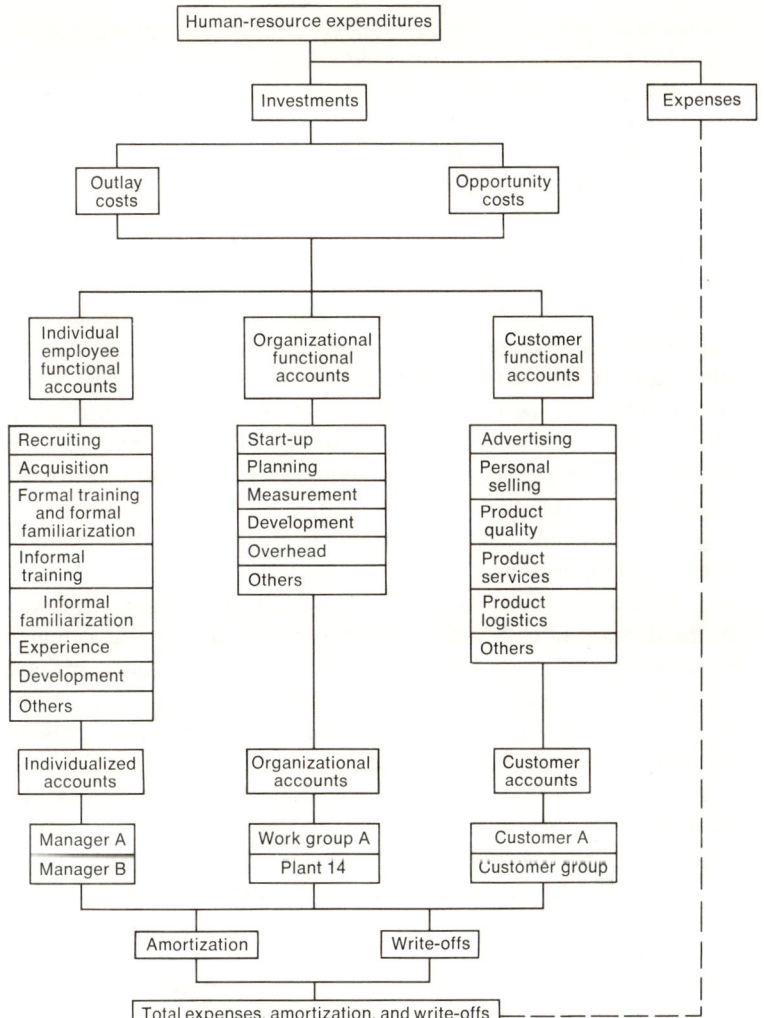

Figure 1. Model of an outlay cost measurement system.
(Source: Woodruff and Whitman, 1970. Reproduced with permission from Robert L. Woodruff, Jr., and Robert G. Whitman.)

Expenditures must, according to Brummet, Flamholtz, and Pyle (1969b), meet the test of offering service potential (to the organization) beyond the current period. Thus salary costs representing the planning and development of work in future accounting periods would be capitalized as an asset under organizational functional accounts, and salary costs for carrying out normal current work activities would be immediately expensed.

Recorded along with human resource totals of individual and organizational accounts is the resource of customer goodwill and relations (see Figure 2). The human resource costs of developing and maintaining customer relations and product service are recorded as assets. Although the reduction of customer goodwill may dramatically reduce sales, appropriate write-off bases for customer accounts provide an additional measurement problem.

Because the cost-outlay system describing human resource investments, obsolescence, and write-offs as they occur only partially fulfills Barry's information needs, positional replacement cost is also used in planning personnel replacement. Adjusted for price level changes, the cost of training and recruiting individuals for vacancies in each of Barry's managerial positions will, it is hoped, be available for planning purposes.

Barry accounts for 100 salaried people distributed among 3 of their 5 geographical locations (see Figure 3).

If Barry can meet its scheduled objectives (see Figures 1, 2, and 3), the demonstrated benefits that accrue from developing a human resource accounting system will be documented for others. Perhaps then personnel management, managerial accounting, and performance appraisal will take entirely different directions. At present, however, systematic data are needed on the system's effect on both individual and organizational behavior. So far, no such data have been reported, nor is there evidence of their being collected. Until data on the effects of human resource accounting are collected, attempts to convince organizations to adopt human resource accounting are inappropriate and premature.

Following the example of the R. G. Barry Corporation, the Montreal office of Touche Ross & Company, Chartered Accountants, developed a system of accounting for its human resources. The system, as described by Alexander (1971), is intended to be used primarily as a managerial information tool for internal decision making.

In its *1969 Annual Report,* Barry listed net investments in human resources totalling $986,094. The net investments were offset by credits of $493,047, representing "deferred federal income taxes as a result of appropriations for human resources," and $493,047 of retained-earnings appropriation for human resources. In addition, $173,569 of human resource expenses were listed as applicable to future periods. Barry included these accounts in pro forma unaudited and uncertified financial statements prefaced by the following caveat:

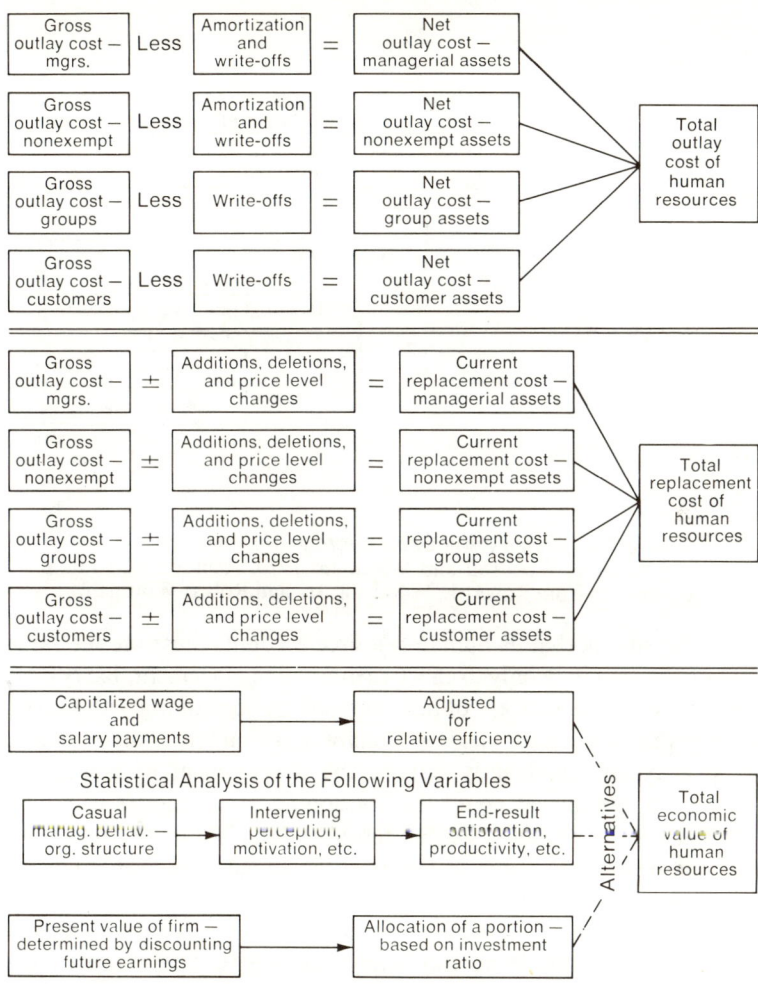

Figure 2. Model of a human resource accounting system. (Source: Woodruff and Whitman, 1970. Reproduced with permission from Robert L. Woodruff, Jr., and Robert Whitman.)

The information presented on this page is provided only to illustrate the informational value of human resource accounting for more effective internal management of the business. The figures included regarding investments and amortization of human resources are unaudited and you are cautioned for purposes of evaluating the performance of this company to refer to the conventional certified accounting data further on in this report [Barry Corporation, 1970].

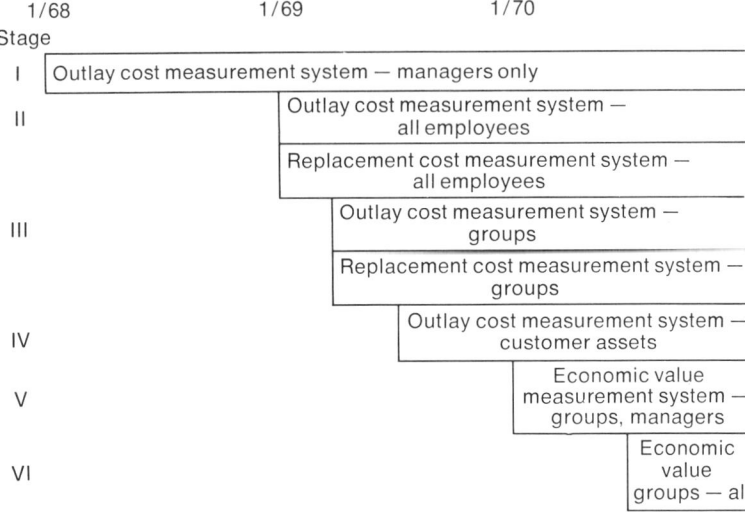

Figure 3. Human resource accounting implementation schedule. (Source: Woodruff and Whitman, 1970. Reproduced with permission from Robert L. Woodruff, Jr., and Robert Whitman.)

By stating that its human resource accounts illustrate the value of human asset data only to effective internal management, Barry does not approach the concept of human resource accounting's usefulness in investment decision making. Confining it to internal management reports could significantly impede the development of human resource accounting, as could the continuing unwillingness of public accounting firms to audit human resource data. Yet these data are no less auditable than many of the assets included in conventional accounting reports. Certified public accountants currently attest to the fair presentation of depreciable fixed assets such as manufacturing plants, productions lines, and heavy equipment. These assets have *estimated* useful lives and write-off periods, and they are carried on financial statements at subjectively determined values. Why then could not accountants certify the method of measuring subjectively determined human resources?

The answer may be found in the traditional position of American public accountants. To demonstrate their willingness to move away from tradition, the Institute of Chartered Accountants in England and Wales, the originator of professional accounting, has consented to attest to the calculations of management's profit forecasts. While this move is a very liberal departure from the traditional practice of accountants in the United States, in which the certification of profit forecasting is not allowed, Willingham, Smith, and Taylor (1970) predict that public demand for audited forecasts may bring about a change even in the traditional American practice of auditing. The rise of a demand for human resource accounting in American firms could take a long time, and audited human resource statements may not exist even in the year 2001.

HUMAN RESOURCE ACCOUNTING IN THE FUTURE

If human resource accounting is to progress beyond its present stage, two requirements must be met. First, research must determine the impact of human resource accounting on organizational effectiveness and on investment decisions. Second, a means of accurately measuring human value must be found. The Barry Corporation's method of measuring human resource value by the costs of recruiting, acquiring, training, familiarizing, and developing personnel assumes an equality of historical cost and current value. It will be several years before Barry can calculate meaningful returns on investment variables. The variables (see Figure 3) are elusive at best, and, even when isolated, the question still remains subject to whether human resource cost is equal to human resource value. The inadequacies of the historical cost method point to the need to develop alternative measures of human value.

Using data collected from two independent samples of claims personnel and sales employees in an insurance company, Flamholtz (1970) determined that replacement cost, compensation, and performance possessed convergent and discriminant validity as measurements of individual value. To demonstrate the advantage of those measures, he developed an operational replacement-cost validation model. Replacement cost, as used in Flamholtz's model, includes the costs of acquiring a new person for an existing position, training the new person to bring him to the performance level expected of his position, and moving the new person's predecessor either out of the organization or to a new position within the organization. Again working with insurance company employees, Flamholtz applied his replacement-cost model to both claims and sales personnel. Replacement costs for claims personnel ranged from $6,000 for a claims investigator to $24,700 for a field examiner, whereas replacement costs for sales personnel ranged from $31,600 for salesmen with low performance levels to $185,100 for a sales manager.

While Flamholtz's replacement-cost model provides a dollar measurement for human value, there is no indication whether it will significantly affect the decision-making of management and public investors. Asking corporate officials to note the amount for which they would be willing to insure individually their key management personnel may produce some data for testing Flamholtz's model. Replacement-cost measurement may provide the same individual value information that key-man insurance totals would. Thus key-man insurance totals could possibly corroborate Flamholtz's replacement-cost data. At present, however, no data are available for evaluating Flamholtz's model.

One weakness of Flamholtz's method is the use of salary data as a measure of values, but, as already pointed out, salaries do not necessarily reflect the input or resource value. Furthermore, Flamholtz's measurement system measures only the value of individual employees and does not measure their value as an effective decision-making team, their morale, or their commitment to the organization. Its failure to measure the effectiveness of the human system that exists within the organization is unfortunate, since in many organizations the ability of employees to work together and their commitment to the organization are the organization's most important assets.

A recent article by Flamholtz (1972a) proposes a model that is one step closer to a theory of human resource value (rather than cost). Although the model is data-free and without empirical support, some preliminary results are listed by Flamholtz (1972b) in another paper.

Another valuation model is presented by Lev and Schwartz (1971), who maintain that human capital values may be presented on the asset side of the balance sheet and the present value of the company's liability to pay wages and salaries on the liability side. Again, with both the Flamholtz and Lev and Schwartz models, the problem of measuring value seems to be overwhelming. A useful measure of human resource value is simply not available.

Perhaps the human system within an organization should not be given a monetary value. It might be more realistic to measure and report on human resources in other terms. Corporations could, for example, systematically assess and report to the public the state of their employees' morale, the commitment of the employees, and their ability to function effectively as a team. Measurement tools could be, for example, attitude surveys and comprehensive organizational diagnoses, including observations and analyses of decision making and the degree of openness at meetings. Some organizations already employ these methods, but they do not report the results to the public. The results from such surveys and observations could even be certified by behavioral science professionals who would specialize in auditing the human system in organizations. If the results were reported to the public along with human resource data, the public would be able to make better, or at least more informed, investment decisions.

Flamholtz's approach does seem to be an improvement over the cost model used by Barry Corporation and the valuation approach suggested by Likert and Bowers (1969). Likert and Bowers have suggested that the value of a firm's human organization could be conservatively estimated at 15 times the total earnings. By this formula, the Barry Corporation, (whose published earnings total $700,-222), has a human resource value of $10,503,330. The Likert and Bowers estimate exceeds Barry's calculation of $986,094 by a factor of 10. Thus the two measures do not appear to be comparable. The Likert and Bowers approach would also seem difficult to apply to a company that suffers a loss. Does a loss mean that human assets have a negative value?

With all the possible attendant tax and regulatory agency problems—property taxes on human assets, immediately increased income taxes resulting from capitalizing rather than expensing training and hiring costs, and historical cost accounting for the AICPA and SEC—the feasible course for human resource accounting advocates is either to demonstrate beneficial managerial reporting or to have accountants attest to pro forma (that is, not submitted to the IRS for tax purposes) human resource amounts. Business organizations may legally keep two sets of expense records, one for income tax reports and one for financial reports to shareholders. Just as British chartered accountants attest to future income projections independent of their certifications contained in published financial statements, accountants could certify separate statements of human resource values.

Aside from all the problems associated with measuring the value of human resources and assessing their behavioral impact, the overwhelming task for all the human resource researchers is to demonstrate the utility of such a system. At this time, we *think* that the world of work would be better off if business organizations had a human resource accounting system, but we do not *know* it. Human resource accounting researchers must demonstrate the utility of their work, otherwise human resource accounting may pass on as just another managerial fad, and the R. G. Barry Corporation may be the only business organization to publish the results of implementing a human resource accounting system. To date, the necessity or usefulness of such data has not been demonstrated. Indeed, one study (Elias, 1970) indicated that investor decisions were not appreciably affected by the inclusion of human asset accounting data in financial statements.

Just as accounting practice must change if human resource accounting is to develop, so must management practice and thinking. A number of studies have pointed out that, although managers give lip service to progressive and democratic management, they tend to behave in traditional ways; they say they recognize the value of people, but they hesitate to measure that value. Managers tend neither to perceive their subordinates as particularly competent nor to value very highly their subordinates' skills, and their resistance to democratic management seems rooted in their low opinion of their subordinates (see Miles, 1965, 1966; Haire, Ghiselli, & Porter, 1966). Overall human resource accounting is not particularly compatible with traditional, authoritarian management. Thus human resource accounting will become a common practice only when superiors begin to value their subordinates' skills more highly and practice participative management more widely.

The concept of evaluating managers on the basis of their use of all assets (monetary, physical, human) will probably provide the attraction for more companies to adopt human resource accounting, especially if the human resources of an organization can be suitably measured. The measurement problem is serious, but it is not new. As early as 1922 a prominent accounting scholar noted:

> In the business enterprise, a well-organized and loyal personnel may be a more important "asset" than a stock of merchandise. ... At present there seems to be no way of measuring such factors in terms of the dollar; hence they cannot be recognized as specific economic assets [Paton, 1922].

If the obstacles to measuring human assets can be overcome, the proposed benefits of human resource accounting may be realities by the year 2001.

SUMMARY

Human resource accounting identifies and tabulates the value of human assets within an organization. At present, the value of a firm's human resources does not appear on its balance sheet nor in the profit-and-loss statement of its annual report. The R. G. Barry Corporation has, however, undertaken an experimental program with the purpose of assessing the value of its human assets along with its financial and physical assets.

The value of an organization's human assets could be made public on a continuing basis, thereby helping investors and stockholders to make more informed investment decisions. However, since investments in physical resources are taxable, the value of human resources might also be taxed either as income or as property. An organization could either list and depreciate the amount of human resources as expenditure or list them as an asset. From the organization's point of view, however, paying taxes on human resources is dysfunctional. Another possibility is to use human resource accounting for internal management purposes only, and herein lies its greatest usefulness to the organization. Human asset data can be of great help to management in evaluating the efficiency and effectiveness of its personnel programs and in formulating policies and practices bearing not only directly on personnel functions but also on other functions with more indirect effects on employees.

Regardless of how such information is used, no completely adequate means is yet available for measuring human resources. The historical method, used to determine the value of physical resources based on original cost, is inadequate. For example, it does not consider the changing resource value of individuals. Furthermore, disclosure of human asset data either to an employee or to his supervisor can have negative side effects. On the other hand, informing an individual of his value could often have the beneficial effect of raising his self-esteem or increasing his bargaining power both inside and outside the firm.

The R. G. Barry Corporation uses a measurement system based on a cost model. The system measures investments in management personnel on both historical-cost and replacement-cost bases. Likert and Bowers (1969) suggest a valuation approach to measurement. In their model, the value of the human organization is set at 15 times the amount of earnings. A serious difficulty with this approach is that if an organization loses money, its human resources are assumed to have negative valuation. Moreover, multiplying earnings by a constant yields no information beyond that already available with earnings alone.

Flamholtz suggests a better approach than either Barry's or Likert and Bowers'. His proposals, one a replacement model and another a conditional value model, provide information on the dollar value per person and take into account such factors as costs for acquiring a new employee, training him to the level of performance required by the position, and transferring the previous holder of the same position either within or outside the organization. This system, like all others, has yet to demonstrate its utility for purposes of managerial decision making.

As more sophisticated accounting methods are developed to take account of an organization's and, ultimately, society's investment in human resources, management thinking and practices will need to keep apace. Lip service currently given by most managers to the value of people is meaningless; managers must respond constructively to the possibility of auditing the impact of change on the value of the organization's most valuable resource, the human resource.

REFERENCES

Adams, J. S. Towards an understanding of inequity. *Journal of Abnormal and Social Psychology,* 1963, **67,** 422–436.

Alexander, M. O. Investments in people. *Canadian Chartered Accountant,* 1971, July, 38–45.

Argyris, C. Management information systems: The challenge to rationality and emotionality. *Management Science,* 1971, **17**(6), B275–B292.

Bakke, E. W. The human resources functions. *Management International Review,* 1961, **1**(2), 16–24.

Barry Corporation. *1969 annual report.* Columbus, Oh.: Author, 1970.

Brummet, R. L., Flamholtz, E. G., & Pyle, W. C. Human resource measurement—A challenge for accountants. *The Accounting Review,* 1968, **43**(2), 217–224.

Brummet, R. L., Flamholtz, E. G., & Pyle, W. C. Human resource accounting: A tool to increase managerial effectiveness. *Management Accounting,* 1969, **51,** 12–15. (a)

Brummet, R. L., Flamholtz, E. G., & Pyle, W. C. *Human resource accounting: Development and implementation in industry.* Ann Arbor, Mich.: Foundation for Research on Human Behavior, 1969. (b)

Elias, N. The impact of accounting for human resources on decision making: An exploratory study. Unpublished doctoral dissertation, University of Minnesota, 1970.

Federal tax course. Englewood Cliffs, N.J.: Prentice-Hall, 1973.

Festinger, L. A theory of social comparison processes. *Human Relations,* 1954, **7,** 117–140.

Flamholtz, E. G. The development and implementation of a replacement cost model for human resource valuation. *Accounting and Information Systems Research Program.* Los Angeles: University of California, Graduate School of Business Administration, 1970.

Flamholtz, E. G. Toward a theory of human resource value in formal organizations. *The Accounting Review,* 1972, **47**(4), 666–678. (a)

Flamholtz, E. G. Assessing the validity of a theory of human resource accounting: A field study. *Journal of Accounting Research: Empirical Research in Accounting—Selected Studies, 1972* (forthcoming). (b)

Grady, P. *Inventory of generally accepted accounting principles for business enterprises: Accounting research study number 7.* New York: American Institute of Certified Public Accountants, 1965.

Guion, R. *Personnel testing.* New York: McGraw-Hill, 1965.

Haire, M., Ghiselli, E. E., & Porter, L. W. *Managerial thinking: An international study.* New York: Wiley, 1966.

Hekimian, J. C., & Jones, C. H. Put people on your balance sheet. *Harvard Business Review,* 1967, **45**(1), 105–113.

Hermanson, R. H. *Accounting for human assets.* East Lansing, Mich.: Bureau of Business and Economic Research, 1964.

Horngren, C. T. *Cost accounting: A managerial approach* (3rd ed.). Englewood Cliffs, N.J.: Prentice-Hall, 1972.

Lawler, E. E. *Pay and organizational effectiveness: A psychological view.* New York: McGraw-Hill, 1971.

Lev, B., & Schwartz, A. On the use of the economic concept of human capital in financial statements. *The Accounting Review,* 1971, **46**(1), 103–118.

Likert, R. *The human organization: Its management and value.* New York: McGraw-Hill, 1967.

Likert, R., & Bowers, D. G. Organizational theory and human resources accounting. *American Psychologist,* 1969, **24**, 585–592.

Likert, R., & Seashore, S. E. Making cost control work. *Harvard Business Review,* 1963, **41**(6), 96–108.

Miles, R. E. Human relations on human resources. *Harvard Business Review,* 1965, **43**(4), 148–163.

Miles, R. E. The affluent organization. *Harvard Business Review,* 1966, **44**(3), 106–114.

Paton, W. A. Accounting theory. Unpublished doctoral dissertation, University of Michigan, 1922.

Pyle, W. C. Human Resource Accounting. *Financial Analysts Journal,* 1970, September-October, 69–78.

Schultz, T. W. Investment in human capital. *American Economic Review,* 1961, **51**, 1–17.

Sprouse, R. T., & Moonitz, M. *A tentative set of broad accounting principles for business enterprises.* New York: American Institute of Certified Public Accountants, 1962.

Thorndike, R. L. *Personnel selection: Test and measurement technique.* New York: Wiley, 1949.

Vroom, V. H. *Work and motivation.* New York: Wiley, 1964.

Willingham, J. J., Smith, C. H., & Taylor, M. E. Should the CPA's opinion be extended to include forecasts? *Financial Executive,* September 1970, 80–82, 88, 89.

Woodruff, R. L. What price people? *The Personnel Administrator,* 1969, **14**(1), 17–20.

Woodruff, R. L., & Whitman, R. G. The behavioral aspects of accounting data for performance evaluation at the R. G. Barry Corporation. In T.

J. Burns (Ed.), *The behavioral aspects of accounting data for performance evaluation.* Columbus: Ohio State University, College of Administrative Sciences, 1970.

SUGGESTED READING

Accountants' reports on profit forecasts. *Accountancy,* June 1969, 467–469.
AICPA code of professional ethics. New York: American Institute of Certified Public Accountants, 1967.
Argyris, C. *Executive leadership.* New York: Harper & Row, 1953.
Brummet, R. L., Pyle, W. C., & Flamholtz, E. G. Accounting for human resources. *Michigan Business Review,* 1968, **20**(2), 20–25.
Brummet, R. L., Pyle, W. C., & Flamholtz, E. G. Human resource accounting in industry. *Personnel Administration,* 1969, **32**(4), 34–46.
Campbell, D. T., & Fiske, D. W. Convergent and discriminant validation by the multi-trait/multi-method matrix. *Psychological Bulletin,* 1959, **56**, 81–105.
Campbell, J. P., Dunnette, M. D., Lawler, E. E., & Weick, K. *Managerial behavior: Performances and effectiveness.* New York: McGraw-Hill, 1970.
Electronics review: Companies, musical chairs. *Electronics,* 1968, **41**(17), 45–47.
Fairchild Camera sued by Motorola on staff: Details of suit given. *Wall Street Journal,* August 29, 1968, 4.
Flamholtz, E. G. The theory and measurement of an individual's value to an organization. Unpublished doctoral dissertation, University of Michigan, 1969.
Flamholtz, E. G. Role of human resources accounting in manpower planning and utilization. *Accounting and Information Systems Research Program.* Los Angeles: University of California, Graduate School of Business Administration, 1970. (a)
Flamholtz, E. G. Should your organization attempt to value its human resources? *Accounting and Information Systems Research Program.* Los Angeles: University of California, Graduate School of Business Administration, 1970. (b)
Flamholtz, E. G. A model for human resource valuation: A stochastic process with service rewards. *The Accounting Review,* 1971, **46**(2), 253–267.
Investment statistics laboratory. *Daily Stock Price Index,* July-September, 1968, **117**, 231.
Morse, N. E., & Reimer, E. The experimental change of a major organizational variable. *Journal of Abnormal and Social Psychology,* 1956, **52**, 120–129.
Moody's industrial manual: American and foreign. New York: Moody's Investor's Service, 1969.
Motorola Incorporated. *1969 annual report.* Franklin Park, Ill.: Author, 1970.
Pyle, W. C. Monitoring human resources—On line. *Michigan Business Review,* 1970, **22** (4), 19–32. (a)

Pyle, W. C. Accounting systems for human resources. *Innovation,* 1970, **10,** 46–54. (b)
Sprouse, R. T., & Moonitz, M. *A tentative set of broad accounting principles for business enterprises.* New York: American Institute of Certified Public Accountants, 1962.
Woodruff, R. L. What price people? *The Personnel Administrator,* 1969, **14** (1), 17–20.
Woodruff, R. L., Whitman, R. G., & Brummet, R. L. Discussion: R. G. Barry human resource accounting. In T. J. Burns (Ed.), *The behavioral aspects of accounting data for performance evaluation.* Columbus: Ohio State University, College of Administrative Science, 1970.

CHAPTER 10

Auditing Change: The Technology of Measuring Change

Nicholas Bond
California State University at Sacramento

Patrick Goldring, an imaginative social analyst, believes that the life style in developed countries is approaching that of a broilerhouse chicken. In *The Broilerhouse Society* (1969), he even provides a comparative checklist of B characteristics (broilerhouse foods, broilerhouse jobs, broilerhouse leisure patterns) and non-B features on which can be scored an individual's resemblance to the ideal broilerhouse inmate. He goes on to describe office work in the broilerhouse society:

> The time is approaching when the handful of men and women marooned among automatic data-processing units in city offices will sigh for the departed days when flocks of twittering miniskirted girls brought romance and color to otherwise dreary working life. There will still, perhaps, be the bored, endlessly nail-filing girl in reception and the private secretary to answer the phone and fend off callers. But the invoice typist, the copy typist, the shorthand typist, the filing clerks and all the rest of the decorative office army will be gone. . . .
> As machines take over more routine functions, these last remaining executives, too, will pack up their office files and go home. When one

hundred percent car ownership and increasing population makes travel to town an impossible undertaking, there will be no reason why the executive should not work at home, if he still has any work to do. The conference phone-link enabling executives to hold a discussion without leaving their offices in six different cities is already a commonplace. . . . Transfer of documents by photowire or high-speed tape can easily be arranged [Goldring, 1969, pp. 56–57].

Skillfully and humorously presented, Goldring's broilerhouse society is a plausible, if uninviting, prospect.

Other behavioral scientists do not foresee such an unpleasant future, and according to them, the computer-based cybernetics revolution, although increasingly apparent, will not advance at a galloping pace. They regard the vision of automation's inevitable creation of a broilerhouse society as only fantasy.

However, all views of the future must take into account the occurrence, rate of onset, and ultimate effects of change. Furthermore, predictions about the future often designate some variables alleged to be critical to the change process. There exists, therefore, a need to develop a change measurement technology based on measurement models and change indicators.

> Such indicators would give a reading both on the current state of some segment of the social universe and on past and future trends, whether progressive or regressive, according to some normative criteria. The notion of social indicators leads directly to the idea of monitoring social change. If an indicator can be found that will stand for a set of correlated changes, and if intervention can be introduced (whether on the prime, indicative variable or on one of its systemic components), then the program administrator may have been provided a powerful analytical and policy tool [Sheldon & Moore, 1968, p. 4].

Two main classes of change data can be identified. One is the standard statistical series collected regularly by governmental and private agencies—for example, the decennial census, monthly reports on the labor force, the GNP and industrial sector statistics, and the Federal Reserve financial summaries. These data may initially be gathered for specific reasons (such as allocating Congressional seats), but they can have many other uses. Change is assessed primarily from time-series observations: data of one point in time are compared with data of a later point in time, and the difference or change is noted. For a finer analysis, subsets of data can be compared for their deviance from the central tabulations, and explanatory hypotheses can then be framed by classifying the subset variables. The time-series method is especially well suited to assessment of large structural changes in a whole society. Ordinarily, the investigator who studies such tabulations has little or no control over the phenomena he is observing, and the human subjects appearing in the tabulation for one period will not necessarily be the same as those appearing in comparable data from another period. Some American statistical series date from 1790.

The second type of change data is gathered from planned projects designed to produce specific changes in a relatively small group of persons, generally within a short time. Many such projects —for example, the Headstart and Job Corps programs—often are subject to critical public review, and thus are under pressure to achieve immediate, positive results.

The current proliferation of change projects has led to the increased recognition of the need for, and difficulties of, precise change measurement. For example, populous states now have central offices for coordinating and evaluating research on the effects of federally supported educational programs. Some projects allocate 10 percent or more of their funds for evaluation. Though the emphasis of this discussion is on work and work-related changes, the logic of change assessment is much the same for many different areas of study. For example, measuring and interpreting change in family size over the decades, in the long-term trends in the striking behavior of factory workers, and in employability as a result of technical training or growth as a result of therapy are all logically related enterprises.

TIME-SERIES OBSERVATIONS OF LONG-TERM CHANGE

Most observers would expect that the number of hours worked per week has declined steadily since the early years of the century, but consider the following data for American male factory workers:

Year	1900	1929	1940	1967
Hours per week	59	44	38	41

From 1900 to 1929 the number of hours worked per week decreased. However, from 1929 to 1967 the number of hours worked has remained almost the same; the trend stabilized during that period. This example illustrates the essence of time-series observation of change: the chosen index is simple and noncontroversial; the data stretch over a convincing period of time; the trend is obvious, and interpretation of the data does not require elaborate statistical machinery.

Sometimes a time-series observation reveals constancies that are startling. For example, the following figures show the percentage of income of American urban families contributed by the husband:

Year	1900	1935-1936	1960	1965
Percentage	80	82	80	81

During a 65-year period, when real income in the United States increased to more than twice that of 1900, the percentage of the husband's contributions to total family income remained constant. One possible interpretation is that families tended to adopt an income goal that is a fixed percentage over the husband's earnings.

There are similar consistencies in percentage of income spent on taxes (about 12 percent) and savings (about 6 percent) in the United States during a 25-year period following the onset of World War II. An informal taxation tolerance level seems to have settled at about 12 percent.

Sometimes a confusing array of time-series data will make sense when the data are ordered according to some outside variables. The GNP-growth figures for Western European countries present a mixed pattern, but, when they are arranged with other data, as in Table 1, the relationship between the GNP and other variables emerges. Countries with high unemployment still have many people working in agriculture; furthermore, the gains in national productivity (here defined as increase in GNP per inhabitant) ranged from 20 percent for Ireland to 85 percent for Germany. This increase in productivity is apparently related to a labor shift from agriculture to manufacturing and services. That a significant labor shift cannot be realized in countries already having relatively low rates of agricultural employment may help to explain the relatively low productivity increases for Britain and Belgium. Also indicated is a strong relationship between increases in productivity and increases in foreign trade. The GNP growth rate was slower for the 1955–1960 period than for the 1950–1955 period. However, it cannot be inferred that growth must taper off; comparable figures from the 1960–1964 period showed that the productivity boom continued, and overall European GNP growth during that period was about 18 percent (Holmberg, 1966, p. 169).

A productivity increase presumably is due to the utilization of more capital resources and to technological improvement; of these two factors, technology is the more important. Thus assembling a series of productivity indexes (goods and services produced per worker) is one way to measure technological change. Somewhat surprisingly, these indexes reveal a steadier, slower technological change rate than some social analysts would seem to suggest. Bell (1968) summarized six studies in which all of the indicators pointed to a technological change rate of approximately 2.5 percent per year. Despite the dazzling technology developed during the past 20 years, this rate is still only slightly higher than it was in the early decades of the century.

Other tabulations for the industrial sector further illuminate

Table 1. Relationship between GNP-per-Inhabitant, Labour Force in Agriculture, and Volume of Exports

Western European countries (by rate and direction of change in unemployment levels)	Volume increase in GNP/inhabitant (%)			Proportion of labour force in agriculture (%)		Increase in volume of exports (%)
	1950 to 1955	1955 to 1960	1950 to 1960	1950	1960	1950-60
a Continuous low unemployment:						
Norway	14	12	28	31	23	69
Sweden	13	14	29	20	14	72
Switzerland	23	17	44	17	11	96
Great Britain	14	9	24	6	4	19
b. Declining unemployment to low level:						
Denmark	6	22	29	25	19	100
West Germany	46	27	85	25	14	330
c. Diminishing but high unemployment:						
Austria	39	27	76	33	23	210
Belgium	15	9	25	11	8	102
France	20	18	41	28	21	104
The Netherlands	24	15	43	14	10	107
Italy	29	29	67	40	28	204
d. Continuous high unemployment:						
Finland	24	13	40	46	36	111
Greece	37	27	74	48	53	156
Ireland	13	6	20	41	36	76
Portugal	17	15	35	50	44	44
Spain	?	?	?	50	42	96
Turkey	18	19	40	77	75	45

Source: Holmberg, P. The relationship between full employment and technological change in Western Europe. In J. Stieber (Ed.), *Employment Problems of Automation and Advanced Technology*. Copyright 1966 by St. Martin's Press. Reprinted by permission of St. Martin's Press and Macmillan, London, and Basingstoke.

Bell's findings. High production increases have occurred in such industries as coal mining, railroads, and agriculture, which, in response to either declining or slowly growing demand for their products, cut back employment and introduced technological methods already known but not widely diffused—diesel power, strip mining, and mechanized agriculture (Bell, 1968, p. 196). If there is a latent, or not widely diffused, technology available, it is likely that greater productivity will be sought through utilization of the technology and by a smaller work force, with high wages and other added benefits for those workers who remain in that sector. The findings of studies on the diffusion lag between technological innovation and its adoption by industries indicate that (1) innovations are exploited nearly twice as fast in consumer applications as in industrial ones; and (2) rates for technological diffusion are similar in the middle and later stages of market penetration.

The overall figures for technological change, then, are not dramatic. The rate of technological change has increased in the past decades and will probably continue to increase. However, the current rate at which technological innovations are utilized throughout a sector does not indicate drastic increase in rate of technological change in the future. There have been, however, striking changes in the labor force, and if these changes continue to occur on a broad enough scale, basic structural changes in the society also can be postulated.

Perhaps the most dramatic change in the labor force has been the emergence of "knowledge workers" as a large segment of the labor force. In less than a decade (1963–1970), the proportion of the "scientific population" in America (scientists and engineers) has risen from approximately 3.5 percent to about 4.7 percent of the total population, and for the same period, the number of science doctorates has increased by over 50 percent; approximately half of those Americans in the 18 to 21 age group are in college. On the assumption that by 1972 about 3 percent of the people in the world would be doing work that is primarily intellectual, Bell (1968) predicted that the population of scientific workers would be nearly 100 million. He also predicted that by 1975 about one-fourth of the American labor force will have had 4 years of college, with professional and technical workers making up more than half of this educated segment of the working population. On both absolute and relative scales, these figures are impressive.

What is not shown in overall figures like these, however, is the concentration of the top scientific and engineering workers in relatively few places. When 10 universities do more than a third of the nation's university research, and 21 universities do more than half of the research, then Bell's three-class Scientific City begins to emerge: an elite class of creative and administrative leaders, a middle class of engineers and teachers, and a third (the largest) group of technicians and junior faculty. It ought to be possible to confirm or to extend such a three-group model via time-series indexes designed to measure dimensions of the differentiation among classes. Evidence that members of the elite group "draw closer together" over time and that mobilities across group lines tend to attenuate would indicate change.

It is easy to become euphoric over some of these numbers and to foresee indefinite growth in the need for technical specialists. In 1971, however, the job opportunities in nearly all technical occupations had dropped sharply from the previous year. The federal cutbacks in university support contracts and in aerospace research and development were so severe that many observers feel that there is now a glut of PhDs in chemistry, biology, and physics. A year or two of cutbacks in these areas would temper some of the projections for the Scientific City. Perhaps a major task for Scientific City inmates will be designing a systematic means for using the talent available within the gates.

Ordinarily, it is not difficult to decide whether a trend or peak exists in a time series, since for broad structural changes (or constancies) the trend will be obvious before it is analyzed. In 1950, only 29 percent of all women over age 14 were in the labor market. By 1970, the rate for all women was 39.6 percent, a gain of nearly one-third over the 1950 figure. The Census Bureau Report, from which these figures were taken, thus provides very few tests of significance for the various trends noted (U.S. Census Bureau, 1972). Controversies encountered in time-series analysis often emerge from data selection rather than from doubt that a genuine trend exists.

The selection of a time-series index gives rise to criterion problems. These problems exist in all change-tracking efforts, and though they can be managed, they cannot be solved. For example, if only one or a few numbers are taken as the indicator of a multidimensional process, fractional measurement will be the result (Etzioni & Lehman, 1967). Qualitative dimensions are not especially apt to be ignored. GNP figures do not account directly for such productivity as growth in educational level, personal security, or aesthetic awareness, nor do they include many hidden but definite costs. A partial solution to the fractional measurement problem is to measure as many dimensions of the process as practicable, and to interpret change effects on the basis of this multidimensional measurement. This method is sometimes called an overdetermination strategy. Other criterion problems arise from measurement stability, transformation of raw data units into standardized units, differing subjective importance of various possible indicators, and contaminated scores (for further discussion of criterion problems, see Campbell & Stanley, 1963; Campbell, 1967; Dunnette, 1966; and Sheldon & Moore, 1968).

EXPERIMENTS AND QUASI-EXPERIMENTS

Most visions of society demand planned change. Families in even a fully developed broilerhouse society will have to limit themselves to two or three children. Broilerhouse inhabitants will furthermore have to learn to be satisfied with machine-dispensed food and around-the-clock work schedules. In other words, present behaviors must change. Consider Bell's concept of the postindustrial society, for which he notes five key dimensions: (1) a service economy; (2) a preeminent technical class; (3) the impetus of theoretical knowledge; (4) self-sustaining technological growth; and (5) the creation of a knowledge technology. Bell's own analyses suggest that the postindustrial society is already here, but changes in any of the five dimensions could perhaps be accelerated by appropriate intervention. For example, planned change can possibly improve the occupational prospects of urban youth, perhaps by introducing special work or teaching programs, by constructing new career ladders, or by subsidizing employers for implementing development programs. But if planned change is to be implemented effectively, methods to evaluate and measure such change must be perfected.

Classical Experimentation

When I first started consulting on behavior-change projects some 15 years ago, I thought that a social scientist should be able to set up a satisfactory evaluation design in a free afternoon. Sometimes I had a free afternoon and was encouraged to make the attempt. What you ought to do, I would tell my clients, is to set up an experiment. Arrange for one group to receive change treatment (for example, training, counseling, persuasion, agency support) and an equivalent or control group not to receive it. Pretest and posttest scores for both groups can then be obtained and compared. If the client seemed to receive this advice favorably, I would then go on to my favorite

Table 2. The Solomon Four-Group Plan

	Experimental group	Control groups		
	A	B	C	D
Pretest	Yes	No	Yes	No
Treatment	Yes	Yes	No	No
Posttest	Yes	Yes	Yes	Yes

recommendation: the Solomon four-group plan (Solomon, 1949), which consists of one experimental and three control groups arranged as shown in Table 2. If subjects are randomly assigned to the four groups, and proper controls are maintained, the Solomon plan implies that a major treatment effect and three potential contaminant effects can be distinguished as follows:

Treatment effect:	Compare Posttest B with Posttest D
Test effect:	Compare Pretest C with Posttest C
Passage of time effect:	Compare Posttest D with Pretest A
	Compare Posttest D with Pretest C
	Compare Posttest D with average of Pretest A and Pretest C
Interaction effect:	Compare Posttest A with Posttest B
	Compare Posttest A with Posttest D

This classic four-group plan does facilitate comparison, and when it is accompanied by statistical tests, it is often recommended to social science and education students as the primary method of treatment evaluation. Unfortunately, this design and its variants have flaws. Simple passage of time and the treatment experience are assumed to affect independently the final outcome scores. However, some interaction between these two factors inevitably will take place, thus destroying some of the significance in comparisons of Posttest D with Pretests A and C. Serious practical problems emerged, too, when Belasco and Trice attempted to apply the four-group plan to two projects. The random assignment process guarantees, one would assume, that the starting points for all groups are the same. Yet, in one of their studies, A scores and C scores (there were about 30 subjects in each group) were significantly different on the pretest (Belasco & Trice, 1967). It then follows that perhaps B and D were originally different, too, and the entire comparison system collapses except for the rather uninteresting test effect on Group C.

Experimental logic dictates that conditions remain constant. As a change program progresses, however, certain modifications and improvements of the change agent, and perhaps of the subjects, occur. Thus to a project sponsor, classic experimental design may seem unrealistic.

Furthermore, the four-way plan demands large numbers of persons if satisfactory samples are to represent each group. For some projects, such as routine training programs for military recruits, number of participants would not be a serious problem, but for others, the large numbers could be burdensome or impractical.

Still another difficulty, encountered in almost any strict evaluation design, is administrative disapproval of the random assignment of people to conditions. Counselors do not regard their people as interchangeable, and they do not readily trust randomness in a test plan. The following is an account of a youth-work program that tried to carry out a controlled research plan:

> In essence the program required random assignment of trainees to the various program components. . . . With major decisions affecting a trainee's assignment delegated to a table of random numbers, the counselors came to believe their training and skills had become superfluous . . . Some of the counselors reacted by improvising ways of minimizing the impact of random assignment on some trainees . . . Many requests for exceptions were made by counselors, and most were accepted by the study director [Herman & Munk, 1968, p.171].

Agencies participating in change programs can sabotage evaluations in other ways. Patrick Suppes, who tested computer-aided instruction (CAI) in elementary mathematics, reports an interesting case. Part of Suppes' experimental plan was to provide 8 minutes per day of arithmetic practice by means of a computer-driven console. Every student at the experimental school had this CAI experience, and every control student in another school was denied it. The design was basically a two-group comparison, shown as A-C on the Solomon plan. The control school, however, soon initiated a program of 25 minutes per day of manual drill on the same arithmetic problems. The control group's posttest scores were a little higher than those of the experimental group; but as Suppes observes, this finding only means that 25 minutes of manual drill is better than 8 minutes of CAI drill. The strict comparison originally planned could not be made (Suppes & Morningstar, 1969).

Some of these experimental difficulties can be overcome or offset in various ways. In some circumstances, the pretest could be eliminated, thus leaving a two-group (B-D) comparison at the end. The larger numbers of subjects in each of the two groups should increase the likelihood of equivalent starting points. Arranging subjects into subgroups or "strata" might improve the match and increase the sensitivity of comparisons even further (but see Meehl, 1969, for a critique of post facto matching). There seems to be no easy resolution of the difficulties of imposing random assignment and standard treatment, though randomness could perhaps be achieved through deception—that is, by announcing that group assignment is made on some publicly acceptable basis when actually assignment is random.

The outlook for the traditional, controlled experimental designs, then, is rather pessimistic. Perhaps such designs are suited for only a minority of project situations involving people, such as measuring effects of a technical training course which has already been well standardized and debugged. In real world settings, where the change agent is dealing with complex or threatening variables and objectives, the practical control difficulties may not be worth the effort.

If controlled experiments are not feasible, what are the alternatives? Evaluation studies that have tried to follow the classic experimental plan offer some clues. In a Baltimore project (Belasco & Trice, 1967), alcoholics treated in a therapeutic milieu were not, in general, affected positively by the treatment. However, of the patient total of 378, some 20 percent did show improvement. Those who showed some improvement seemed to fall into three classes: "improvers," "maintainers," and "AA joiners." It turned out that "improvers" tended to have personality and demographic traits that were different from those in the other two groups. A similar situation emerged in a supervisor training study (Belasco & Trice, 1967). When evaluated by traditional design comparisons, training effects were slight. But some supervisors did change favorably as a result of the training, and some even appeared to change simply by taking the pretest. Moreover, as revealed by questionnaires, those who changed favorably after training exhibited personality-trait patterns different from those of the supervisors who were affected by testing only. Thus response to planned change is individual, and individual differences can be exploited by the change agency. Knowing and using information on individual differences should, then, improve the likelihood of treatment success, and treatment assignment in some projects should not be random but should be made on the basis of information about susceptibility to treatment. Such information, if not initially available, could perhaps be obtained from pilot tests.

Hyman and Wright (1965) urge the comparative design whereby several treatments are available and every participant gets some type of treatment. They offer this design as an answer to the ethical problem of giving some subjects no treatment at all, and they point out the advantages of exploring effectiveness over a great range of therapeutic procedures. Exposing subjects to different treatments is compatible with the comparative design and, in fact, is at present being used in computer-aided instruction (CAI). For example, math students are given access to a variety of aids, and, to a certain extent, the students can choose from the aids to design their own assistance formats. The computer then matches specific materials in these assistance formats to the students' past performances and learning histories.

Cooley and Glaser (1969) are working with computer-aided instruction with Pittsburgh school children. Their CAI system is essentially a process of adapting the instruction to the peculiarities of the individual student's progress. The TASKTEACH concept (Rigney, Towne, & Langston, 1972) also provides a highly interactive mode of adapting to individual differences. In this approach, tasks are arranged and taught in hierarchical lists. Students can move ahead to higher-level tasks if certain contingencies are realized.

Planned change projects, then, require flexibility both for experimenting with change agents and for recognizing individual variability in response. What other characteristics should the evaluation model have? Baker (1967) proposes an interdisciplinary approach, with many small-scale experiments serving to guide the choices of the next treatment. Campbell (1967) believes that the achievement of massive treatment effects is the main objective; the effect can be analyzed after it is obtained, and perhaps it then can be further exploited.

The traditional experiment as a method of evaluation can be criticized also for its narrow scope. An experiment usually settles on a single criterion dimension, and the whole effort depends on observations of that dimension. But in most situations of interest, the criterion should be multidimensional; while there is no logical reason why an experimental investigation cannot observe several criterion dimensions, in fact the change agent usually favors or fixes on a single criterion. Odiorne (1965) notes that an experiment should be part of a continuous feedback process, rather than just an isolated event or demonstration. When an experiment has been completed and the results dutifully presented, the really difficult tasks can begin—modifying the change processes themselves.

Finally, experiments often fail to focus on the real goals of an organization. To demonstrate that a special two-year carpentry apprenticeship yields significant skill improvement may be of no real value if the apprenticeship program has an extremely high drop-out rate and is very expensive to run. Experiments can indicate whether the average performance under treatment A is superior to average performance under treatments B or C. But the real question may not be whether the treatment A is more effective, but rather, what levels of performance can be expected from nearly every person at an acceptable cost.

Quasi-Experiments and Behavior Control

When large numbers of subjects are unavailable for random assignment, and when strict experimental controls cannot be imposed on a project, it is still possible to determine the effects of factors by means of quasi-experimental designs. Campbell and Stanley (1963) delineate a number of quasi-experimental possibilities. A quasi-experiment can be performed with a single individual or a small group. While no control group is present, the A-B-A-B reversal design permits a kind of control by withdrawing treatment and then reinstating it.

The reversal design was applied to the change problem of a crying child in a school classroom (Hart, Allen, Buell, Harris, & Wolf, 1964). A child was crying loudly about 8 times per day (the A or baseline condition). Extinction treatment (the teacher ignored the cries) appeared to produce a reduction in frequency, and thus an A-B change, but this reduction could have been due to any number of other factors. Accordingly, the treatment was withdrawn and the A condition (responding to the child's cries) was reinstated. Frequency of crying rises to nearly the previous A level. When the extinction treatment was introduced again, the frequency dropped; the behavior seemed to be under the control of the treatment. The case became more convincing as more reversals were demonstrated.

Another quasi-experimental variant, described by Wolf and Risley (1970), introduces the change agent in one setting but not in another, and then uses the second setting as a control for the first situation. Wolf and Risley wanted to reduce undesirable behavior (leaving seats and talking out) in a fourth-grade classroom. They first tried the experimental treatment in the math period. Treatment consisted of dividing the pupils into two groups and telling them they were to play a game. Each undesirable out-of-seat or talking-out response was marked on the blackboard. If neither team got more than five marks, everyone received certain privileges (for example, extra recess or being first in the lunch line). If both teams received more than five marks, the team with fewer marks received the privileges. This scheme seemed to reduce markedly the undesirable behaviors.

The argument for using a multiple-baseline is that in the reading period, during which there was no game to extinguish the behaviors, the behaviors tended to remain at a high level, even though the students and the teacher were the same as for the math period. The fact that behavior control was effected only in the math period indicates that the reduction of undesirable behavior did not occur merely by chance. When Wolf and Risley introduced the treatment during the reading period, they again effected the desired changes. Even without this later intervention in the reading class, the greater control of behavior in the math class made a convincing case that the treatment was effective.

Large federally funded projects generally are created to produce changes that are more complex and significant than these small changes in classroom behavior. Yet how many projects rely on the quasi-experiment to indicate whether their variables actually produce the desired change? Perhaps some small-scale evaluations should be required early in the life of a project; if evidence of desired change cannot be demonstrated on even a small scale, then the variables to be manipulated in the project would be suspect.

Change Scores

There are several ways to assess change from one occasion to another. Raw gain, or the difference between pretest and posttest scores, is frequently used; for instance, in the Suppes CAI study mentioned above, mean gains for the experimental and control math pupils were presented. The larger mean gain for the experimental group was then offered as evidence of CAI effectiveness. Raw gains, though, are often correlated negatively with initial score, and, when such a correlation occurs, there is the possibility that a curvilinear relation exists between amount of knowledge and measured test score. Lord (1958) says:

> ... the gains of the good students do tend to be numerically less than those of the poor students. However, who is to say but that a gain from an initial true score of 65 to a final true score of 70 may not in every important sense be "greater" than the numerically larger gain from 45 to 55? The former gain, for example, may represent more hours of

study or more effort on the part of the teacher or perhaps a more important insight than the latter, numerically larger, gain [p. 435].

Cronbach and Furby (1970) distinguish four situations in which it may seem desirable to estimate gains or differences from one occasion to another. They suggest that individual gains or change scores are seldom useful and that attention should be directed to the final posttest score and to the relationship among all scores. Consider, for example, the evaluation of a neighborhood youth corps work-training program. Suppose that, in a standard A-C two-group experiment, a portion of the applicants who appear at a training center is randomly assigned to training, and the remaining portion is not. A pretest score X, perhaps a conglomerate of personal history and attitude items representing employability status, and a posttest score Y for each subject on these same items are administered. There may also be some other pretreatment information, such as vocabulary or years completed in school, designated W. Cronbach and Furby recommend first determining which linear combination of X and W best predicts the final score Y, and then performing analysis of covariance adjustments on the Ys. An adjusted Y that is higher for the experimentals than for the controls would be evidence in favor of the training experience. The extent of the adjustment would depend on how high the correlation was between the final score Y and the combination of X and W; if the correlation was very low, then the experimenter would be operating on the Y scores only. For a one-group experiment in which each individual acts as his own control, the recommendation is to compare the X average with the Y average, not to compute individual change scores.

A change project may also test for what kinds of people show greatest gains. Two subjects have identical pretest scores X, but one achieves a much higher Y. Why? In order to answer this question, the experimenter needs some information other than X; perhaps W data will suffice. Cronbach and Furby (1970) suggest a regression approach in which the final score Y is regressed on estimated pretest score X and ancillary score W. "... It appears that nothing is gained by referring to change measures in this context. The relationships of true scores can be investigated without estimating true scores for individuals [p. 79]."

For a third type of change inquiry, Cronbach and Furby postulate the situation in which the deviant subjects are to be identified. A deviant in a training study is one who learns much faster (or much slower) than was predicted; a deviant in a psychotherapy study is one whose self-concept approaches the ideal self much more quickly than anticipated. To select deviants, regression equations are set up to predict final status for each individual, and this prediction is compared with estimated final status. In addition to X scores, all the early W information should be included in making the Y forecast. As a matter of fact, Cronbach and Furby recognize that change is often multidimensional, and they urge multiple measurements on both ends of a change attempt. Thus their equations include a Z variate, which might be a retention test of Y. A variety of W-X-Y-Z relationships can be explored.

A fourth possible use of difference scores is to develop an index of some theoretical construct. The experimenter can postulate some dynamic variable, such as personal growth, and attempt to operationalize it by writing various difference scores as part of the definitional network. But, as Cronbach and Furby ask, why fix on Y-X? Perhaps Y-$.6X$ or Y-$.2X$ would turn out to be a better weighted relation between the variables. "There is little reason to believe and much reason to disbelieve the contention that some arbitrarily weighted function of two variables will properly define a construct. More often, the profitable strategy is to use the two variables separately in the analysis so as to allow for complex relationships [Cronbach & Furby, 1970, p. 79]."

It is believed that the Cronbach and Furby recommendations will have a salutary influence on statistical practice in change projects. As a result of their work, probably fewer raw gain comparisons will be reported from now on. Their focus on posttest, or Y, scores in experimental studies accords well with such designs as the multiple-baseline and reversal, and adjusting the Ys by covariance should be feasible when there is much W information on individuals and behavior control is not achievable. The special case, or the deviant group, has always been a problem in change measurement, and the idea of a general residual gain for identifying such deviants ought to be pursued; until now, experimenters have had little opportunity to test the validity or usefulness of knowing who those people are who make extraordinary (unpredicted) progress. The Cronbach and Furby formulas should encourage some empirical work in this direction.

ALTERNATIVE CHANGE-EVALUATION MODELS

Besides time series and experimentation, there are many other ways to monitor change. A few of the many possibilities are examined below.

The Legal Model

Guttentag (1970) suggests that a scientific interpretation can be viewed as a process whereby two adversaries present their case, each attempting to make the best possible argument for his position. There are set processes for admitting evidence; legal methods (usually analogical) for inferring from the evidence. Legal rationales for classifying a given case under one rubric or another could be applied also to change projects.

To an outsider, the legal approach to deciding matters of fact often seems rigid and arbitrary. But since the legal system has always dealt with real-world complexities, the process might be expected to maintain a steady focus on relevant issues, thus providing an alternative to experimental methods, which Guttentag (1970) has criticized as being precise but irrelevant. At present, fully developed project evaluations based on the legal model do not exist; maybe some should be attempted and compared with other evaluations of the same projects. It is expected that evaluations based on the legal model would be oriented toward certain idiosyncratic achievements and limitations, rather than toward overall changes.

Ecobehavioral Measurement

In observing a school classroom, Guttentag (1970) noted that activity "... did not stretch out in a homogenous mass but instead developed in blocks or segments. These segments have internal integrity and boundaries. They are units with a time-space locus, microenvironments, and they coerce the behavior of their inhabitants." Thus if an observer wants to know what is happening in that schoolroom (and similarly, in a neighborhood or society), he would have to identify the beginning and end of these segments, understand their immediate concern or business, and determine their importance to the participants. Such ecobehavioral units define the real environment in the classroom, and at least certain features of that environment could be scored and watched for change.

It is not known whether the ecobehavioral model can make a unique contribution to project studies. Kounin predicted children's behavior by relating dimensions of a teacher's style to the ecology of the classroom (Kounin, Friesen, & Norton, 1966). Ecological changes, then, might be suitable criteria in many project settings. An ecobehavioral analysis would at least take explicit account of factors contributing to the social climate.

Social-Area Analysis

A city is divided into tracts; for each tract, a number of data items are tabulated, including marriage, housing, health, education, court, and welfare statistics. Baseline levels on each performance index are then established for each tract; program effectiveness is assessed by initiating the program in some tracts and not in others. If the project is designed to reduce delinquency, then specific indexes of truancy, teenage arrests, and incarcerated youth should be below baseline. It might happen that other indexes not directly identifiable as delinquencies would also be affected by the program.

This approach is really a multidimensional variant of the multiple-baseline design mentioned earlier. Or it could become an A-B-A-B reversal scheme if the program could be applied and withdrawn on demand. Probably the most interesting methodological feature would be the combination of various data items into composite indexes to represent global changes. Massive changes are probably not to be expected without massive program efforts; hence the few studies based on the social-area model have been rather inconclusive.

The Representative Case

Change in a single individual can be highly informative if the individual is especially suitable for testing the effects of certain manipulations. The subject is not randomly selected. Rather, the subject is carefully selected on the basis of his possession of particular characteristics that are the variables to be studied. If a change project is directed to the dynamics of hostile attitudes toward new career ladders, the observer would choose an individual who has already demonstrated such hostility. Data collection would then attempt to document hostile reactions to manipulated or natural variables. For example, program administrators often assume that information about career opportunities will reduce skepticism and promote positive interest; a representative case study could test the effects of such information.

An example of a representative case study is Zinker's study of a woman dying from cancer (see Shontz, 1965). The change to be observed was the degree of the patient's personality disorganization as she approached death. In terms of Maslow's hierarchy of needs, it would be supposed that, as death neared, the higher needs (esteem, self-actualization) would become less salient. To measure such changes, interview data from the patient were tabulated into a hierarchy-of-needs score for each interview session; other data were available, too, such as weekly psychological ratings by hospital staff. Although physiological needs of this patient were frustrated as death neared, love and a sense of belonging were apparently stable and relatively satisfied throughout the several months of the study. Thus, facing imminent death is not necessarily an experience that produces regression of needs in the Maslow schema.

A major objection to the representative case study method is that an individual may be unique, and consequently the effects observed cannot be generalized. However, if the process of interest (need-hierarchy structure in the dying patient, or hostility in the underemployed) is tracked in a clearly representative individual, one or a few cases may be sufficient for some evaluative purposes.

A practical difficulty with the representative-case method is the response bias induced by the investigator. Technical precautions such as rotated or uninformed observers can help; the subject himself, even though he knows the general purpose of the project, can still be naive about some of the specific responses that are being tabulated. Shontz (1965) gives a thorough and generally favorable critique of the method, along with examples of its use for studying drug effects, dream interpretation, and clinical states. He also suggests ways to make the method more powerful—by providing for times when the behavior of interest should not appear and by differentiating subclasses of the critical behavior, for example.

Large change projects, before they become irrevocably committed to a particular set of variables, might benefit by a test of the effectiveness of change treatments in one or two representative cases. If the project does not produce change in a single individual, perhaps there are individual differences in responses to the effectiveness of the program, or perhaps the entire program should be reexamined. At the very least, the investigator should consider the possibility of the program's overall ineffectiveness.

Statistical Optimization

Not all statistical models require the treatment plan of the fixed experiment. Various schemes, often called adaptive or learning models, respond to the data as they are collected. Consider the evolutionary model proposed by Box (Box & Draper, 1969). This model does more than just test for effects; it is designed to locate a point of optimum yield for the variables under consideration and to prescribe new levels (of the treatment) on the basis of early results. This method has been applied in the chemical industries and seems to lead to genuine cost savings over nonoptimized processes. Dimensional requirements are stringent, however, and the variables must be quantitatively scaled so that the response surface can be defined and examined for maximum points.

A similar model is Cornfield's adaptive procedure for conducting clinical trials (Cornfield, Halperin, & Greenhouse, 1969). Two treatments—A and B—are designed. As evidence accumulates to indicate which treatment is superior, an increasing proportion of patients are assigned to the more effective treatment. Cornfield postulates that cost, in this situation, is defined in terms of two factors: (1) the proportion of patients assigned to the wrong treatment; and (2) the absolute size of treatment difference. Patients are thus allocated to the treatments so as to minimize cost. If the decision-maker has an estimate of the treatment difference, he can use this information at the beginning by assigning appropriate numbers of patients to treatments A and B. This procedure, as Cornfield notes,

> ... might ease the ethical problem involved in trials on human subjects. The usual ethical justification for not administering an agent of possible efficacy to all patients is the absence of definite information about its effectiveness. However satisfactory this justification may be before the trial starts, it rapidly loses cogency as evidence for or against the agent accumulates during the course of the trial. But any solution, such as the present one, which permits adaptive behavior, i.e., the allocation of proportionately more and more of the future patients to the apparently better treatment, at least reduces this ethical problem. [Cornfield, Halperin, & Greenhouse, 1969, p. 766].

The adaptive control design is analogous to a black box; inside the black box is a complex machine. It is not understood exactly how the machine runs, so optimal input settings cannot be prescribed in advance. However, an output measure and also quantitative indexes on each of the inputs are available. Suppose the system starts to run. To improve the output, an observer can randomly cause variation in each of the inputs, observe the effects on the output, and keep adjusting the inputs as the feedback indicates. It is hoped that eventually the input variables that cause pronounced effects will receive the most weight, ineffectual factors will be weighted out, and the system will progress toward maximum output. There are even adaptive configurations that can be said to "learn," in the sense that the weighting can produce more than one input pattern and then discriminate among unknown signals via the learned weights.

One such adaptive model, Opcon, was realized as a practical device more than a decade ago. In a way, Opcon is a physical realization of the statistical notion of evolutionary surface. Opcon attempts to optimize chemical processes by making step-by-step changes in one variable, allowing the system sufficient time to adjust to the change, and then measuring the effect. After the effect is determined, a decision is made concerning the next change in the variable, as in which direction the change should be. This process continues until an optimal relationship exists between the input variables and the outputs.

The Dow Chemical Company applied the Opcon system to a pilot plant for the production of styrene. A complete optimizing run could be achieved in several days, and each new setting was allowed to run for an hour or more to let the plant stabilize. Of course, attempts to apply this method to human change would undoubtedly require more time for implementation, would be more ambiguous in their effects, and might never stabilize. But a step-change adaptive model might be worthwhile, and the random variation of the amount of treatment deserves consideration, even though it is seldom attempted with people.

As exciting as these adaptive schemes are, they are apt to be more inspirational than immediately useful. The instability of the social environment and the unreliability of the measurements used suggest that even the most powerful adaptive techniques might not provide any significant system improvement. But such methods as the purposive, but random, variation in parameters and the learning of contingent patterns via adjustive monitoring might be used in certain kinds of planned change efforts. As an example, consider the Negative Income Tax proposal for direct money payments to poor families. There is a basic floor for family income, say $3,300 a year. If a family has no earned income, it still receives $3,300 annually. For each additional dollar of earned income, the allotment of free money is reduced slightly; perhaps each additional earned dollar causes a loss of 30 cents in free money. Thus the reduction in support is arranged so that the family is always slightly better off when it earns outside income. A key question is whether work behavior changes as a result of the free money payments.

Starting in 1967, field tests were tried on the effects of negative income tax alternatives (Kershaw, 1972). An early finding of these studies is that work behavior of supported families is not much different from comparable families who do not receive such support; about 31 percent of the supported families increased their earnings by more than $25 per week, compared to 33 percent of the control families who received no such support. Introduction of payments apparently was not a disincentive to work. As such programs are publicized, however, the responses to them may change; and as the affected people adapt to the payment plan, there may also be need for administrators to adjust income floors, payments, and support reduction rates in an adaptive way.

Probabilistic Information Processing

Edwards has proposed a specific decision configuration of humans and computers (see Edwards & Phillips, 1964). The procedure is to employ individuals in those tasks for which they are best suited (or for which they are absolutely essential) and to use computers for high-speed processing of the information generated by the individuals. Individuals must provide utility and likelihood values, for instance, but these might be best assembled and multiplied by the computer. Suppose that the desired output is a diagnosis, and that a diagnosis was made when probabilities were assigned to each of the possible diagnostic categories. There are many cues in the real world which might aid this diagnosis. The human's job is to estimate the conditional likelihood of obtaining each data cue under each diagnostic category. A Bayesian computer routine would then calculate the "best" diagnosis.

A system like Edwards' could be of use in many projects involving people. Counselors in youth programs often observe, for instance, that it is difficult to predict which of the applicants will stay with a given work program long enough to gain any real experience. Nearly every big city has tried some kind of hospital trainee project; individuals may be offered jobs as dietary aides or laundry workers. Drop-out rates are high, and only a small number from the original group of trainees may eventually be hired for jobs; yet some do complete the program. A diagnostic program for providing Bayesian "success likelihood" on each participant should be feasible for such training programs; the conditional probabilities could be updated as more cases were processed and followed up. Changes in the likelihood of success would be taken as evidence of program effectiveness. The same approach could be used to identify those families who will respond appropriately to a negative income tax plan.

Preliminary tests show that under appropriate display conditions, the probabilistic information processor (**PIP**) does yield output probabilities and that these probabilities may be more valid than regular, unprocessed estimates made by experienced judges. The possible gains of applying PIP to human resources are promising enough to encourage serious trial.

Simulation

A physical, algebraic, or other representation of a process may be called a simulation if it can imitate some of the behavior of the process. Certain disciplines, such as aerodynamics, employ analog models, but the only practical analog simulations of complex human behavior are those that imitate continuous tracking tasks. Digital simulations store information about the time required to complete each step in a process, the likelihood of successful completion, the effects of one task on another, and so on. To accomplish a simulated run throughout the whole process, the stored information is sampled according to some random-number plan, and the overall performance data are combined. A run ends when the task is completed or when the allowed time runs out. By changing some of the stored distributions, the observer can explore many aspects of performance. Simulation allows the observer to push the limits of a configuration without the dangers and expense of the real process. Among those processes successfully simulated are the human behaviors involved in landing an aircraft, riding a bicycle, and the ordering behavior of a department store executive.

If the structural relations that determine complex social behaviors were known, they too could be simulated. Bell (1968) foresees simulation models of whole societies in his Scientific City. Early social planners thought that a social planetarium would improve democracy because citizens could visit the planetarium on Sunday afternoon, insert social changes into it, and observe the consequences.

Simulation of complex social units may soon be possible, as the Forrester central-city project suggests. Forrester (1971) simulates a city by means of 3 "level variables" and 22 "rate variables." The level variables are (1) class of population (labor, management, the underemployed), (2) housing (one type for each population class), and (3) industry (new, mature, declining). The rate variables prescribe how the three basic components change over time. All these factors are stored in a computer program. Once the initial conditions are set, the program structure will cause the rate variables to operate with the level variables, and thus produce a running history of the city.

Forrester has already computer-tested certain proposals for revitalizing the city. His computer runs indicate that job training programs and low-rent housing attract low-income workers to the city and that training projects may hasten the exodus of trained people from the city. Thus the intervention may make matters worse. To discover those policies that would be effective, the simulation would try many combinations of policies and rate variables; in all likelihood, some new variables and relationships would have to be invented, too.

A large-scale simulation like Forrester's is bound to be inaccurate or incomplete in some of its structural relations, boundaries, and predictions. Forrester believes, however, that the model is concordant with certain gross historical data, and that changes can be made without abandoning the basic concept. The main trouble with simulation is that the output is so critically dependent on the values and relations that are put into the model. An example is the Club of Rome world simulation for the next few decades. This model produced very pessimistic predictions when Forrester (1971) inserted his resource and technological assumptions; by the end of the century, resources will be depleted, population will decrease, and the average standard of living will be sharply reduced. But Boyd (1972) obtained very optimistic projections from the same model by changing some of the input parameters regarding technology. It appears that if simulation of social change is to be more than an intriguing academic exercise, the inputs should be anchored in real-world observations and continuously updated. More credence could be placed in those simulations that were based on reliable statistical values and variance estimates.

Provisional Development

In direct reaction to the decision theory and the cost-effectiveness movement is a change strategy that might be called provisional development. It comes from several sources in political science, economics, and engineering; in fact, Hirschman and Lindblom (1962) describe the remarkable and independent convergence of certain ideas from these three disciplines.

At first glance, the provisional approach seems to be irrational. It denies, for example, the truth of two widely accepted propositions: (1) public policy problems can best be solved by attempting to understand them; and (2) there exists sufficient agreement to provide adequate criteria for choosing among possible alternative policies. The argument against these propositions is multifaceted, but its essence is that complexity and uncertainty simply preclude a total synoptic view of certain problems. The information for getting good parameter estimates is just not available; the number of conceivable policies is too large to deal with; objectives are blurred, and they change unpredictably from one time period to another. Consequently, in many situations, understanding is impossible to obtain.

The approach then prescribes marginal change, intensive exploration of a small number of possible policies, remedial instead of optimal policy, and simultaneous means-end choices. In economic terms, such a philosophy would favor unbalanced growth, with the imbalances being corrected by increased resource mobilization. Thus if a developing country wants to achieve growth in both industrial and agricultural production, it might be best to place emphasis upon one aspect heavily at first, and then, forced by troubles in the neglected sector, to mobilize for the other activity.

The same arguments are also applicable to development projects wherein it is better to carry along various programs and live with the confusion and inefficiency because the achievement may ultimately be more balanced than it appears to be early in the project. The argument is especially persuasive when the main objective is eventual, rather than immediate, radical improvement.

Among the interesting aspects of the provisional approach is its explicit and even cheerful acknowledgment of man's limitations and the world's uncertainties. Hirschman and Lindblom ask the key question, "... as long as we know that a system is going to be out of balance anyway when the subsystems develop, what type of unbalance is most likely to be self-correcting? [1962, p. 221]" They also recognize that extreme unbalance and rigid marginalism can have destructive effects. There ought to be, it appears, some blend of provisionalism and centralized planning in every important project.

EXPECTATIONS

It appears that long-term change analysis will continue to focus on the invention of suitable indexes, their combination into theories of structural change, the informal analysis of discontinuities, and cross-classification schemes for interpreting changes. There is also a good chance that analysts will give more attention to some of the statistical techniques for projecting time-series observations into the future.

Large-scale projects will probably not typically attempt to carry out broad experiments in order to prove project worth or to discover the potent variables. Instead, the small-scale, but revealing, demonstration of behavior control, via treatment introduction and withdrawal, will be the principal method of project study. As the criterion of behavior control gains more recognition, projects designed for people will necessarily become more concerned with the selection of subjects and with individualized treatments.

Serious attempts to implement decision models and optimization schemes should indicate whether probabilities and outcome values can be scaled so as to permit the models to be worked. Occasional successes can be expected, and even where the synoptic approaches fail, some of their parameter estimates will provide useful change measurement.

SUMMARY

A technology for measuring change and its effects is developing. Several methods, already available, show promise for auditing change as we move toward the year 2001. Time-series analysis is the collection of descriptive statistics for a long period in order to map trends or changes associated with social interventions. Generally, however, interpretation of such trends requires a degree of intuition. The method is beset with criterion problems because the investigator has no direct control over variations in the phenomenon being studied.

Other approaches for detecting change involve various experimental or quasi-experimental designs. A project may be undertaken in order to effect a particular change. For example, a new teaching method may be undertaken with the hope of changing the usual rate of student learning. The investigator wants to know whether change occurred; and, if it did, whether or not it was the result of the new method or treatment. Even the most rigorous of classic experimental design, the Solomon four-group design, suffers shortcomings: many subjects are required; the passage of time is not necessarily independent of treatment effects; random assignment of subjects is difficult and somewhat uncertain; results obtained cannot be used immediately to modify the design to yield further information; and, most serious, some participants may even sabotage the experiment.

Because of the rigidity of most classic designs and the near impossibility of conducting such experiments in areas of most significance in the real world, innovative quasi-experiments have been developed and used successfully. Of these, the multiple-baseline and reversal design appear more promising. However, both the experiment and the quasi-experiment often fix on just one criterion, do not observe all critical variables, fail to focus on the real goals, do not allow sufficiently for early results to influence decisions later in the experiment, and do not adequately take account of individual differences. In short, both the experimental and quasi-experimental designs need greater flexibility and greater allowance for individual differences.

Several other approaches exist for measuring and monitoring change. These include the legal model, ecobehavioral measurement, social-area analysis, the representative case, statistical optimization, decision theory, probabilistic-information processing, simulation, and provisional development. The legal model focuses on relevant issues. Ecobehavioral measurement analyzes homogeneous blocks of behavior, identifying the beginning and the end of each behavioral segment. Social-area analysis divides a city or social unit into blocks and collects data from various areas; it is a variant of the multiple-baseline design. Prior to committing a large resource to the design or study, the representative-case approach selects for study a person or a small group of people. However, the individual or small group may be unique, and the results may be misleading. In certain respects, the representative case study is analogous to a pilot study. The statistical-optimization approach feeds back into the system that information which has been gathered so that the system can change in an optimal direction. Change is monitored and modified to effect an optimal outcome. Decision systems combine the probabilities and utilities from human sources by means of computer algorithms and produce diagnostic likelihoods and optimal strategies. Simulation is the imitation of the behavior without the expense of the real process. Provisional development assumes the world is uncertain and much is unknown, and it attempts to initiate unbalanced growth that will lead eventually to balance and improvement.

REFERENCES

Baker, F. B. Experimental design considerations associated with large-scale research projects. In J. Stanley (Ed.), *Improving design and statistical analysis.* Chicago: Rand McNally, 1967.

Belasco, J. A., & Trice, H. M. *Assessing change in training and therapy.* New York: McGraw-Hill, 1967.

Bell, D. The measurement of knowledge and technology. In E. H. Sheldon & W. E. Moore (Eds.), *Indicators of social change: Concepts and measurements.* New York: Russell Sage Foundation, 1968.

Box, G. E. P., & Draper, N. R. *Evolutionary operation: A statistical method for process improvement.* New York: Wiley, 1969.

Boyd, R. World dynamics: A note. *Science,* 1972, **177,** 516–519.

Campbell, D. T. Administrative experimentation, institutional records, nonreactive measures. In J. Stanley (Ed.), *Improving experimental design and statistical analysis.* Chicago: Rand McNally, 1967.

Campbell, D., & Stanley, J. Experimental and quasi-experimental designs for research on teaching. In N. C. Gage (Ed.), *Handbook of research on teaching.* Chicago: Rand McNally, 1963.

Cooley, W. W., & Glaser, R. The computer and individualized instruction. *Science,* October 1969, **166,** 574–582.

Cornfield, J., Halperin, M., & Greenhouse, S. E. An adaptive procedure for segmental clinical trials. *Journal of the American Statistical Association,* 1969, **64,** 759–770.

Cronbach, L. J., & Furby, L. How we should measure "change"—or should we? *Psychological Bulletin,* 1970, **74,** 68–80.

Dunnette, M. D. *Personnel selection and placement.* Belmont, Calif.: Wadsworth, 1966.

Edwards, W., & Phillips, L. D. Emerging technologies for making decisions. In G. L. Bryan & M. W. Shelly (Eds.), *Human judgments and optimality.* New York: Wiley, 1964.

Etzioni, A., & Lehman, E. W. Some dangers in 'valid' social measurements. In B. Gross (Ed.), *Annals of Social and Political Sciences,* 1967, **373,** 1–15.

Forrester, J. W. *World dynamics.* Cambridge, Mass.: Wright-Allen, 1971.

Goldring, P. *The broilerhouse society.* New York: Weybright & Talley, 1969.

Guttentag, M. Model and methods in evaluation research. New York: City University of New York Graduate Center, 1970.

Harris, C. W. (Ed.) *Problems in measuring change.* Madison, Wisc.: University of Wisconsin Press, 1963.

Hart, B. M., Allen, K. E., Buell, J. S., Harris, F. R., & Wolf, M. M. Effects of social reinforcement on operant crying. *Journal of Experimental Child Psychology,* 1964, **1,** 145–153.

Herman, M., & Munk, M. *Decision making in poverty programs.* New York: Columbia University Press, 1968.

Hirschman, A. O., & Lindblom, C. E. Economic development, research and development, policymaking: Some converging views. *Behavioral Science,* 1962, **7,** 211–222.

Holmberg, P. The relationship between full employment and technological change in Western Europe. In J. Stieber (Ed.), *Employment problems of automation and advanced technology.* London: St. Martin's Press, 1966.

Hyman, H. H., & Wright, C. Evaluating social action programs. In J. D. Halloran (Ed.), *The uses of sociology.* London: Sheed & Ward, 1965.

Kershaw, D. N. A negative-income-tax experiment. *Scientific American,* 1972, **227,** 19–25.

Kounin, J. S., Friesen, W. V., & Norton, A. E. Managing emotionally disturbed children in regular classrooms. *Journal of Educational Psychology,* 1966, **57,** 1–13.

Lord, F. M. Further problems in the measurement of growth. *Educational and Psychological Measurement,* 1958, **18,** 437–454.

Meehl, P. *Nuisance variables and the ex post facto design.* Minneapolis: University of Minnesota, Department of Psychiatry, PR-69-4, 1969.

Odiorne, G. S. A systems approach to training. *Training Directors Journal,* 1965, **19,** 3–11.

Rigney, J. W., Towne, D. M., & Langston, E. T. *Computer-aided performance training for diagnostic and procedural tasks.* Los Angeles: University of Southern California, Electronics Personnel Research Groups, Technical Report 70, September 1972.

Sheldon, E. H., & Moore, W. E. (Eds.) *Indicators of social change: Concepts of measurements.* New York: Russell Sage Foundation, 1968.

Shontz, F. C. *Research methods in personality.* New York: Appleton-Century-Crofts, 1965.

Solomon, R. L. An extension of control group design. *Psychological Bulletin,* 1949, **46,** 137–150.

Suppes, P., & Morningstar, M. Computer-assisted instruction. *Science,* October 1969, **166,** 343–350.

U. S. Census Bureau Report. Cited in the *Sacramento Bee,* October 15, 1972.

Wolf, M. M., & Risley, T. R. *Reinforcement: Applied research.* In R. Glaser (Ed.), *The nature of reinforcement: Part II.* Pittsburgh: University of Pittsburgh Research and Development Center, 1970.

SUGGESTED READING

Bennis, W. G. Theory and method in applying behavioral science to planned organizational change. In J. R. Laurence (Ed.), *Operational research and the social sciences.* London: Tavistock Publications, 1966.

Cronback, L. J., & Gleser, G. C. *Psychological tests and personnel decisions.* (2nd ed.) Urbana: University of Illinois Press, 1965.

Fleishman, E. A., & Hempel, W. E., Jr. Changes in the factor structure of a complex psychomotor test as a function of practice. *Psychometrika,* 1954, **19,** 239–252.

Fishburn, P. *Decision and value theory.* New York: Wiley, 1964.

Harris, C. W. (Ed.) *Problems in measuring change.* Madison: University of Wisconsin Press, 1963.

Kaufman, A. *The science of decision-making.* New York: McGraw-Hill, 1968.

Lebergott, S. Labor force and employment trends. In E. H. Sheldon & W. E. Moore (Eds.), *Indicators of social change: Concepts and measurements.* New York: Russell Sage Foundation, 1968.

Roberts, L. G. Pattern recognition with an adaptive network. In L. Uhr (Ed.), *Pattern recognition.* New York: Wiley, 1966.

Stevens, S. S. Ratio scales of opinion. In D. K. Whitla (Ed.), *Handbook of measurement and assessment in behavioral sciences.* Reading, Mass.: Addison-Wesley, 1968.

Stieber, J. (Ed.) *Employment problems of automation and advanced technology.* London: St. Martin's Press, 1966.

Suchman, E. A. *Evaluative research: Principles and practice in public service and social action programs.* New York: Russell Sage Foundation, 1967.

Index

Accommodation, 107
  of individual to job, 107, 113
  of job to individual, 103–105, 107, 113
Accountability, 109
Acquinas, St. Thomas, 18
Advertising, 75–76
American Institute of CPAs' Accounting Principles Board, 156
Artistic freedom, 78–79
Assembly-line work, 47
Attendance, 123–124
  absenteeism, 40, 115, 116, 117
  bonus for regularity, 124
Attitudes toward work, 1–2, 4–5, 30, 35–36, 38, 41–46, 47, 49, 105–106, 126
Automation, 49, 59, 74, 178–179
  of knowledge and energy distribution systems, 72
  workers displaced by, 147
Automobile production, 46–47, 91–92

B-characteristics, 178
Barry, R. G., Corporation, 3, 4, 156, 158, 161, 164–169, 170, 172
  1969 Annual Report, 165, 169
Bass, Bernard M., 10, 11, 69–89, 134–152
Behavior modification, 190–191
  counter conditioning, 124

Behavior modification (continued)
  extinction, 125, 190
  modeling, 122, 125
  operant conditioning, 122–125
  shaping, 122–124
Bell, D. (*see also* Scientific City), 182–184, 185
Bellamy, Edward, 134–135
Biosocial theory (*see* Smith, Karl U.)
Blue-collar workers, 70, 147
Bond, Nicholas, 11, 178–206
Bowers, D. G., 171–172, 174
Broilerhouse Society, The, 178–179, 184
Bryan, Glenn L., 1–11
Bureaucracy, decline of, 143

Cable television, 137
Change, controlled experiments to study, 185–190
Change, quasi-experiments to study, 190–193
Change, as a social value, 76–77
Change data, 179–180
Change-evaluation models, 194–202
  ecobehavioral measurement, 194, 204
  legal, 194–204
  simulation, 200–201, 204
  social-area analysis, 204
  statistical optimization, 196–199, 204

Change-evaluation models (continued)
  probabilistic information
    processing, 195–200
  representative case, 195–196, 204
Child labor, 2, 7
Common Market, 145
Communication, 137–138
  and EDP, 149
Community Mental Health Centers
  Act of 1963, 97
Community services, 7, 93
  new careers in, 94–97
Computer-aided instruction (CAI),
  187, 189, 191
Computer simulations, 140
Conglomerates, 143
Consumer behavior, 60–61, 66,
  75–76
Cox, Harvey, 75
Crowding, 74
Cultural lag, 65

Decentralization:
  functional, 143
  geographic, 137
  organizational, 144
Deferred gratification, 56, 76
Depersonalization of worker, 3, 5,
  16, 74–75
Demographic changes, 70–71
Discrimination learning, 125
Dominance hierarchies, 34
Dow Chemical Company, 198
Drucker, Peter, 21–22, 26–27
Drugs, 77
Dubin, Robert, 10, 53–68
Dunnette, Marvin D., 10, 53,
  90–112
Durkheim, Emile, 58

Ecobehavioral units, 194
Ecology, 58, 194
Education:
  changes in, 84
  of employees, 62
  free schools, 7
  goals of, 61
  lifelong work-study, 7
  and resource conservation, 92

Education (continued)
  university training for
    management, 148–149
  as youth's job, 5
Electronic data processing (EDP),
  72, 75, 138, 139–141, 143,
  147–148, 178
  Bayesian computer routine, 99
Environment and work, 31–33,
  36–37, 50
Environmental-difficulty hypothesis,
  50, 51
Equal employment opportunities,
  86
Expectancy theory, 122, 125–126
Exploitation of worker, 100

Fairchild Semiconductor Company,
  155
Family, changes in, 83–84
Federal Tax Course, 157
Financial Accounting Standards
  Board, 156
Fine, Sidney, 10, 90–112
Flamholtz, E. G., 170–172, 174
Focal institutions, 54–55, 66
Freud, Sigmund, 54
Friedman, Georges, 47
Fringe benefits, 118, 128–130

Galbraith, John, 142
Generation gap, 69, 77–78, 86
Goldring, Patrick, 178–179
Gompers, Samuel, 15
Government:
  changes in, 85–86
  as regulator of economy,
    145–146
Gross National Product, 71, 129,
  181, 189
Guilds, 16
Guttentag, M. 194

Hallowitz, Emanuel, 98
Headstart, 180
Health, 93
  careers in, 97–103
Health Policy Advisory Center, 99
Heneman, Herbert G., Jr., 9, 12–28
Hippies, 75

Hogan, C. Lester, 155
Hough, Leaetta, 90–112
Housewives, 8
Human resource accounting,
    153–175
  external reporting of, 154–156
  in the future, 170–173, 174–175
  historical cost method, 169–170
  internal reporting, 158–160
  and market value, 155
  need for, 153–155
  problems with, 160–164
  in sports, 155–156, 162
  tax control of, 157–158
Human resource conservation, 132

Industrial Revolution, 18, 26, 147
Industrialization, 17, 46–48
Ingroup-outgroup relations, 33–35,
    49–50
Innovation (*see* Technology, as
    leading to change)
Institute of Chartered Accountants
    in England and Wales, 169
Interdependence of society, 58–60
Internal Revenue Service, 157, 158
Internationalism, 144–145
Intrinsic rewards and work, 31,
    37–38, 122, 132

Job:
  concept of, 2–4
  enlargement, 141, 149
  performance, 130, 159–160
  satisfaction, 3
  semi-skilled, 73
  skills, 102–103, 107, 121–122,
      132, 160
  social aspects, 119–120
  training, 94–100, 113–114,
      148–149
Job Corps, 104, 180

Kelly Girl, 63
Kennedy, John F., 97
Knowledge explosion, 70–72
Knowledge, as foundation of
    economy, 22
Knowledge workers, 183

Labor unions, 18–20, 146–147
Laissez-faire entrepreneurship, 2
Lawler, Edward E., III, 11,
    153–177
Leavitt, H. J., 139
Leisure, 22–24, 39, 76
Lev, B., 171
Likert, R. 171–172, 174
Lincoln Hospital Project, 97, 99, 106
Looking Backward, 134–135
Lorton Reformatory, 101
Luther, Martin, 18, 26

Managers, 148–149, 160
  changing roles, 139–140
  evaluated, 173
  as evaluators, 173
  malpractice by, 163
  university training of, 148–149
Marginal workers:
  definition, 115
  motivating, 114–122
Maslow, A. H., hierarchy of needs,
    195–196
McClelland, D. C., 120
McLuhan, Marshall, 76
Mead, Margaret, 38
Mechanical solidarity, 58
Meritocracy, 64, 78
Middle-class values, 102
Militants, 146–147
Military, the, 59, 66, 85
Military-industrial complex, 66
Mobility of labor force, 62–63, 82,
    127, 162
Mobutu, President Joseph, 34
Moore, Wilbur, 23
Motivation of the worker, 116–126,
    163
Motorola Company, 155
Multi-equal institutions, 55–66, 67
Multiple baseline, in
    quasi-experiments to study
    change, 190–191, 195, 203
Mumford, Emily, 10, 90–112

Nader, Ralph, 61, 145
Negative income tax, 198
Neighborhood service center
    program, 98

Neighborhood youth corps, 192
New Careers, 105–106, 107–111
New Careers Bulletin, 100
New Industrial State, The, 142
Nonwork, 22, 23–24, 129, 131

Office of Mobilization of Economic Resources, 94
Ogburn, W. F., 65
Opcon system, 198
Operant conditioning (*see also* Behavior modification), 122–125, 132–133
Organic solidarity, 58, 66
Organization man, 64
Organizational size, 143
Organizational structure, 58
Osgood, Charles, 41–45, 50

Packard, Vance, 76
Para-professionals, 93, 96
Peace Corps, 145
Perceptual style, 32
Perlman, Selig, 20
Planned change, 185
  individual response to, 188
Pollution control, 70, 93–94
Population growth, 70–71, 86
Porter, Lyman W., 10, 113–133
Professionalism, 100
Project groups, 141, 144, 149–150
Protestant Reformation, 81
Protestant work ethic, 75, 77, 81

Real time, 140
Recreation, 92–93
Religion, and work, 14, 15, 17–18, 23, 81–82
Replacement cost, of employee, 170–171
Resource conservation industry, 91–94, 106
Retirement, 4, 8, 64, 118, 147
Return on investment (ROI), 159
Reversal design, 190
Revolution of rising expectations, 75–77, 145
Reward administration:
  expectancy theory, 125–126

Reward administration (continued)
  modeling and social imitation, 125
  operant conditioning, 122–125
Rewards, and work, 114, 124, 126–131, 132–133
Rhode, John Grant, 11, 153–177
Risley, T. R., 190–191
Rosett, Henry, 10, 90–112
Ryterband, Edward C., 10, 11, 69, 89, 134–152

Sabbaticals, 130
Scholastics, the, 18
Schwartz, A., 171
Science revolution, 71–72
Scientific City, 183–184, 200
Scientific population, 183
Second careers, 8, 70
Secondary jobs, 3–4
Securities Exchange Commission, 156, 158
Self-actualization, 80–87
Self-selection, of jobs, 109
Semantic differential, 41–43
Seniority, 63
Sex differences, and work, 4–5, 41
Shaping (*see also* Behavior modification), 122–124
Simulation, 204
  Club of Rome world simulation, 201
  of complex social units, 200–201
Situation ethics, 81–82
Skills, 64, 104–105, 107
Slave labor, 64
Smith, Karl U., 21, 26–27
Social class, and work, 17, 39, 132, 146–147
Solomon four-group plan, 186, 203
Specialization, 14, 46–47, 56–57, 73
Spock, Benjamin, 5
Subcontracting, 63
Supervision (*see also* Managers), 138–141
Suppes, Patrick, 187

T-group phenomenon, 74
TASKTEACH concept, 189

Index   211

Team identification (*see also* Project groups), 109
Technological imperative, 71–75, 149
Technological innovation, 72
Technological revolution, 91–92
Technological specialists, need for, 184
Technology, as leading to change, 13, 14, 16, 21, 106, 146, 181, 183
Tennessee Valley Authority, 74, 145
Thorndike, R. L., 161
Time-series data, 170–180, 180–185, 202, 203
Time-series index, selection of, 184–185
Touche Ross & Company, Chartered Accountants, 166
Training, on the job, 114, 192, 189–190
Triandis, Harry C., 9, 29–52
Turnover, 63, 101, 115, 162

Unconditional reinforcement (*see also* Behavior modification), 123
Underemployed workers, 106, 115
Unions (*see* Labor unions)
U.S. Census Bureau Report, 184
U.S. Navy, 33
University of Michigan Research Center, 61
Urban development, 82, 92

Variable-ratio reinforcement schedule, 128, 131
Veblen, T., 60–61
Vocational training:
  evaluation of, 98–99
  for existing careers, 100–103
  for new careers, 94–100
Vroom, V. H., 121, 164

Wages and salaries, 60, 109, 110–111, 116–118, 124, 132, 141, 147, 162, 181
Welfare, 56–57, 59–60, 64, 85, 117
Whisler, T. L., 139
White-collar jobs, 70

Wilensky, Harold, 23
Wolf, M. M., 190–191
Women, in labor force, 59, 60, 93, 184
Work:
  concepts, 12–18, 20, 21, 26–27
  cultural differences in, 29–51
  definition, 1, 13, 24–25
  as drudgery, 17
  in the future, 7–9, 134–135
  rewards from, 122–126
  and social meaning, 48–59
  synonyms, 13
  voluntary, 9
Work, in other cultures:
  Afghanistan, 38
  Africa, 13, 39, 41
  Amazon, the, 30
  Bolivia, 20
  Bulgaria, 40
  Burma, 35
  China, 13, 14, 15, 36–37, 38
  Communist countries, 13, 14, 40
  Ecuador, 39
  Eskimos, 32, 43
  medieval Europe, 39
  Finland, 35
  ancient Greece, 23, 26, 40, 42–43
  India, 36, 40, 42
  Japan, 84
  Kashmir, 39
  Lapland, 37, 41
  Malaya, 37, 41
  Manus' concept of, 38
  Mongolia, 36–37, 41
  Nigeria, 35
  Oceania, 30
  Okinawa, 37, 38, 39
  Roman Empire, 23, 36, 39
  South America, 15
  South Pacific, 36
  ancient Sumeria, 15
  Thailand, 37, 38, 41
  Tikopia, 30
  Triobriand Islands, 35
Work-life expectancy, 22
Work and nonwork, decreasing distinction between, 91, 149
Work and nonwork cycle, 61–62
Work rate, 40, 48

Working hours, 39, 128, 132, 134, 136
  change since 1900, 180
  cubic day, 5
  daily cycle, 56
  shorter work week, 5
  temporal segregation, 56
  time off, 129–130
  twenty-five hour day, 5
  weekly cycle, 56
Working years (*see also* Retirement), 61
  first, second, and third careers, 8